EUROPEAN TRADE POLICIES AND THE DEVELOPING WORLD

Edited by L.B.M. Mennes and Jacob Kol, both Faculty of Economics, Erasmus University, Rotterdam

European Community trade policies are contradictory in some areas in that the European Community has established very high external tariff barriers for some commodities whereas at the same time EEC governments profess that they are keen to help third world countries develop by liberalising world trade. This book explores some of the complications of trade between the European Community and the developing world. It looks at how patterns of world trade are changing, how European Community protectionism affects developing countries and how special deals and exceptions are brought about in some cases. It examines how different European Community countries differ in their approach and concludes by examining how the situation may develop.

EUROPEAN TRADE POLICIES AND THE DEVELOPING WORLD

Edited by L.B.M. Mennes and Jacob Kol

Routledge
Taylor & Francis Group

LONDON AND NEW YORK

First published 1988 by Croom Helm Ltd
Published 1990 by Routledge
2 Park Square, Milton Park, Abingdon, Oxon, OX14 4RN

Simultaneously published in the USA and Canada
by Routledge
605 Third Avenue, New York, NY 10017

*Routledge is an imprint of the Taylor & Francis Group, an
informa business*

British Library Cataloguing in Publication Data

European trade policies and the developing world.
   1. Developing countries – Foreign
   economic relations – European Economic
   Community countries 2. European Economic
   Community countries – Foreign economic
   relations – Developing countries
   I. Mennes, L.B.M. II. Kol, Jacob
   337.1'42   HC59.7
   ISBN 0-415-05083-9

Library of Congress Cataloging in Publication Data

European Trade policies and the developing world.

   Includes index.
   1. European Economic Community countries — Commercial
policy. 2. Developing countries — Commercial policy.
I. Mennes, L.B.M. II. Kol, J.
HF1492.E87   1987   382'.3'094   87-8969

ISBN 13: 978-0-415-05083-8 (hbk)

CONTENTS

PREFACE

As this preface is being written, the Punta del Este meeting has just given the go ahead signal to a new trade round. A good deal of attention has been paid to the fact that this will encompass trade in agriculture and in services, two areas where very high levels of protection persist in many countries. Perhaps not as clearly noticed has been the strong involvement of countries of the South in the negotiations that have led to the decision. The evolution was already noticeable in the Tokyo Round. This time, these countries have held up the round until their basic demands were met. It is clear that they will continue to play an essential role in the coming negotiations.

This attitude marks a change from the initial decades that followed the creation of the GATT, when developing countries focused their efforts principally on securing special and differential treatment, that would exempt them from respecting the rules set by that organization. In this they were by and large successful - it turned out at the same time that permission to protect was not much of an asset in a world where countries that adopted inward looking trade strategies have been poor growers. First the East Asian countries, then the so-called "New Nics" turned with considerable success to policies that emphasize a reliance on world markets. Many countries in the South have reduced obstacles to trade and, in spite of some backsliding which the debt crisis has caused in part, the trend to more open trading strategies is unmistakeable. Also India, in spite of its strongly protectionist intellectual tradition, has moved decisively in that direction - and done very well. And now even Mexico, for some years the last major developing country to hold out against the GATT, has decided to join that organization.

This change in attitudes reflects the remarkable expansion of these countries' shares in international trade, especially for manufactures. The initial fears that developed countries would close up their markets to competition from "low wage" producers were unfounded. There have been protectionist measures, but they have not prevented the South from increasing steadily its market shares, which are in any event still much too low to have much impact on employment in the rich countries.

Much has been happening, therefore, to motivate a book such as this. The Hague Group, of which this is the first publication, takes its origin in a research project of the World Bank, that sought to shed light on the evolution of penetration on developed countries markets by developing countries, by means of novel data constructed by the group, (1) and undertook also a broad study of the political motivations of protection policies in developed countries. This "Market Penetration Group", as it came to be called, included economists from eleven developed countries, of which four were non-European.

It is the decision of its European members to continue to work together that gave rise to the Hague Group. The Netherlands Minister for Development Cooperation, and the World Bank again, have generously provided the support that has made the group's cooperation feasible.

The Hague Group has three aims. It is policy oriented, and intends to carry out research that is useful to decision-makers. It believes that to be useful, such work needs to have a strong empirical content: several of the papers use newly created data and models, to the construction of which the authors have contributed. The group's approach, finally, is not merely descriptive: its work makes wide use of the modern techniques of quantitative analysis.

All the papers are policy oriented. Martin Wolf's paper emphasizes the risks that are inherent in the slow drift of the world trading order away from the multilateralism on which the GATT was founded. For different reasons, both the European Community and developing countries have furthered that trend, and their "unholy alliance" may move the world even further down this slippery road in the coming trade round. Jean Waelbroeck and Jacob Kol aim at understanding the very rapid growth of developing countries exports. Will markets remain sufficiently open to allow these to grow as swiftly as in the past? What industries can expect to suffer from the developing countries next "market penetration breakthroughs"? Mathew Tharakan investigates the use made by the European Community of antidumping and countervailing duties, an instrument of trade protection whose importance has grown by leaps and bounds since a code of conduct was established in the Tokyo Round. Wouter Tims reviews the impact on the developing countries of the European Communities' Common Agricultural Policy (CAP) - a topic which will be one of the focal points of the coming trade negotiations. Ad Koekkoek and Loet Mennes consider some potential effects of liberalizing the Multi Fibre Arrangement (MFA). This was renewed this summer without considerable change, but the shape of the following one may turn out to be an issue on which the next Round will founder. Carl Hamilton stresses the silliness of the "article 115 of the Rome Treaty" trade restrictions, through which EC members have sought vainly to compartmentalize their markets for textiles and clothing. These restrictions, one of the Community's sacred cows, are a leading obstacle to the creation of a truly unified common market. David Greenaway's, and also Brian Hindley's papers, evaluate the very high cost to consumers of the politically convenient voluntary export restraints which, like other trading nations, the European Community has been using heavily. Patrick Messerlin's study goes beyond the traditional definition of protection to encompass protective devices that are not covered by the next round's agenda: it will provide food for thought for the diplomats of the future. Alexander Sarris finally, explains why the recent entrants to the Community may have good reason to push the EC into a negotiating stance that is unfavourable to the developing world.

There is nothing new under the sun, and these topics have been studied before. What the book contributes, in addition to the ability of every latest study to reflect the most recent events and facts, is its reliance on new sources of information. Jean Waelbroeck and Jacob Kol's paper is based on the novel data set on production and trade which was created by the "market penetration group", and has been continued since then by the OECD. Mathew Tharakan uses a custom built data base of the anti-dumping and countervailing duties decisions taken by the European Community; he uses a new analytical approach, due to Michael Finger, that rests on a theoretical distinction between the "high track" protection that is decided under strong political pressures, and the "low track" measures that are governed by quasi-legal rules. Wouter Tims' paper is the first application to the study of European Community agricultural protection of the IIASA general equilibrium model of world agriculture, with the construction of which he has been involved. Here also, a large empirical research effort has been undertaken, brought to completion by a strong IIASA team, which combined the production of original data, econometric estimation, and sophisticated modelling. Ad Koekkoek and Loet Mennes compile new measures of the comprehensiveness of the EC version of the Multi Fibre Arrangement. David Greenaway's paper uses a small model of the sectors which he has investigated, while Brian Hindley's is based on his new data on prices of video cassette recorders across the world. Patrick Messerlin's rests on a patient compilation of the diverse and heterogeneous information available on protection in France. Alexander Sarris, finally, has undertaken a quantitative analysis of the way in which, after its entry into the European Community, Greece was to a substantial extent able to replace by other taxes the tariff protection which it had to give up.

History is never complete. The developing countries are growing twice as fast as those of the North, and are shifting to more open trading strategies. Their share of international trade will continue to rise. "Market penetration" will continue, the domestic producers who lose will clamour for protection while those who gain keep silent. European governments and the European Community will feel forced to get involved.

The Hague Group has no reason to fear that it will have no more to do. Indeed, the preparation of its next study has begun.

Jean L. Waelbroeck

Note
1. This data set is being kept up to date by the Organization for Economic Cooperation and Development (OECD).

Chapter One

INTRODUCTION: TRADE POLICIES AND THEIR EFFECTS

L.B.M. Mennes and Jacob Kol

1. PROTECTION IN THE INDUSTRIAL COUNTRIES

1.1 The rise in protectionism

Since the mid-1970s there has been a considerable increase
in protectionist pressures. (1) In particular international
organizations like the GATT, the OECD, the World Bank and
the IMF have repeatedly warned against increasing
protectionism and its negative effects on the world
economy.

In its 1984/85 annual report the GATT admits that the
greater part of world trade continues to take place under
the rules and disciplines of the GATT. But it also
emphasizes that a growing number of measures is being
taken which contravene countries' commitments under the
GATT. According to the GATT, this trend is nowhere more
evident than in the spread of agreements whose purpose is
to restrict competition by sharing markets. Such agreements
like voluntary export restraint agreements, orderly
marketing agreements, consultation agreements, etc., are in
fact discriminatory quantitative restrictions on either
imports or exports which are inconsistent with countries'
GATT obligations. These instruments are increasingly
applied in the context of a sectoral approach to resolving
trade problems, showing that many governments prefer
bilaterally managed trade to multilateral liberal trade. (2)

Similarly, the OECD expressed its concern about
mounting pressures on the open multilateral trading system.
(3) According to the OECD, since the late 1960s, tariff and
non-tariff protection from imports in the OECD countries
has concentrated on a small number of industries: textiles

1

and clothing, footwear, some light consumer products and steel. In recent years the scope of protection has both widened and deepened in the following ways:

- protection has been extended to previously less or un-affected industries such as automobiles, consumer electronics and machine tools;
- within the protected industries, the share of trade subject to control has increased;
- a growing range of countries is subject to discriminatory controls on their exports;
- the share of these countries' exports subject to control has risen.

With respect to the evolution of trade policies towards developing countries, the OECD observes that, also after implementation of the Tokyo Round, tariffs confronting developing countries' exports of manufactures to the industrial countries remain above those applying to intra-OECD exports. Moreover, non-tariff barriers facing major developing countries' export products have also spread and tightened in recent years. Examples are the second renewal of the MFA in 1982 and new or strengthened quantitative restrictions in areas like steel, consumer electronics and footwear. Requests for protective measures against low-cost imports have mushroomed and although only few have resulted in actual actions, the mere threat of further restrictions has an adverse impact on the trading and investment climate.

The OECD emphasizes in particular that by far the most important effect of protectionist policies has been to accelerate the product and geographical diversification of developing countries' exports of manufactures. The more advanced NICs have been particularly successful in diversifying out of industries most affected by restrictive trade measures: into other labour-intensive industries; into unrestrained sub-product areas within industries where protection exists; into new geographical markets; and into industries which are less labour-intensive and more intensive in the use of skill, especially engineering skills and/or capital. This point will be taken up again later on in this paper.

Also the IMF notes that although governments in most industrial countries have made efforts to resist protectionist demands, trade restrictions increased, mainly in the form of discriminatory non-tariff barriers (4). Recently, according to the IMF, there has been an increased tendency in industrial countries to broaden and sharpen trade legislation, particularly in order to deal with "unfair" foreign competition. Examples are the 1984 Trade and Tariff Act of the USA and the New Commercial Policy Instrument adopted by the European Community in September 1984.

As the most striking aspects of trade relations and measures affecting developing countries the IMF mentions: the nominal tariff reductions under successive GATT rounds have been less significant on products of interest to the developing countries; the structure of tariffs in industrial countries which impedes the development of higher value-added industries in developing countries; the extension of tariff preferences to developing countries under the General System of Preferences which has been beneficial in trade terms, although various factors limit the benefits; and the increase in countertrade arrangements in trade with or within developing countries. According to recent estimates such countertrade arrangements account for between 8 and 10 per cent of the external trade of members of the GATT. (5)

Like the other institutions also the World Bank emphasizes the growing use of non-tariff barriers against developing countries' exports. The Bank warns that increased protectionism in industrial countries against developing countries' exports reduces the export earnings that developing countries would otherwise obtain. That is detrimental to their capacity to import and therefore a threat to efficient economic growth. In addition, it has a negative effect on developing countries' capacity to serve their debts and adversely affects their terms of trade. In this respect it must be emphasized that the most severe trade interventions in industrial countries aimed at developing countries are almost all directed primarily against major debtor countries (with the exception of the MFA). (6)

To quantify the overall extent and significance of non-tariff restrictions on imports is a notoriously difficult exercise. Most studies have focused on identifying the share of trade subject to non-tariff barriers, without quantifying the degree of restriction involved. Moreover, the studies concerned come to quite different conclusions due to differences in methodologies and in definitions of non-tariff barriers.

The most detailed study in this respect - by the World Bank - shows that a much larger share of industrial-country imports from developing countries is subject to non-tariff barriers than of imports from other industrial countries: 27.0 compared with 17.1 per cent in 1983. (7)

There is no doubt that at present protectionist pressures are a continuous threat to the world trade system and particularly to developing countries' growth. On the other hand, there is evidence that actual protection has increased relatively less than the pressures for protection. (8) In a recent survey on industrial protection in developed countries Balassa and Balassa conclude that in contrast with tariff protection, non-tariff protection in the industrial countries has indeed increased, but that the protectionist measures applied by these countries after 1980 were chiefly oriented against each others' exports, with imports from developing countries largely escaping the effects of the new measures. (9)

This is to a large extent confirmed in the World Bank study mentioned above. The evidence there shows that between 1981 and 1983 new non-tariff barriers were imposed on a large number of small trade flows from developing countries and a smaller number of large flows from industrial countries. This does not mean, however, that developing countries were exempt from the rise in protectionism, for their main exports (such as textiles and clothing) experienced considerable tightening of the existing trade restrictions. (10)

1.2 Protection and exports from developing countries

Regarding the impact of the new protectionism on the volume of world trade and developing country exports, views are different. According to Bergsten and Cline, both protectionist pressures and actions have failed to show up in a serious retrenchment of international trade. (11) They show that the slowdown in the volume of world trade and the volume of non-oil OECD imports which actually occurred in 1980 and 1981 is fully explained by the reduction in world growth.

In a survey of a programme of studies on the impact of developing countries' exports of manufactures on the markets of the principal industrial countries Hughes and Waelbroeck observed that the actual impact of the "new protectionism" of the 1970s appeared not to have been as large as was initially thought probable. (12) Similarly, Hughes and Krueger came to the conclusion that, at least in the 1970s, protectionist actions were not sufficient to prevent those developing countries with open economies from significantly increasing their share of world markets. (13) How much more they could have done in the absence of protectionist measures, is an open question. However, given the full employment that prevailed in those economies, it is doubtful whether expansion at a significantly more rapid rate could have occurred. Also Balassa, in a recent paper on the prospects for trade between developed and developing countries, concludes that the deceleration of the growth of manufactured imports from the developing countries can be attributed to the decline in growth rates in the developed countries rather than to increased protection. (14)

Another study on the effects of protection on developing countries' manufactured exports and an assessment of how vulnerable these exports might be to future restrictions is by Hughes and Newbery. (15) Their main conclusion is that during the period 1973-83 the newly industrializing countries were able to sustain high rates of growth of manufactured exports despite protectionist actions. There is some evidence that protection forced the largest four Far Eastern newly industrializing countries to switch some of their exports from industrial countries to other destinations, perhaps thereby allowing other developing countries to obtain high rates of growth of exports to industrial countries, or perhaps displacing them from other markets.

A further conclusion of this study is that there is a group of medium middle income countries - Malaysia, Thailand, Philippines, Indonesia, Morocco, Tunisia, Turkey, Colombia, Uruguay, Paraguay, Chile, Jordan and Syria - which has had higher export growth than the newly industrializing countries during this period, though the large poor traditional exporters and the small middle income exporters have performed rather poorly. This suggests the possibility that protection may have assisted the second rank exporters, both by restraining the market shares of the most successful newly industrializing countries, and by raising the profitability of exporting manufactures for some countries. The increased profitability is due to the increase in the price level in the importing country which imposes quota or other constraints; in this way rents are being generated for countries receiving a quota or being exempt from restrictions.

Finally, protectionism has not been very effective in reducing imports into the developed economies, and to the extent that it was successful, it probably reduced industrial countries' exports of manufactures by as much, or more, than it reduced imports. Moreover, it harmed the poorest developing countries disproportionately.

Hughes and Newbery emphasize that although manufactured imports from developing countries have been growing fast they still represent - with the exception of clothing - a small share of apparent consumption in the industrial countries: not more than 4 per cent in 1981. This is confirmed in the paper by Waelbroeck and Kol in this volume who show that at the 2-digit and 3-digit SITC level the rates of market penetration by developing countries into the EC, the USA, and Japan are still very low, except for textiles and clothing and miscellaneous manufactured goods. (16) Waelbroeck and Kol conclude that the room for further expansion of the exports of developing countries is considerable, provided that they can increase and diversify supply. This conclusion is confirmed when considering data at the 4-digit and 5-digit SITC level.

This conclusion is different from results obtained by Cline, who presented a number of simulation exercises indicating that generalization of the East Asian model of export-led development across all developing countries would result in untenable market penetration into industrial countries. (17) The validity of some of Cline's arguments and policy conclusions was doubted by Ranis. (18) Ranis' main points were that Cline had overstated substantially the increase in developing countries' manufactured exports to the industrial countries likely to result from the adoption of the export-oriented developing strategy followed by the so-called Gang of Four, and that he had exaggerated the protective response to such an increase on the basis of inadequate empirical analysis. In his reply Cline admitted that his simulation exercises were an extreme scenario for manufactured exports from developing countries, implying an annual growth rate of these exports of some 30 per cent for the period 1982-90, though equal to the annual manufactured exports growth rate of South Korea during 1960-79. (19) Cline repeated that such growth rates would lead to high market penetration rates in the industrial countries which would certainly provoke new protection. On the other hand, Cline's updated calculations show that developing countries can probably expand their manufactured exports at real rates of 10 to 15 per cent annually without provoking problems of market absorption and protection.

2. THE EFFECTS OF TRADE LIBERALIZATION

May one conclude that the revival of protectionism is not a matter of great concern? According to Corden there are three considerations against such a conclusion. (20) First, the adverse effects on trade may come later, since investment in export-oriented activities will be inhibited and since some of the measures concerned are only recent. Secondly, the pattern of trade may have been distorted, even though world trade has not decreased. Thirdly, in the absence of the recent protectionist policies, trade would have expanded much faster than GNP, so that a shift to more export-oriented growth is being hampered. With respect to this last point one should note that as world trade has begun to expand again since 1983, the ratio of world trade volume growth to world output growth has remained below its long-run level, probably reflecting the persistent dampening effects of increasing protectionism in recent years. In addition it should be noted that there is so far no better explanation of the inadequate international transmission of the recovery than the world wide continuing deterioration of trading conditions. Without more open international markets, the recovery-in-progress may be only a brief one. (21)

2.1 Simulation studies
Next, the question comes up what impact trade liberalization might have on the world economy and on the developing countries in particular. The effects concerned can be conceived of either in partial or general equilibrium terms. Studies using a partial equilibrium framework are quite numerous. (22) Their results show in general significant welfare effects, like those reported in a recent IMF-study. (23) In the latter study it is found that a complete, non-discriminatory removal of import restrictions (including non-tariff barriers) in seven categories of imports of agricultural and manufactured goods by industrial markets would lead to a sharp increase in developing

country exports. Depending on the strength of the supply response these exports could increase by roughly 4-9 per cent in real terms. Although the model used in the IMF-study is static, and neglects changes resulting from terms of trade changes, economies of scale and intra-industry trade, it does show, according to the authors, that trade liberalization can have significant beneficial effects on developing country exports.

No doubt, by employing partial analysis one neglects important general equilibrium effects of trade policy changes on trade, employment and therefore welfare. There is, however, a growing literature on numerical general equilibrium trade policy models; these models are being used to analyse the effects of various trade policy options for both developed and developing countries, and of proposals for multilateral and bilateral trade initiatives.

One of the first of such studies, consisting of fully integrated models of world trade and production, is by Klein and Su. (24) They use Project Link to study the effects of 5, 10, and 20 per cent tariff increases on the manufactured imports of 13 OECD countries. The main results under the 5 (20) per cent protectionist scenario are that after two years world trade declines by 4.2 (15.1) per cent; real GNP in developed and developing countries is lower by 0.2 (0.8) and 0.5 (1.3) per cent respectively. Inflation rates and world trade prices rise under all scenarios.

If one considers the welfare effects of complete trade liberalization in all countries, recent results obtained by Whalley suggest that in that case world income, although increasing by almost 0.5 per cent would be redistributed from the developing to the industrial countries; developing countries' GNP would decrease even by some 3.3 per cent. (25) This result is due to a deterioration of the developing countries' terms of trade after trade liberalization. Such a deterioration is explained by higher average rates of protection in the developing countries and by the smaller amount of trade involving the developing countries compared with trade among the industrial countries.

In an earlier study, however, Brown and Whalley had obtained somewhat different results, i.e. abolition of all tariff and non-tariff barriers in all countries would increase the welfare of both developing and industrial countries, but by not more than a few tenths of percentages of GNP. (26) In case of a unilateral elimination of protection by the industrial countries the welfare effects for the developing countries can be expected to be somewhat more substantial: an increase in their GNP by some 2.5 per cent.

In another study on trade liberalization Whalley emphasizes that gains or losses to any region from changes in trade policies tend to be small when calculated as fractions of GNP. (27) This seems due to the fact that trade distortions affect a relatively small part of total activity; and where the distortions themselves are often relatively small, they can be expected to have small distorting effects. If these gains and losses are compared with the distorting effects of domestic policies, such as taxes and domestic regulations most of the effects appear smaller by several orders of magnitude. This is especially so for developing countries, many of which have domestic policies that produce major distortions and have large losses associated with them. (28)

On the other hand, Whalley's analysis shows that countries should actively seek multilateral trade liberalization or at least agreements preserving previous accommodations to the threat of a global retaliatory trade war achieved at the successive GATT rounds in the past. If the present cooperative arrangements in the setting of world trade policies are not continued and the threat of a global retaliatory trade war became reality, the current estimates of trade elasticities suggest high retaliatory tariff and non-tariff barriers and considerable world welfare losses.

Deardorff and Stern use the Michigan model of world production and trade to assess post-Tokyo Round tariffs. (29) They estimate that the latter elimination would result in a 3.7 per cent increase in world exports but have hardly any effect at all on developing countries' exports. Economic welfare would increase in the USA and Japan but decline in the EC except for Ireland, Italy, the Netherlands and the United Kingdom; the US dollar and other major currencies would depreciate somewhat and consumer prices would fall to a small extent in the USA but to a much greater extent in most other industrial countries. The effects on the major developing countries would in general be comparatively small; for all developing countries together GDP would increase by 0.06 per cent.

Deardorf and Stern emphasize that these results are due to the fact that tariffs are already low and that in case also non-tariff barriers would be removed the effects would be significantly larger and more beneficial to developing countries.

2.2 Some refinements and comments

The results of the Deardorff-Stern study were rejected by Balassa who argued that tariff protection by industrial countries on industrial goods imported from developing countries was twice as high as suggested by the aggregate data and that the export supply elasticities in developing countries were seriously underestimated. (30)

In addition, according to Balassa, the Deardorff-Stern model does not incorporate the phenomenon of trade in differentiated products in the form of intra-industry specialization. Balassa argues that for these reasons Deardorff and Stern seriously underestimate the benefits developing countries may obtain through the elimination of tariffs by the industrial countries.

Balassa's last point was confirmed in a recent study by Richard Harris, where he presents an empirical general equilibrium model of a small open economy with an imperfectly competitive sector. The details of industrial organization in the non-competitive sectors include economies of scale, explicit price-setting firms, and product differentiation. (31) The results of some general equilibrium simulations on trade liberalization are compared with those of a competitive model implemented on the same data set. The major conclusion is that the estimated welfare gains from trade liberalization are substantial in the industrial organization model and about four times larger than the gains estimated from the competitive model. Furthermore, intra-industry adjustment appears to be an important avenue for resource allocation in the industrial organization model.

In a recent discussion on the results of a number of general equilibrium trade policy models it was concluded that for the larger countries trade policy is less important than for smaller countries. And for smaller countries where scale economies are not fully exploited - for instance because these countries are denied access to large foreign markets - trade policy becomes correspondingly more important. It may even be that for many smaller developed and developing countries, trade policy may be the single most important policy issue with which they are confronted. Another conclusion is that the impact of trade policies on the terms of trade may be considerable. If so, there occurs a major difference between the national and global interests.

The national interest may lie in protection, while the global interest is in the elimination of protection and the sharing of the joint gains from trade. (32)

In another general equilibrium model for analysing the macro-economic impact of alternative trade and fiscal policies in the OECD on developing countries' output, terms of trade, debt and debt service, van Wijnbergen shows that trade intervention against developing countries not only shifts their terms of trade adversely, but also leads to higher interest rates, deteriorating their debt service burden. In other words, in case of trade intervention against them, developing countries suffer twice. First, their static, intratemporal terms of trade deteriorate; second, they are confronted with higher real interest rates, i.e. their intertemporal terms of trade suffer also. As van Wijnbergen demonstrates, in case of a substantial increase in OECD protection against developing countries, considerably negative effects can be expected with respect to real interest rates as well as to GDP, export and import growth in both developed and developing countries. (33)

2.3 The effects on economic policy decisions

Regarding the effects of trade liberalization - or of increasing protectionism - two additional observations are in order. First, there is more than sufficient reason to have fear for the negative effect that industrial countries' protection - particularly on the part of the EC - has on the attitude of developing countries vis-à-vis the liberal international trading system as it is embedded in the GATT. The international trading system created after World War II was based on the principle of non-discrimination. However, in order to secure stability in trade policy it was necessary to permit action to increase protection or violate other norms in certain conditions; this was done in the form of various clauses permitting protection for balance of payments reasons, infant industry protection, etc.

There is no doubt that the EC follows policies of preferential liberalization and discriminatory protection. But also the developing countries are addicted to the idea of special and differential treatment. Both country groups base these trade policy preferences on the belief that discrimination is a beneficial element in international trade policy; they share the fear that comparative advantage does not work among unequals where one has to deal with an apparently irresistible competitor. In this sense Martin Wolf speaks of an "unholy alliance" of the developing countries and the EC, leading to the destruction of the legitimacy of non-discrimination as a guiding principle of the international trading system. (34) This deplorable development will only be enforced by increasing protectionist pressures in the economically strongest country group.

Secondly, and related with the previous point, there is considerable danger that continuing protectionism will induce developing countries not to continue or adopt export-oriented growth strategies, because they expect that growth of their exports will be denied to them. In this respect it must be emphasized that export growth is one of the results of an export-oriented growth strategy; but there is much more at stake than just an increase in exports.

This is convincingly pointed out by Krueger who argues that it would be implausible to attribute the increase in growth rates in countries adopting an export-oriented strategy directly to increased exports. (35) The growth rates of these countries suggest that something more than the direct impact of exports was at work in accounting for the superior growth performance. Krueger mentions three sets of dynamic factors bearing on performance differences: Technological factors like the nature of production functions, including the extent of indivisibilities and economies of scale, the presence of infant industry considerations and the spread in factor intensities across activities. Economic factors as people's responses to incentives and direct controls, the impact of industry structure on behaviour and the flexibility of the economy. Political-economic factors related with the fact that government policy instruments for regulating and controlling are less likely to achieve the intended results than those that create incentives for individual persons to carry out desired courses of activity.

The relative importance of each of these three sets of dynamic factors is still unknown. But, as Krueger emphasizes, insofar as the superior performance of export-oriented policies has been the result of the economic and political behavioural factors, rather than the technological factors, openness itself, rather than export growth, contributes in an essential way to rapid increases in output and productivity. The significance of this consideration in evaluating the prospects for developing countries' future growth in case of a potentially slower expansion of world trade is evident. If openness creates rapid growth due to competition and the nature of policy instruments used, the benefits from an export-oriented strategy will be less with slower growth of world trade, but not very much less.

This consideration does obviously not imply that world trade growth is not important for developing countries; both openness as well as export growth contribute significantly to superior economic performance in case an export-oriented strategy is followed. For this reason trade liberalization, in particular by the industrial countries, is an important instrument for encouraging developing countries to adopt export-oriented growth strategies.

3. EUROPEAN TRADE POLICIES AND THE DEVELOPING WORLD

In the preceding two sections we have considered the issues of protectionism and trade liberalization. It can be concluded that protectionist pressures in most industrial countries in the past several years have been high; on the other hand actual protection against developing countries' exports seems to have increased relatively less than the pressures for protection. Regarding the issue of trade liberalization, one can derive from the available evidence that for various reasons trade liberalization - particularly on the part of the industrial countries - is an important contribution to developing countries' possibilities of growth.

The studies presented in the remainder of this volume fit in with the general framework of protectionism and trade liberalization. They deal with European trade policies and their effects on the developing world, and can best be classified in three categories: general studies, sector studies, and country studies. The general studies are on: the erosion of the liberal international economic order due to the destruction of the legitimacy of non-discrimination as a guiding principle of the international trading system (Wolf); EC trade policy and the possibilities for manufactured exports from developing countries (Waelbroeck and Kol); the sector- and country-incidence of anti-dumping and countervailing duty cases in the EC (Tharakan). The sector studies deal with the following subjects: the effects of the EC Common Agricultural Policy on the developing countries (Tims); the working of the Multi Fibre Arrangement and the effects of liberalization (Koekkoek and Mennes); the attempt to control imports of textiles and clothing from outside the West-European free trade area into particular national markets (Hamilton); the costs and benefits of voluntary export restraints and source specific quotas for non-leather footwear and woven clothing (Greenaway); the political economy aspects of the first voluntary export restraint between the EC as a whole and Japan referring to video cassette recorders (Hindley). Finally, there are two country studies: the first one is on France where it is examined whether French trade policies discriminate against developing countries (Messerlin); in the second study the effects of the accession of Greece to the EC on EC trade policies vis-à-vis developing countries are considered (Sarris).

Martin Wolf discusses in his paper the economic, legal and political aspects of the liberal international economic order which emerged after World War II; the strengths and weaknesses of this order; the way in which the EC has contributed to weakening or even disrupting the system due to its adherence to discrimination; and the affirmative àction in this respect on the part of the developing countries.

In establishing the international trading system after World War II the aim was to end the laissez faire for individual governments which had been the main characteristic of the inter-war period and to replace it with a system of internationally-agreed rules governed by certain norms: a transparent and market-conforming instrument of protection, the tariff; the "binding" of protection; reciprocity; and unconditional non-discrimination. These basic norms serve the essential function of ensuring the existence of a global market. Non-discrimination is central to this system whose principal technique of liberalization is reciprocity and whose principal sanction is retaliation.

The system has had substantial initial successes. But it has a major weakness: it is internally inconsistent. For, the entire structure is to be supported by strict adherence to non-discrimination, but the mercantilism inherent in the system discourages adherence to that principle. This has resulted in two main difficulties. First, the failure to secure and maintain adherence to the principle of non-discrimination. Second, the problem of "administered" protection, or the necessity to permit protection to increase in order to reach agreement.

According to Wolf, the EC has contributed significantly

to the weakening of the system by adopting policies of preferential liberalization and discriminatory protection. It has done so motivated by a fear of competition and economic change. Consequently, preferences have become the principal instrument of foreign policy for the EC, while the tariff has been replaced by discriminatory instruments of protection like the "voluntary" export restraint.

Also the developing countries want an end to the notion of non-discrimination by insisting on two kinds of change: relaxation of discipline imposed on them, and preferences in their favour. In one fundamental respect the addiction of developing countries to "special and differential" treatment derives from the same roots as the EC's preference for preferences. They share the phobia that comparative advantage does not work among so-called unequals.

Thus, the EC and the developing countries have become partners - an "unholy alliance" - in weakening or even disrupting the liberal international economic order by destroying the legitimacy of non-discrimination as a guiding principle of the international trading system.

Jean Waelbroeck and Jacob Kol explore in their paper past trends and future possibilities for manufactured exports from developing countries. For this purpose they consider the three main markets: the EC, the USA, and Japan; the main focus is on the EC.

With respect to trade in manufactures with developing countries, these three main markets show a typical backyard pattern. The EC trades predominantly with the Mediterranean countries; Japan trades in particular with East Asia; the USA concentrates its exports on Latin America, while its imports come mainly from the same area and from East Asia.

Market penetration by manufactured imports from the developing countries is still very low; the EC has the most open market with a penetration rate of 3.5 per cent in 1983. Although market penetration for specific products - mainly textiles and miscellaneous manufactures - can be quite high, import competition from developing countries has not been a major factor in declining employment in the industrial countries. Consequently, there seems to be ample scope for increasing manufactured exports from developing countries provided that these exports match with developing countries comparative advantages and are not contained by protection in the industrial countries.

Regarding the latter issue, the authors conclude that

not so much market penetration but rather the political strength of various industries' representatives constitutes the trigger point for protection. Furthermore, where EC member states still have a significant discretion with respect to their trade policies and show different degrees of openness towards trade with developing countries, the latter could perhaps exploit these differences among EC members in their trade negotiations.

Traditionally comparative advantages of developing countries have rested on the abundance of natural resources and, more recently, of unskilled labour. Primary based manufactures form still an increasing source of foreign exchange, but their share in developing countries' manufactured exports to the industrial countries is declining.

Within the unskilled labour-intensive products textiles, clothing and footwear have formed the bulk of developing countries' manufactured exports. It seems also that the newly industrializing countries gave way to newcomers in these exports. Also, the Multi Fibre Arrangement perhaps has not been so restrictive as is often assumed. Nevertheless, more export success may be expected from labour-intensive products other than textiles and clothing. In the paper a whole range of products is indicated - from food products to radio components - where comparative advantages of developing countries have been proven to exist. With some inventiveness developing countries may be able to create good export opportunities for these products.

In his contribution to this volume, Mathew Tharakan gives a detailed analysis of the country- and sector-incidence of anti-dumping and countervailing duties (AD/CVD) initiated in the EC. These measures are applied in a far more selective and discriminatory way and with less chance for retaliation than other non-tariff barriers under the GATT; hence the temptation to use them in practice. Data on anti-dumping investigations by the EC during 1980-84 show that the majority of these cases was concluded by the acceptance of a price-undertaking on the part of the exporter.

Although imports into the EC affected by AD/CVD cases still comprise less than 1 per cent of total imports, there is a clear upward trend in import coverage.

Regarding the country incidence of AD/CVD cases, Tharakan reports that through 1980-1983 only in the case of five countries the imports under AD/CVD cases initiated in the EC amounted to more than 1 per cent of their total exports to the EC. For individual years the number of countries thus affected has been larger of course and has been increasing. Countries concerned are mainly developing countries (like South Korea, Zimbabwe, Egypt and Taiwan) and centrally planned economies in Eastern Europe.

AD/CVD cases <u>concluded by acceptance of price-undertaking</u> covered more than 1 per cent of total exports to the EC almost exclusively in cases of Eastern Europe centrally planned economies. On the other hand, termination of AD/CVD cases by <u>the imposition of definitive duties</u> were less important, reaching less frequently the level of 1 per cent of total exports to the EC; mainly exports from developing countries were affected.

The sector incidence of AD/CVD cases has shown some fluctuations over time. Nevertheless, two sectors were prominent in the cases initiated, as well as in cases terminated either by price undertakings or definitive duties imposed. These two sectors are: organic chemicals and iron and steel. While these sectors are not usually associated with the comparative advantage of LDCs, imports of certain subcategories of the product groups involved came from LDCs (for example, steel plates from Brazil).

Recent information on 1985 and 1986 shows that AD/CVD investigations and decisions are increasing in number, particularly concerning imports from Japan. Relevant products are: hydraulic excavators, electronic typewriters and photocopiers.

The AD/CVD mechanism in the EC has certain particularities. For instance, EC administrators have greater discretionary powers than US officials specifically in determining "reasonable" profit margins when constructing "normal" values and export prices. Also the possibility of termination of the proceedings by the acceptance of price-undertaking by exporters, which was already mentioned, is a special feature. The high frequency of the price-undertakings is probably due to exporters finding the arrangement profitable while the Commission and the complainants usually see it as a less harmful way to end the proceedings.

Although the share of EC imports affected by AD/CVD procedures has clearly increased since 1980, it is still much smaller than that in the USA. Further, Tharakan finds that it cannot be argued that on the whole the AD/CVD cases in the EC have had a clearly accentuated incidence on imports from developing countries.

The paper by <u>Wouter Tims</u> deals with the effects of the European Communities' Common Agricultural Policy (CAP) on the developing countries. In particular, Tims analyses the effects of liberalizing the CAP in the form of unilaterally removing border protection in the EC.

First, the objectives, instruments and effects of the CAP are outlined. The most significant effects of the CAP took place in the EC's foreign trade. Imports of agricultural products which are also produced in the EC declined, exports increased in some cases very rapidly with significant impact on world prices.

With the purpose to study the effect on the domestic food situation in given countries of alternative policy measures, an internationally linked system of 20 detailed country or country-group models together with 14 simpler regional models was developed by a network of researchers participating in the Food and Agricultural Programme (FAP) of the International Institute for Applied Systems Analysis (IIASA) in Laxenburg, Austria. Tims discusses the purposes and properties of this Basic Linked System (BLS) of national models: it is an empirically estimated general equilibrium system which distinguishes 10 agricultural commodities; a whole range of government policies is covered and government policy reactions as well as behavioural responses of producers and consumers are endogenized; finally, it is not a forecasting tool, but an instrument for policy analysis which can explore simultaneous changes in a number of policies by different governments in terms of deviations from a reference scenario for the years 1990, and 2000.

The BLS is employed for analysing the effects of abolishing border protection in the EC. This is done through removing tariff equivalents - which are calculated as differences between domestic producer prices and the corresponding border prices over a period of five years. The effects relate to price changes at world markets and to changes in trade and production volumes in the countries concerned.

The effects on the developing countries are small and frequently negative. This must be somewhat qualified as a number of products which are of interest to developing countries and subject to market organization by the EC are not considered in the BLS: sugar, fruits, vegetables, fish and grain substitutes used for livestock feed. The negative effects are partly due to the fact that developing countries are themselves important importers of agricultural products which are bound to show higher world prices.

Tims emphasizes that adjustment to a more liberal environment appears to take a longer time than is covered in the BLS model. Moreover, it is important to note that in the present simulation exercise the developing countries are assumed not to participate in liberalization themselves. Abolishing their own agricultural protection may accelerate the adjustment process.

Ad Koekkoek and Loet Mennes consider in their paper some potential effects of liberalizing the Multi Fibre Arrangement (MFA). The MFA had originally various objectives. In fact, it was supposed to prevent a general rush into protectionism which was expected because many developed countries had been taking unilateral, ad hoc actions, against rising textile and clothing imports. But, instead of being reduced over time, as intended, protection in the textiles and clothing trade with the developing countries actually increased.

Nearly all textile and clothing products imported into the EC from the MFA countries are subject to some restriction. But it is very difficult to measure to what extent the MFA actually provides protection. Some studies have tried to measure the price increasing effect of the MFA. A review of these studies indicates that the protective effect of MFA quotas is considerable and on average at least as important as tariff protection. Another approach towards considering the effectiveness of the textile arrangements consists of looking at the trade coverage of the system and the rate of quota utilization. In 1983 87 per cent of extra EC textile and clothing imports, irrespective of origin, consisted of products, which are potentially regulated by the MFA. The average quota utilization in the sensitive product groups, for all developing MFA suppliers together, decreased from 100 per cent in 1978 to 82 per cent in 1983. The data on quota utilization can be interpreted as at least being consistent with some of the known by-product distortions of the MFA. Still the figures show a surprising amount of underutilization.

Koekkoek and Mennes estimate the effects of liberalizing the MFA, by the EC, for the Netherlands, the EC and developing countries. Depending on the assumptions, the annual welfare gain for the EC, for textile and clothing together, is estimated at between 1 and 3 billion dollars. For more than two thirds this consists of a transfer of rents earned by foreign producers under the present system. For the Netherlands the total annual welfare gain is estimated at between 65 and 190 million dollars.

For developing countries an estimate has been made of the effect of liberalizing the MFA by the EC on their exports and employment. For the MFA countries the value of exports would increase by between 2 and 6 billion dollars. The volume of employment in textiles and clothing, in these countries, associated with exports to the EC, some 1.25 million persons, would increase by some 20-45 per cent.

Carl Hamilton demonstrates the futility of a particular intervention in the framework of the MFA, namely the attempt to control imports of textiles and clothing from outside the West-European free trade area (the EC together with the EFTA) into particular national markets.

First, the concept of the tariff equivalent of an export restraint is explained. Hamilton discusses then some issues that arise when restraints are imposed on outside suppliers to customs unions or free trade areas. It is concluded that, under most circumstances, the sub-division of quota levels among member countries of customs unions and free trade areas is irrelevant. This conclusion must be qualified, however, in two respects. First, if individual member countries introduce administrative obstacles to the full utilization of the quota specific to their markets, prices will tend to rise throughout the customs union or free trade area because in fact the aggregate quotas are reduced. Secondly, if the market of one member country were to be sufficiently liberalized to allow external suppliers to take it all, the result would be a dual-price outcome. One price for consumers and another, higher one, for producers able to sell in the rest of the customs union or free trade area.

Next, average tariff equivalents of export restraints on clothing exported from Hong Kong to Western Europe and the United States are presented. It turns out that the countries of the EC had approximately the same combined trade barrier of 32-35 per cent between 1980 and 1983, and that the average tariff equivalent of the export restraints was 14 per cent.

Analysis of the changes in import patterns of the EC and EFTA for textiles and clothing between 1970 and 1979 due to economic integration and bilateral trade restrictions shows in particular for France and Sweden a strong trade-diverting effect, increasing the market shares of especially the non-restrained developed countries. On the other hand, the increases in the shares of imports in domestic consumption in Germany and the UK were captured primarily by developing countries, indicating that bilateral trade restrictions did not have much trade-diverting effects at the time.

The main implications of Hamilton's analysis are twofold. First, the internal sub-division of the overall quota for the EC is unnecessary. Second, action by just one member to restrict imports into its own market, as happens under the so-called "exit from the basket" provisions of the EC's bilateral agreements or invocation of Article 115 of the Treaty of Rome is pointless so long as the same imported products have free access to other EC markets.

Finally, Hamilton considers the intriguing possibility that one of the smaller West-European countries would propose a complete liberalization of restrictions at its border, combined with tighter restrictions on external imports into all other West-European markets so as to allow its producers to exploit the protectionism of other West-European countries. This might show up the absurdity of the current structure of restrictions on imports of textiles and clothing into Western Europe.

David Greenaway makes an attempt to estimate the costs and benefits of voluntary export restraints (VERs) and source-specific quotas (SSQs) for two sectors: non-leather footwear and woven clothing. This is done for the UK, where these instruments are used alongside tariffs to regulate the flow of imports from NICs/LDCs. The reference year is 1982.

The model used to obtain estimates of the deadweight losses and transfers associated with tariffs and VERs is the standard partial equilibrium model. It is well known that in all such models a problem exists with respect to estimating the price raising effect of the quotas. To solve this problem Greenaway follows the usual method of relying on information provided indirectly by transactions in quotas, i.e. quota premiums. This results in estimates of the ad valorem tariff equivalent of the quota premiums equal to almost 15 per cent for woven clothing and 13 per cent for non-leather footwear.

Assuming price elasticities of demand of -1.086 for woven clothing and -0.25 for non-leather footwear, supply elasticities of 1 and 2 for both sectors, and using rates of discount of 5 and 7 per cent, Greenaway obtains estimates of losses from protection which are substantial, even under the assumption that protective instruments remain in force for a comparatively short period and are discounted at a relatively high rate.

For both sectors it is assumed that the benefit of protection is employment preservation. It is estimated that the cost per job saved in both activities is relatively high. Even the most conservative estimates of the costs to the economy exceed annual average wages in the industries concerned.

Greenaway discusses briefly the effects of source-specific interventions on developing countries. Some of the by-product distortions of the restraints concerned may be beneficial to these countries. This may pertain to upgrading, the provision of rents, and the incentive effects on new exporters of artificially inflated prices. No attempt is made at a cost-benefit appraisal of source specific restraints, but Greenaway points out that it is not plausible at all that net benefits will be positive for the developing countries, even if the measures concerned may not have arrested the growth of developing country exports in the aggregate by as much as is sometimes believed.

Brian Hindley discusses in his paper the political economy aspects of VERs. He does so by analysing the first VER between the European Community as a whole, represented by the European Commission, and Japan, which referred to video cassette recorders (VCRs) and to the years 1983, 1984 and 1985. Though Japan is not a developing country, the case is an important one because it is rightly considered as holding lessons for the future conduct of EC trade policy. If the EC adopts such a course in its trade relations with a country like Japan, it may be expected that it will pursue VERs even more enthusiastically in its trade with other and weaker trading partners.

According to Hindley the background of the VER concerned is the fact that in trade policy matters the role of the European Commission - which under the Treaty of Rome is responsible for the external relations of the Community - has been seriously undermined. For, actual commercial policy affecting the Community has to a large extent taken the form of bilateral agreements between individual member states and non-members. The thought that the Commission could restore its authority in matters of trade policy only by negotiation of community-wide VERs must have been attractive, even for officials with relatively liberal views.

Next, information is given on the announced limits on Japanese exports of VCRs to the EC, the relation between these permitted exports and European output (Philips and Grundig), the minimum selling price for Japanese producers and the behaviour of VCR prices in the EC.

During 1984 the level of Japanese VCR exports to the EC agreed for that year was reduced; also the quota for 1985 dropped sharply. Hindley mentions a number of indications that the VER concerned has been driven in an increasingly restrictive direction by the failure of Philips and Grundig to expand their output to the extent envisaged in 1983.

This failure is explained partly by a possible saturation of the EC market for VCRs, partly by the increasing unpopularity of the Philips-Grundig product, and in particular by the lack of incentive provided by the VER for Philips-Grundig to increase output. On the contrary, Hindley thinks it likely that the VER provided the firms concerned with an incentive to reduce output, contributing in this way to increasing their profits or reducing their losses from VCR production.

The welfare losses associated with the VER concerned seem to be considerable. Hindley estimates that each job that the VER is assumed to have created has cost residents of the EC at least 106,000 and probably more than 300,000.

The verdict on the VER on VCRs as an instrument of economic policy is clear. It has discouraged European manufacture of European VCRs; it did increase profits of the European producers, though at welfare costs that are considerable. All this makes the VER concerned not recommendable.

In his country study on France, Patrick Messerlin takes as a point of departure the fact that France is frequently considered as one of the most protectionist countries in the industrial world. In particular his paper investigates the question whether French trade policies - within or outside the EC framework - discriminate against manufacturing exports from developing countries rather than from other industrial countries. To that end, the French system of protection is investigated: tariffs, non-tariff barriers at the border and non-border protection are analysed.

The analysis shows that tariff protection indeed discriminates against exports from developing countries, especially in the eighties, and increasingly so. The results suggest furthermore that the General System of Preferences was not sufficiently powerful to counterweight that evolution.

For various reasons it may be argued that non-tariff barriers are more suited to protect against imports from developed countries than from developing countries. Notwithstanding this, the available evidence suggests that French non-tariff border protection affects imports from developing countries rather than from other industrial countries.

Non-border protection includes domestic taxes on goods not produced domestically, domestic subsidies (among which export subsidies) and public procurements, quotas on domestic sales and the nationalization of enterprises.

Domestic subsidies and export subsidies account for 6.0 and 1.5 per cent respectively of French manufactured value added during 1979-1981. Both forms of subsidies are concentrated in industries competing with developing country exports: steel, electronics and ships.

Public procurements seem to enforce the effects of subsidies, as they are concentrated in the same industries. Also nationalized firms are found predominantly in these industries; this is of importance since nationalization is meant among others to protect against foreign competition. Quotas on domestic sales are on Japanese cars.

It is concluded that in France also non-border protection discriminates predominantly against exports from developing countries.

The second of the country studies is on Greece, one of the new entrants into the European Community. It is well within the scope of the present volume to focus on one of these entrants, because upon accession Greek interests may be in conflict with the EC policy of giving preferences to developing countries' exports.

This point is taken by <u>Alexander Sarris</u> as the central theme of his contribution. First, the pattern of trade and protection of Greece before the accession is analysed. It is concluded that Greece exhibits the pattern of production and trade of a developing, labour-abundant economy. On the other hand, imports from developing countries do not compete particularly with flourishing Greek industries, while developing countries are shown to be important markets for Greek manufactured exports.

The evolution of protection shows a considerable decline in tariff rates for total manufactured imports over the period 1960-1980; the average tariff being lower in 1980 for imports from the EC than from non-EC sources. Domestic taxes, however, counteract this. This leads first of all to a much smaller decline in overall nominal protection than was found for tariffs alone. Furthermore, due to differential domestic tax rates combined with differences in product mix, imports from EC are shown to meet more price increasing obstacles than imports from other sources.

Analysis of the sectoral pattern of protection in combination with figures on market penetration and export propensity shows that the 5 out of 20 manufacturing sectors that experience declines in market penetration and increasing export propensity are precisely the only 5 sectors that are increasingly protected. These sectors are: textiles, wood and cork, rubber and plastics, refinery products and basic metallurgy. On the other hand, two sectors experienced large increases in export propensity while protection decreased and import penetration went up. These sectors are: clothing and shoes and the leather industry. These developments may indicate that these sectors were internationally competitive. The figures on export propensity mark the outward looking strategy followed by Greece: an increase in export propensity over the years 1960-1980 is recorded for 18 out of 20 sectors.

In order to examine possibly conflicting interests between Greece and developing countries in their access to the EC market, the similarity in the structure of the corresponding exports to the EC is analysed. It appears that the major areas where Greece might be in conflict with developing countries are certain agricultural products (mainly fruits and vegetables, wine, tobacco and olive oil) and some manufactures (mainly clothing, shoes and textiles). Within the textiles and clothing group similarity in export structure is found to be considerable, especially in products considered sensitive under the Multi Fibre Arrangement. Consequently, Greek support for an EC policy to liberalize such imports from developing countries is not likely, especially upon accession of Portugal and Spain.

Notes and References

1.   For extensive discussion and documentation see e.g. W.M. Corden, The Revival of Protectionism, published by Group of Thirty, New York, 1984; Brian Hindley and Eri Nicolaides, Taking the New Protectionism Seriously, Thames

Essay No. 34, Trade Policy Research Centre, London, 1983; C. Fred Bergsten and William R. Cline, Trade Policy in the 1980s: An Overview, Chapter 2 in William R. Cline (ed.), Trade Policy in the 1980s, Institute for International Economics, Washington DC, 1983.

2. General Agreement on Tariffs and Trade, International Trade 1984/85, Geneva, 1985.

3. OECD, Costs and Benefits of Protection, OECD, Paris, 1985.

4. Shailendra J. Anjaria, Naheed Kirmani, and Arne B. Petersen, Trade Policy and Developments, Occasional Paper No. 38, International Monetary Fund, Washington DC, July 1985; David Goldsbrough and Iqbal Zaidi, Transmission of Economic Influences from Industrial to Developing Countries, Staff Studies for the World Economic Outlook, International Monetary Fund, Washington DC, July 1986.

5. Group of Thirty, Countertrade in the World Economy, Group of Thirty, New York, 1986.

6. The World Bank, World Development Report 1985, The World Bank, Oxford University Press, Oxford, 1985.

7. Julio J. Nogués, Andrzej Olechowski and L. Alan Winters, The Extent of Non-Tariff Barriers to Imports of Industrial Countries, World Bank Staff Working Papers, No. 789, World Bank, Washington DC, 1986, p. 25.

8. C. Fred Bergsten and William R. Cline, op. cit., 1983, p. 72.

9. Bela and Carol Balassa, Industrial Protection in the Developed Countries, The World Economy, Volume 7, No. 2, June 1984.

10. Julio J. Nogués, Andrzej Olechowski and L. Alan Winters, op. cit., p. 30.

11. C. Fred Bergsten and William R. Cline, op.cit., 1983, pp. 72-75.

12. Helen Hughes and Jean Waelbroeck, Can Developing Country Exports Keep Growing in the 1980s? The World Economy, Volume 4, Number 2, June 1981, pp. 127-147.

13. Helen Hughes and Anne O. Krueger, Effects of Protection in Developed Countries on Developing Countries' Exports of Manufactures, in R. Baldwin (ed.), The Structure and Evolution of Recent U.S. Trade Policies, University of Chicago Press, Chicago, 1983.

14. Bela Balassa, Trade Between Developed and Developing Countries: The Decade Ahead, OECD Economic Studies, No. 3, Autumn 1984, pp. 7-25.

15. Gordon A. Hughes and David M.G. Newbery, Protection and developing countries' exports of manufactures, <u>Economic Policy: a European Forum</u>, Vol. 1, no. 2, April 1986.

16. Jean Waelbroeck and Jacob Kol, <u>The Evolving Pattern of World Trade, EC Trade Policy and Exports from the South</u>, this volume, chapter 3.

17. William R. Cline, Can the East Asian Model of Development Be Generalized?, <u>World Development</u>, Volume 10, Number 2, February 1982.

18. Gustav Ranis, Can The East Asian Model of Development Be Generalized?, A Comment, <u>World Development</u>, Volume 13, Number 4, April 1985.

19. William R. Cline, Reply, <u>World Development</u>, Volume 13, Number 4, April 1985; William R. Cline, <u>Exports of Manufactures from Developing Countries</u>, the Brookings Institution, Washington DC, 1984.

20. W.M. Corden, <u>The Revival of Protectionism</u>, Published by the Group of Thirty, New York, 1984.

21. General Agreement on Tariffs and Trade, <u>International Trade 1982/83</u>, Geneva, 1983.

22. See Chris Milner, Empirical Analysis of the Costs of Protection, in David Greenaway (ed.), <u>Current Issues in International Trade</u>, Macmillan, London, 1985; Shailendra J. Anjaria, Naheed Kirmani and Arne B. Petersen, <u>op. cit.</u>, 1985.

23. Naheed Kirmani, Pierluigi Molajoni, Thomas Mayer, Effects of Increased Market Access on Exports of Developing Countries, <u>Staff Papers</u>, International Monetary Fund, Vol. 31, No. 4, December 1984.

24. Lawrence R. Klein and Vincent Su, Protectionism: An Analysis from Project Link, <u>Journal of Policy Modeling</u>, Vol. 1, No. 1, January 1979.

25. John Whalley, The North-South Debate and the Terms of Trade: An Applied General Equilibrium Approach, <u>The Review of Economics and Statistics</u>, Vol. 6, No. 2, May 1984.

26. F. Brown and J. Whalley, General Equilibrium Evaluations of Tariff-Cutting Proposals in the Tokyo Round and Comparisons with More Extensive Liberalisation of World Trade, <u>The Economic Journal</u>, Vol. 90, No. 360, December 1980.

27. John Whalley, <u>Trade Liberalization among Major World Trading Areas</u>, The MIT Press, Cambridge, Massachusetts and London, England, 1985.

28.   For a recent survey see: John B. Shoven and John Whalley, Applied General Equilibrium Models of Taxation and International Trade: An Introduction and Survey, Journal of Economic Literature, Vol. 22, No. 3, September 1984.

29.   Alan V. Deardorff and Robert M. Stern, The Economic Effects of Complete Elimination of Post-Tokyo Round Tariffs, Chapter 20 in: William R. Cline (ed.), op. cit., 1983; Alan V. Deardorff and Robert M. Stern, The Michigan Model of World Production and Trade, The MIT Press, Cambridge, Massachusetts and London, England, 1986.

30.   Bela Balassa, Comments, Chapters 17-20, in William R. Cline (ed.), op. cit., 1983, pp. 711-722.

31.   Richard Harris, Applied General Equilibrium Analysis of Small Open Economies with Scale Economies and Imperfect Competition, American Economic Review, Vol. 74, No. 5, December 1984, pp. 1016-1032.

32.   Deborah Fretz, T.N. Srinivasan and John Whalley, Introduction, in T.N. Srinivasan and John Whalley (eds), General Equilibrium Trade Policy Modeling, The MIT Press, Cambridge, Massachusetts and London, England, 1986.

33.   Sweder van Wijnbergen, Interdependence revisited: a developing countries perspective on macroeconomic management and trade policy in the industrial world, Economic Policy: a European Forum, Vol. 1, No. 1, Nov. 1985.

34.   For a lucid analysis of this issue see: Martin Wolf, An Unholy Alliance: The European Community and Developing Countries in the International Trading System, this volume, chapter 2.

35.   Anne O. Krueger, Comparative Advantage and Development Policy 20 Years Later, in Moshe Syrquin, Lance Taylor and Larry E. Westphal (eds), Economic Structure and Performance, Essays in Honor of Hollis B. Chenery, Academic Press, Inc., Orlando, 1984.

Part One

GENERAL STUDIES

Chapter Two

AN UNHOLY ALLIANCE: THE EUROPEAN COMMUNITY AND DEVELOPING COUNTRIES IN THE INTERNATIONAL TRADING SYSTEM (1)

Martin Wolf

> With respect to customs duties and charges of any kind imposed on or in connection with importation or exportation or imposed on the international transfer of payments for imports or exports, and with respect to the method of levying such duties and charges, and with respect to all rules and formalities in connection with importation and exportation ..., any advantage, favour, privilege or immunity granted by any contracting party to any product originating in or destined for any other country shall be accorded immediately and unconditionally to the like product originating in or destined for the territories of all other contracting parties.
> The General Agreement on Tariffs and Trade, Article 1, Paragraph 1

1. INTRODUCTION

There emerged after World War II an international economic order, based on liberal principles, under which the world enjoyed an unprecedented period of economic growth and stability. The order was never fully realized. Even its proponents did not fully understand all its implications. And it never lacked for opponents. Nevertheless, however imperfectly achieved, its successes were remarkable and its clear and progressive erosion is creating increasing difficulty.

The principal purposes of the present paper are (i) to discuss the underlying rationale of the liberal international economic order and its inherent and ineradicable fragility; (ii) to demonstrate the salient contribution made both by the European Community and the bloc of developing countries to the weakening of this fragile system; and (iii) to reveal that their contribution to international economic disorder reflects a shared value - a belief that discrimination is a beneficial element in international trade policy.

It is true that the belief in discrimination takes different forms and serves different ends for the two groups. Such differences between them are important, but not as important as what they have in common. Furthermore, the views and practices of these two groups have over time influenced others. In particular, the United States appears to have moved decisively away from its rhetoric in favour of non-discrimination, although, it must be admitted, the practice of discrimination had entered into the policy of the United States, albeit hesitantly, already in the 1950s.

The discussion below starts with a consideration of the economic, legal and political aspects of the liberal international economic order, focusing principally on trade, whereupon the strengths and weaknesses of the actual order established after World War II are examined. There follows a brief consideration of the principal thrust of the European Community's trade policy, focusing on three aspects of the desire to discriminate, namely, preferences as a tool of foreign policy, discriminatory protection as a way of slowing adjustment to uncomfortable change and, over all, discrimination as a sign of self-confessed economic weakness. The discussion then turns to a short review of the goals of developing countries, focusing on the implications of their whole-hearted allegiance to the notion that 'equal treatment of unequals is unjust'. Finally, the consequences of these various pressures for the international economic order are examined and, in particular, whether any means exists to slow what looks to be an unstoppable process of erosion. To anticipate the conclusion: it is difficult to see any way of sustaining the liberal international economic order against the forces now working against it. The dénouement will, however, certainly not be the New International Economic Order espoused so long by the developing countries. It will just be international economic disorder.

2. PRINCIPLES OF THE LIBERAL INTERNATIONAL ECONOMIC ORDER

2.1 Fundamental norms

The international trading system that was established after the end of World War II was based on a liberal conception of the relation between the state and the economy, on the one hand, and among the various participating states, on the other hand. The underlying assumption - principally, that of the representatives of the United States - was that the market - the sphere of autonomous individual action - needed to be protected from the state and in this way states would be protected from one another. In short, the aim was to end the laissez faire for individual governments which had been the main characteristic of the inter-war period and replace it with a system of internationally-agreed rules, at whose heart were certain fundamental norms. Those norms were (i) the use of a transparent and market-conforming instrument of protection, the tariff, (ii) the 'binding' of protection, (iii) the exchange of tariff concessions on a reciprocal basis, and (iv) their generalization to trade among all contracting parties by means of the principle of unconditional non-discrimination.

In considering the rationale for the liberal international trading system below, two specific questions will be considered. What are the underlying values that justify the whole endeavour and what is the economic rationale for the norms of the international trading system?

2.2 Underlying values

The rationale for the system is liberal in two respects. First, there is the assumption that economic activity would and should be organized by spontaneous, competitive action. Secondly, there is an attempt to remove international economic relations from politics, the view being that discretionary political interference, especially discrimination among suppliers, can only lead to damaging international conflicts and, what is more, these conflicts are virtually always over policies which are impoverishing to all parties. In short, the effort was made to take trade policy from the weaponry of the sovereign nation state.

The attempt may look naive, but the naiveté is understandable, especially given the experience of unbridled nationalism in two great wars and the years in between. The idealism turned out to be somewhat less naive in retrospect than at the time. The onset of the Cold War ensured that universal participation would not occur. The failure to ratify the International Trade Organization also materially reduced the interest of the relatively few independent developing countries in what became the General Agreement on Tariffs and Trade. Consequently, the institutions of the trading system were, at least initially, almost entirely in the hands of the developed democracies. It seems no less than elementary common sense for countries sharing common values and participating in a common system of defensive alliances to attempt to regulate their affairs so as to minimize conflict over economic policies, especially over policies which are usually damaging to the practitioners themselves. On what other basis should allies, which are also liberal democracies, wish to organize their mutual economic relations?

2.3 **Economic aspects**

What justifies the underlying rules of the liberal international order from the economic point of view? Over the past decade or so the implications of the system were spelled out in the work of the late Jan Tumlir, formerly Director of Research at the GATT, who also endeavoured to place the trade or 'real' side of the international rules alongside the rules established for monetary policies. His thumbnail sketch is as follows:

> In the period since World War II, national economic policies were made compatible, both internally and between countries, by the adherence of governments to international rules articulated in Bretton Woods, Havana and Geneva. On the monetary side these rules ensured relative stability of national price levels, and thus also of exchange rates, and on the trade side they secured stable and non-discriminatory access of all exporters to at least the large markets of the developed countries. (2)

What would be achieved by the adherence of major countries to the fundamental norms of the international trading system? The answer is stability in change. The price mechanisms of each participating economy would be tied together in a global system, so facilitating (i) coordination of economic activity throughout the global economy, (ii) signalling of changing opportunities and (iii) autonomous adjustment by private decision-makers, wherever located, to those changes. (3)

From the perspective of orthodox neo-classical economics it is not easy to understand the wisdom of the norms of the liberal international trading system. The problem for economists arises at two levels. First, there is nothing in those norms to ensure that trade policy will be 'optimal' as conventionally understood. In other words, there is nothing to ensure free trade or even impose control on the structure of protection. (4) Secondly, in the presence of other unremedied distortions in national economies, even an agreement on free trade would not necessarily be optimal. The general theory of the second best would, therefore, tell the analyst that there is no a priori reason why a willingness to adhere to these norms would lead to an improvement in welfare over what would obtain in a world where they are ignored.

Insistence on the presence of all the conditions for an optimum is solely destructive. The conclusion must be that economics does not allow one to advance any general propositions about what policies lead to an improvement in economic welfare, since conditions in the actual world are so enormously far from the desiderata of perfect competition, perfect foresight, absence of externalities and complete markets. Subject to such requirements economics becomes entirely sterile.

A more relevant vision of economic life is usually referred to as 'neo-Austrian'. For present purposes the distinction between neo-classical and neo-Austrian perspectives is simply stated: the neo-classical view would be that there is a clear case for the unhindered market only if the optimal conditions hold; the neo-Austrian view would be that there is a clear case for the market because they cannot conceivably hold. Indeed, if they did hold, one might just as well not have the market since it would then not be particularly difficult to plan the economy. The market, in other words, is simply the best 'second best' institution for economic progress, especially given the ineradicable failures of government.

Two important ideas in the neo-Austrian tradition have been developed in the work of Joseph Schumpeter and Friedrich von Hayek. The first of these is 'creative destruction'. The economy, Schumpeter argued, is characterized by a ceaseless flow of interrelated but largely unpredictable changes born out of the pursuit of new opportunities and the need to adjust to their exploitation.(5) The second, due to Hayek, is the way the market leads to the development and use of widely dispersed information. The coordination of economic activity is achieved through the market in a way that is parsimonious in the need to centralize the most costly of all resources, relevant and up-to-date information.(6)

The appropriateness of this way of looking at the problem of economic rationality to the norms of the liberal international trading system is evident. If the world economy is to function at all, the most important information - information about relevant changes - must be disseminated and adjustment to those changes occur. With a system of bound tariffs there is, indeed, a 'deadweight efficiency loss'. Nevertheless, information about economic change is distributed throughout all the linked economies and the normal reactions of profit-seeking firms ensure coordination of supplies. Furthermore, in the absence of particularly perverse distortions in national economies, adjustment can also be expected to occur in each economy in the direction required by economic developments elsewhere.

Contrast the situation with pervasive quantitative restrictions. Quantitative restrictions fragment the market. Under binding quantitative restrictions potentially tradeable commodities in the protected economy behave like non-traded goods and their prices are likely to tell one nothing whatever about developments in the global economy. The likelihood is that the structure of an economy protected by quantitative restrictions will, over time, deviate ever further from that required to exploit the international division of labour in an efficient manner. Deadweight losses will tend to grow. The fully tradeable sector of each economy will tend to shrink in relation to the whole and adjustment to external change will, correspondingly, fall on a smaller proportion of total activity and so become increasingly difficult, leading to still more quantitative restrictions. Yet it is inconceivable for any national economy that efficient development can occur without taking advantage of opportunities to trade. At the limit, if quantitative restrictions become sufficiently pervasive it would be necessary to agree to a global plan for trade à la Comecon. (7) To state the possibility is to indicate its absurdity. The difference between a policy based on bound tariffs (or stable levels of subsidisation for that matter) and one of quantitative restrictions (or variable levies, which have an equivalent effect) is that bound tariffs, although undoubtedly distorting, <u>stabilize</u> the conditions for the global market process, while quantitative restrictions fragment the market and so <u>terminate</u> the process.

One aspect of such a liberal international trading system needs to be noted. It is particularly valuable to small, economically dynamic countries. It is valuable to small countries because they are likely to be dependent on trade, while incapable of securing satisfactory access for the goods and products of their citizens on the basis of political self-help alone. It is valuable to dynamic countries because it is they who most need the automatic accommodation to their growing exports that would result from the pursuit of profit by buyers and sellers in the market. What is new is almost always viewed as disruptive. If change has to be negotiated between gainers and losers, political forces usually ensure that it will be slowed. It is for this reason that, as 'managed trade' has come to the fore, it has been seen as a way of preserving traditional patterns both of trade and international relations, while curbing the impact of 'disruptive' new-comers. That, in a nutshell, is what makes the idea of 'selective safeguards' so seductive.

This, then, is the economic rationale for the use of bound tariffs which, in addition, automatically ensure that protection is transparent. Consequently, these policies guarantee the existence of a global market. Free trade would almost certainly be better and lower tariffs would be better than higher ones. Nevertheless, the basic norms of the liberal trading system serve the essential function of ensuring the existence of a global market. Since 'optimal' markets have never existed, while actual market economies, with all their imperfections, have generated most of the economic development there has ever been, it seems reasonable to assert - inductively - that the existence of global markets is itself of great value, even if they are not optimal.

3. ON THE BINDING OF LEVIATHAN IN THE LIBERAL TRADING SYSTEM

3.1 Nature of the constraints

The principal economic function of the norms of the international trading system is to ensure the existence of an international market economy. The objective is a modest one because of the limited restraints over sovereign discretion that can be agreed among a large number of countries. One may define an efficient international agreement as one that embodies the minimum conditions for the existence of an international market economy, but permit discretion to sovereign governments beyond the requirements of that minimum.

The executive agreement on trade policy that emerged after World War II can be seen as the natural result of conditions at the time. In view of the strong political forces for maintenance of protection in all countries, there was no possibility of making a commitment to principles of liberal trade binding in each country's domestic law. Similarly, there was no possibility of agreeing to a common international legal process like that subsequently created in the European Community. The failure to ratify the ITO may be taken as demonstrating that any radical curtailment of sovereignty was then infeasible. Indeed, a common legal process has proved difficult enough to maintain in the vastly more homogeneous area of Western Europe from which the European Community emerged. There were really only two alternatives: either an international agreement among the executive branches of government, to be interpreted diplomatically for the most part, or pure unilateralism. While attractive to academic economists, the experience of the 1930s and the need to gain some liberalisation fairly quickly made the unilateral approach rather unattractive. (8)

3.2 Enforcement of the constraints

An international trading order is a collective good in two senses. First, countries that do not contribute cannot be excluded from at least some of the benefits and, secondly, provision of a full measure of the good requires a cooperative effort among several governments. Theory suggests that provision of a public good will be inadequate, unless there is coercion or, as Mancur Olson of the

University of Maryland has put it, 'selective incentives'. (9)

There is one situation in which international trading order would be supplied both voluntarily and adequately. If a sufficiently large number of countries were to act on a view that free trade is <u>unilaterally</u> optimal, provision of the collective good would create no problem because the providers would not see it as imposing a cost on themselves. In the close to ninety years after the repeal of the Corn Laws there was little difficulty in this regard with respect to the United Kingdom. But this was not true elsewhere and the United Kingdom could hardly create an open international economy on its own. What happened in the nineteenth century, therefore, was international bargaining on the basis of reciprocity.

Belief in the virtues of unilateral liberalism has never been widespread. It certainly was not in the aftermath of World War II. It appears that a government will act consistently on the basis of a belief in unilateral liberalism only if it consists of Platonic Guardians (as in contemporary Hong Kong or Singapore), or if the interests of exporters are exceptionally effective (as in nineteenth century Britain) and understanding of the underlying economics is widely spread, or if there is at least a strong commitment to the provision of a stable structure of liberally-defined property rights. Failing these somewhat exceptional situations, the only practicable means of liberalization has been international bargaining on the basis of reciprocity. The essence of the post-War trading system, therefore, was the attempt both to achieve a policy limited to the use of the tariff and to liberalize and stabilize those tariffs by exploiting the mercantilism of its participants as revealed in the demand for reciprocity.

Reciprocity alone does not make for an international trading order. Since small countries have little power to retaliate, there is a danger of discrimination in which large powers only permit liberal international exchange where one another's citizens are concerned. There is also a danger of purely unilateral determinations of reciprocal fairness, with resulting bitter disputes.

Non-discrimination is, accordingly, central to a system whose principal technique of liberalisation is reciprocity and whose principal sanction is retaliation. In an essentially mercantilist system it is non-discrimination that creates a global order. (10) The essential points can be stated quite simply. By virtue of non-discrimination purely bilateral bargains become available to all participants, even those with little effective capacity to negotiate. Furthermore, the commitment to non-discrimination puts the retaliatory power of the strong behind the complaints of weak. Non-discrimination, in other words, creates a system of collective security out of what would otherwise depend on the power of individual states. It disciplines mercantilism.

3.3 Fragility of the constraints

It is impossible to avoid admiration for those who have thus created an international trading system out of mercantilism (as had largely been the case in the nineteenth century as well). The system was parsimonious in its fundamental principles and, so long as non-discrimination continued to operate, could be reasonably effective. But the success resulted from a Faustian bargain. Liberalization was achieved at the price of constantly re-emphasizing an erroneous, essentially pre-economic, view of international trade.

The most obvious problem created by the dependence on retaliation is simply that it is unreliable. That retaliation is costly to the free trader is obvious, but it is costly even for a mercantilist, especially if it is non-discriminatory. There is the danger of cycles of retaliation and there are risks to the whole pattern of international relations. In consequence, retaliation will never be predictable, just as was found of the collective security systems so popular in the inter-war years. Often the policies of small countries will be ignored because they do not matter very much, while there will be unwillingness to incur the wrath of a major power. Ultimately, therefore, retaliation is far from an effective sanction and, as a result, the survival of the open international trading system will depend in large measure on voluntary provision by countries addicted to mercantilist ideas that tell them that such provision is against their own individual interests. Consequently, international economic order will in the end tend to be under-provided.

The problem with the mercantilist basis of the system goes deeper even than that it provides a somewhat ineffective sanction. It is internally inconsistent. The entire edifice is to be supported by strict adherence to non-discrimination, but the mercantilism inherent in the system discourages adherence to that principle. Why, countries ask, should they retaliate against one another over discriminatory policies not aimed at their own exports? Are they not, indeed, likely to benefit from such policies? Why should the benefits of non-discriminatory access be afforded to countries that do not 'play the game'? Again, why should there be liberalization when the markets on offer in return are negligible, but also why retaliate against protection of insignificant markets? It is not difficult to see that mercantilism is unlikely to prove consistent with a commitment to non-discriminatory and generally liberal policies in a world of many countries with very divergent characteristics.

The problem is insoluble, at least within the context of an executive agreement of the kind in effect since World War II. Awareness of the grim results of undisciplined protection in the past - especially in the 1930s - has helped to encourage adherence to the basic norms but such a memory is a depreciating asset. The existence of a hegemonic power can also bolster the system if it recognizes that its defection from the rules is against its own unilateral interest, being likely to lead to a general collapse, as indeed happened in the 1930s after passage of the Smoot-Hawley tariff in the United States. But these are merely palliatives.

The problem remains that the economy is global but government is not. Under mercantilism, however, individual national governments do not normally see it as in their interest to follow policies conducive to global order. The system rests on a fertile error, mercantilism, disciplined by a general principle, non-discrimination, but the former actually undermines the force of the latter. Constant harping on mercantilist concepts not only weakens adherence to the ideas of unilateral liberalism but casts doubt on the wisdom of non-discrimination. Without mercantilism there would be no retaliation and so no discipline, but with it there is likely to be discriminatory retaliation and protection. The edifice is built on sand.

3.4 Successes and failures of the post-war trading system

Given the difficulties involved, the establishment of the liberal international trading system after World War II was more successful than might reasonably have been expected. Nevertheless, the ideal and the reality inevitably diverged. In particular, it would be wrong to assert (i) that a substantial number of the individuals and governments involved had a clear conception of the international economic order adumbrated above; or (ii) that there was any one country in which such a group was entirely dominant; or (iii) that the concept was put into effect in a fully satisfactory way.

On the contrary, it is clear that the participants, both individuals and governments, had very distinct objectives and purposes. There were, inter alia, clear differences on the relative weight to be placed on legal norms and rules as against liberalization of trade barriers per se, conflicts over the significance of the norm of non-discrimination and doubts about the wisdom of subordinating domestic policies to international constraints. Equally, it proved impossible to establish the agreement on commercial policy in any strong form, in at least two senses: first, the texts - not only of the draft charter of the ITO but even of the more narrowly circumscribed GATT - are full of inconsistencies, loopholes and escape clauses and, secondly, it proved impossible to achieve either ratification of the ITO or - subsequently - full application of the GATT. Furthermore, not only was much of the progress towards liberalization achieved in the context of the clearly discriminatory programmes of the Organization for European Economic Cooperation but, more fundamentally, the liberal international trading order described above was never fully achieved, even for trade in goods. Most notably, agriculture was never liberalized and neither discrimination nor quantitative restrictions ever disappeared entirely. (11)

None of this is a decisive objection to our discussion both of the concept of the liberal international trading order and even of a falling away from its partial achievement. First, the liberal order was the only coherent concept on offer. Secondly, the underlying ideas were reasonably clearly understood by a number of the key actors from the United States, especially in the State Department, and that alone counts for a great deal. (12) Finally, the first decade or so was clearly one of rapid movement in the direction of liberal and non-discriminatory trade - at least among the major developed countries - and the fifteen or so years thereafter were ones in which the summary description given above of how policy was to be conducted is, at the least, not a caricature. Indeed, one may well hold that the actual achievement of the GATT system far exceeded what might reasonably have been expected, given the rejection of the ITO by the Congress of the United States and the continued resistance to many of its underlying ideas in so many countries. It is the exchange rate system agreed at Bretton Woods and not the trade order that has been indubitably consigned to the dustbin of history.

Nevertheless, after substantial initial successes, the system has been cumulating difficulties and those difficulties reflect both the underlying sources of fragility already discussed and the particular form in which the agreement was reached, what Richard Gardner, the American author of a standard work on post-war economic reconstruction, has castigated as 'legalism', the danger of 'exalting agreement in form over agreement in substance'. (13)

One aspect of the problem has been the difficulty in securing and maintaining adherence to the principle of non-discrimination. Without non-discrimination, however, there is little to discipline the operation of the mercantilist instincts of large powers against smaller ones.

The second major problem may be seen as that of 'contingent' or 'administered' protection. (14) It is the problem of securing the desired stability in trade policy. In order to reach agreement it was necessary to permit action to increase protection or violate other norms in certain conditions. The attempt was made to control such actions, but they had to be allowed. There were clauses permitting protection for balance of payments reasons (Article XII), infant industry protection (Article XVIII), emergency protection (Article XIX), quantitative restrictions against imports of agricultural products (Article XI), protection against dumped or subsidized goods (Article VI), discrimination against particular, generally new, contracting parties (Article XXXV) and finally discrimination in the case of customs unions and free trade areas (Article XXIV). Furthermore, there were many important areas of trade policy never adequately covered - agriculture, in particular - and new policies that evolved to escape the internationally-agreed disciplines, especially voluntary export restraints.

A system intended to stabilize conditions of trade by binding and lowering the tariff has bound only the tariff but has failed to stabilize conditions of trade. The various loopholes and escape clauses have operated in the context of an unwillingness to adjust to changes originating abroad and are associated with a rejection of the notion of comparative advantage in favour of the mercantilist intellectual framework of the GATT. To take one apparently paradoxical example, the American countervail against the adjustment-resisting subsidies of others has itself protectionist force, especially as cases can be resolved on the basis of voluntary export restraints. (15) In short, within a generally mercantilist intellectual framework undisciplined by strict adherence to the principle of non-discrimination, it has proved difficult to stabilize protection. In this fundamental sense the underlying rationale of the system has failed, it being more appropriate to refer to an international trading non-system, a patchwork of ad hoc arrangements.

It is in the light of these general considerations that the ways in which the European Community and developing countries have contributed to international trading disorder can be assessed.

4. DISCRIMINATION AND THE EUROPEAN COMMUNITY (16)

4.1 Some common threads

There appear to be certain underlying threads in the adherence of the European Community to discrimination which can be followed back to the inter-war period, most notably in the policies of France and the United Kingdom. Those threads are, first, an unwillingness to liberalize on an unconditional most favoured nation (MFN) basis when confronted with an apparently irresistible competitor, itself deemed highly protectionist. During the inter-war period and the first ten years or so after World War II that competitor was the United States. Since then it has been Japan and, still later, the Asian newly industrializing countries (NICs). The second thread, closely related to the first, is the fear of general uncompetitiveness that emerges as a desire for a chasse guardée where exports can be sold on favourable terms. In the case of the United Kingdom, for example, the final descent into protection in the 1930s went along with the creation of Imperial Preference, a major obstacle to American plans for non-discriminatory trade immediately after World War II. France, too, put considerable efforts into preferential trade with its colonies and dependencies. The third and again related thread is the desire to use commercial policy as a way of securing foreign policy goals, a direction followed with enthusiasm by France after World War I and again after World War II (both on its own and, later, through the European Community), by the United Kingdom from the 1930s and - during the 1930s - most notably by Germany and Japan. (17) Last but not least, there is an objective again related to the others: the desire to manage the politically difficult process of economic change by blaming one, or maybe a few, irresistibly and - if it can be plausibly alleged - 'unfairly' competitive countries, against whom discriminatory protection can then readily be justified.

It is evident that through these different motivations runs a fear of competition and economic change, justified by a primitive mercantilism.

4.2 **Preferences as imperialism**

As mentioned, the United Kingdom and France have been the important protagonists of systems of preferential trade for former colonies and dependencies. The aim has been to preserve a particular political tie after independence and promote the development of countries for which these developed countries feel responsible. The present day fruit is the Lomé Convention with fifty-nine African, Caribbean and Pacific countries. (18) At the same time, the Community offers less favourable preferences to developing countries as a group under the Generalized System of Preferences (GSP).

Then the Community as a whole has been concerned to minimize the effect of its formation and enlargement on a number of countries in the Mediterranean with a history of close economic relations to parts of Western Europe. The consequence has been the so-called Global Mediterranean Policy, which is itself the sum of independent association agreements with twelve countries bordering on the Mediterranean (Algeria, Morocco and Tunisia - the Maghreb countries; Egypt, Jordan, Lebanon and Syria - the Mashreq countries; and Israel, Yugoslavia, Turkey, Malta and Cyprus. (19)

Finally (or rather first of all), the Community is part of a free trade area in manufactures which embraces the European Free Trade Association. Accordingly, the European Community is not only itself a discriminatory trading arrangement, if looked at as a collection of separate countries, but is embedded in concentric circles of discrimination. In consequence, the MFN tariff agreed in multilateral trade negotiations under the GATT applies to just seven countries (Australia, Canada, Japan, New Zealand, South Africa, Taiwan and the United States - in effect, the English-speaking developed countries (less the United Kingdom) - plus Japan and Taiwan). (20)

The European Community's MFN tariff applies then to seven countries, but closer investigation reveals that two of them are Japan and Taiwan, with both of which a host of discriminatory export restraints are in effect. The MFN tariff is also of little relevance to Australia, New Zealand and Canada, with their strong comparative advantages in agricultural exports that face prohibitive barriers and mineral exports that face none. What is the bound MFN tariff? It is largely the tariff applicable to the United States. As such the United States faces a higher tariff than many of its competitors, but it is not, in general, subject to quantitative restrictions. In short, the European Community's trade policies may often be negotiated in the GATT, but have little to do with its fundamental norms.

There is no doubt that preferences are the principal instrument of foreign policy for the European Community. They may even be the logical instrument for an economic giant, lacking confidence in itself and, at the same time, having little political power. It is inevitable, however that any change in the preferential status accorded one country - enlargement of the Community, for example - alters the position of everyone else in the hierarchy. Accordingly, the Community finds itself desperately improvising in an attempt to avoid upsetting those whose benefits in the preferential hierarchy turn out to be different from those anticipated.

It is difficult to see any sense in the use of trade policy as an instrument of foreign policy, except for the pleasure that may be given to policy-makers by the ability to manage relations of economic dependency. It is inevitable that a policy based on discrimination will itself upset many countries and that changes in the hierarchy of discrimination will further upset them. (Note that the group of countries facing the MFN tariff includes all the European Community's principal allies, but it is against them that much of the discrimination works.) It is questionable, at least, whether the happiness of those preferred offsets the irritation of those who are not, especially since margins of preference are inevitably unstable. Almost every country outside Western Europe has a reason to feel discriminated against in relation to some competitor. Furthermore, trade policy is not only an instrument which is bound to make someone feel victimized by every favour, but it is also an extremely inflexible instrument. No preference is worth having unless it is stable. If the Community wishes, therefore, to provide something worth having it must inevitably lose its future freedom of action in foreign policy.

For the preferred the policy is something of a poisoned chalice. Their privileged access to the markets of the European Community depends on ex gratia favours which can be - and, indeed, frequently have been - reversed. The required stability of international market access is irremediably lost. This is the inevitable effect of such a policy, given the underlying logic of the liberal international trading system, whose aim was to remove the sorts of manipulation for reasons of foreign policy now indulged in by the European Community.

4.3 Discrimination and resistance to adjustment

The European Community follows policies of preferential liberalisation and discriminatory protection. Of the two the latter is the more significant because of the damage that can be done thereby to the basic structure of a liberal trading system. Among the most important discriminatory instruments of protection is the so-called 'voluntary' export restraint (VER). In this case, what happens is that the automatic accommodation to change inherent in the bound tariff is withdrawn but, in compensation, the importing country gives to the exporter the implicit quota rent as a bribe to form an export cartel against its own citizens. Such a policy for dealing with difficult adjustment problems may preserve the semblance of past agreements to liberalize tariffs within the framework of the GATT, but seriously undermines their significance.

While apparently originating in the United States, the voluntary export restraint became an important element in the policy of the European Community and its members for sectors (other than agriculture) faced with severe pressures to adjust, including textiles and clothing (under the multi-fibre arrangement (MFA)), footwear, steel, automobiles and commercial vehicles, and consumer electronics. (21)

Why discrimination? One needs to understand the way internal and external pressures interact. Reassignment of income among producer groups, while attractive both to those doing the reassigning and to the beneficiaries suffers from one great defect. (22) If visible, it tends to create resistance. In other words, constitutionally-disciplined, open reassignment is limited by what can be passed through a parliament. There is little doubt, to give just one example, that the European Community's Common Agricultural Policy would collapse if all the implicit transfers had to be voted explicitly. The solution to the problem is evident, to employ trade policy, so making the taxation covert - and the more covert the better.

The use of trade policy for this end is made more necessary by the strong resistance within the European Community to the obvious alternative, direct subsidization of producers. Subsidies come from national exchequers, since that is where the revenue is collected. Competitive firms, especially if they have relatively ungenerous governments, then feel at a disadvantage within European Community markets. The solution is to combine subsidization with protection, which benefits all firms and, at the same time, reduces the need for such relatively visible means of support as subsidies.

It is at this point that external factors become important. There is one element of the post-war design which has remained current in Western Europe and also, though perhaps to a diminishing extent, in the United States, and that is the emphasis on cooperative solutions and, in particular, on minimizing external conflict. It is in this light that the European Community (or its members) tries to introduce its protectionist arrangements (except perhaps for agriculture). Other things being equal, the Community tries to avoid disrupting existing patterns of trade and undermining relationships with particularly important countries, especially the United States. The Community also wishes to avoid either overt violation of GATT or the complex and often bitter process of negotiation involved in compensating many suppliers for a change in a bound tariff. Where unauthorized action by individual member countries is concerned covert action is necessary, in any case, because they are not supposed to take trade policy actions on their own account. Finally, where disruption is occurring because of the emergence of new competition it is sometimes considered desirable to minimize conflict even with that supplier.

What is needed then is a discriminatory form of restriction that avoids these difficulties. There appear to have been two solutions. The most popular has been the VER, which is invisible, can be targeted and provides compensation to the exporters under restraint. Because it is increasingly recognized, however, that VERs are costly to the Community, use of the tariff seems to be becoming more common, but only where the concern is about exports from one or at most very few suppliers and especially where the supplier in question is the one that the Community does not wish to help at all, Japan. Important cases of such use of tariffs are those on Compact Disc Players and Video-Cassette Recorders.

The tariff is the more desirable policy, but it is only under special circumstances that a tariff can be narrowly targeted. In important sectors like textile and clothing, and steel and also where no European Community policy is agreed - as for motor vehicles - the Community (or its members), following an earlier lead of the United States, finds itself turning the logic of the liberal international trading system on its head. Instead of non-discrimination and automatic accommodation, there is discrimination and resistance to the process of adjustment; instead of the tariff, an instrument of protection that is compatible with the market, there are quantitative restraints; instead of visible policies, there is covert assistance; and instead of stability and predictability in protection, there is constant change in protective margins and a wide net of potential restraints.

5. AFFIRMATIVE ACTION AND THE DEVELOPING COUNTRIES (23)

5.1 'Equal treatment of unequals is unjust'

The developing countries also want an end to the notion of non-discrimination, under the principle of affirmative action that 'equal treatment of unequals is unjust'. They have proposed two kinds of change: relaxation of discipline imposed upon them, in order to pursue autonomous policies of protection, and preferences in their favour, in order to help their infant exports.

The underlying logic of the position of developing countries derives from hostility to the liberal, market-based principles of the international order itself. Such policies were associated in the minds of the new elites with the values of imperialism. Independence carried with it the need for an ideology at once modern and resistant to Western liberalism. That ideology consisted of an amalgam of nationalism and socialism (both Western ideologies).(24) At the same time, newly-independent developing countries argued that the developed world owed them help to make up for centuries of exploitation. The developed countries were willing to cede these claims, so long as granting them did not impose any significant domestic political cost.

In one fundamental respect the addiction of developing countries to the idea of 'special and differential' treatment derives from the same roots as the European Community's preference for preferences. They share the phobia that comparative advantage does not work among unequals. Developing countries, too, fear irresistible competition for their industries, in their case advancing a 'pauper capital' argument for the right to protection and the need for preferential market access. The tragedy is that policies motivated by these fears tend to prove a self-fulfilling prophecy. The historic irony is that it was in the 1960s, when the performance of a few outward-looking developing countries was showing the bankruptcy of these ideas and the failures of most of the rest were demonstrating the dangers involved in their pursuit, that the developing countries succeeded in making them a part of the legal structure of the international trading system.

5.2 'Help' and international discipline

For the mercantilist liberalism is costly, but in return one gains the benefit of the liberalism of others. Developing countries asked for favours in just these terms and developed countries were perfectly happy to oblige in one respect, that is to waive the demand for liberalism in developing countries. Indeed, as Robert Hudec of the University of Minnesota has pointed out, it was always politically easiest for the developed countries to 'help' by removing constraints on the developing countries. (25)

Over time the arrangement has evolved in rather peculiar ways. Because of the imperative of universal membership developed countries have welcomed the participation of developing countries in an international arrangement whose fundamental values those countries deny and whose disciplines they reject. Ostensibly, therefore, the benefit of non-discriminatory access to the markets of developed countries should be available to the developing countries, without any constraint whatsoever on the policies they adopt.

This is not what has actually happened. Developing countries are contracting parties of the GATT, but do not contract, and developed countries offer 'help' to developing countries which does not help. They give the appearance but not the reality of concessions to the demands of developing countries, that is, preferences where developing countries are not competitive offset by discriminatory protection where they are. Both developed and developing countries agree that the norms of the GATT should not apply to trade between them, though in opposite senses.

5.3 **Preferences** (26)

The desire to be free of GATT discipline may be described as the demand to be able to damage oneself. The demand for preferences, however, is a demand for a real benefit. Unfortunately, it is not presented and, because of the nature of the GATT, really cannot be presented as a mutual benefit. Developed and developing countries agree that preferences are a transfer owed by the former to the latter. In other words, preferences are a form of aid and, to the extent that their benefits depend on trade diversion, so reflecting the element of preference, they are, indeed, a form of aid. It is not surprising, therefore, that developed countries approach preferences in terms of a rational protectionist's intellectual framework. They minimize the domestic political and - from the mercantilist point of view - economic cost by ensuring that preferences become tariff-quotas, often combined with quantitative restrictions (especially in textiles and clothing) whenever the developing countries appear unduly successful. On this basis there is every reason to doubt whether preferences offer any significant economic benefit to developing countries.

5.4 **From contract to status**

The initial idea was that of contract. Each country pledged to bind itself by adherence to certain common norms, rules and procedures judged of value to each and to all. In return, citizens of each member would receive the benefit of non-discriminatory access to the markets of all the others. It may be noted, in passing, that there was an element of conditionality in the non-discrimination. One had to be a

Contracting Party to avail oneself of that basic benefit.

The desire to make GATT universal, not just a 'rich man's club', combined with the demands of the developing countries, has changed the logic of the system. It is now a good exemplar of the modern tendency to a sort of feudalism in reverse. In a feudal legal system status varies across well-defined social classes. Under traditional feudalism the law tends to become more favourable the richer and more powerful the class concerned. Reverse feudalism gives the special exemptions to the disadvantaged. Some issues are the same in both, however, above all how to define and adjust status.

Within the GATT status is self-defined. Almost anyone can be privileged. But this creates a difficult problem for those at the top of the hierarchy. The logic of the GATT is that discipline is costly. It follows, therefore, that the advanced developing countries are seen as 'free riders'. As the earlier discussion of the fragility of the system has suggested, however, voluntary provision of a public good is unlikely to survive resentment about a host of successful 'free riders'. It is for this reason that the problem known as 'graduation' cannot be avoided within the GATT system.

6. DEAD END?

The post-war effort to recreate a liberal international trading system on the basis of mercantilist ideas and multilateral institutions turned out to be a remarkable success. Its stability did, however, demand adherence to non-discrimination, the importance of which is shown by the way discriminatory systems of trade policy have tended to endure and proliferate. With their growth the right to produce and sell becomes a privilege granted after negotiation among governments on the basis of power and political convenience. The role of developing countries and the European Community has been particularly important. They do not resort to discrimination as a necessity but either proclaim it as a good or even demand it as a right. The destruction of the legitimacy of non-discrimination as a guiding principle of the international trading system may, therefore, be seen as the main achievement of the 'unholy alliance' of the developing countries and the European Community. Can it be supposed that any enduring and workable structure for world trade will be constructed on the foundation of that quintessentially seventeenth and eighteenth century combination - mercantilism plus discrimination?

Notes and references

1.   The author would like to acknowledge the helpful comments of Dr Richard Blackhurst of the GATT Secretariat, Professor Robert E. Hudec of the University of Minnesota, and Mr Philip Hayes of the Trade Policy Research Centre. The paper was originally presented at a workshop on 'European Trade Policies and the South' that was held in The Hague on 13-14 September 1985 and was sponsored by the Netherlands Minister for Development Cooperation and the World Bank. The author is grateful for the comments of those present at the workshop. The views expressed are those of the author and do not necessarily reflect those of the Staff or Council of the Trade Policy Research Centre.

2.   See Jan Tumlir, 'International Economic Order: Can the Trend be Reversed?', The World Economy, March 1982, pp.33-34. See also Tumlir, Protectionism: Trade Policy in Democratic Societies, AEI Studies, No. 436 (Washington: American Enterprise Institute, 1985). The author would like to take this opportunity to record his intellectual debt to Dr Tumlir and the loss suffered as a result of his untimely death by all those attempting to understand, explain and defend the liberal international economic order. An earlier work of great importance is Lionel Robbins, Economic Planning and International Order (London: Macmillan, 1937). See, in particular, ch. 9 on 'International Liberalism'.

3.   See Tumlir, 'Can the International Economic Order be Saved?', The World Economy, October 1977, p. 4. See also two important studies co-authored by Dr Tumlir for the GATT Secretariat: Richard Blackhurst, Nicolas Marian and Tumlir, Trade Liberalization, Protectionism and Interdependence, GATT Studies in International Trade No. 5 (Geneva: GATT Secretariat, 1977) and Blackhurst, Marian and Tumlir, Adjustment, Trade and Growth in Developed and Developing Countries, GATT Studies in International Trade No. 6 (Geneva: GATT Secretariat, 1978).

4.   On the optimal conditions for trade policy and their relation to domestic market distortions, see W.M. Corden, Trade Policy and Economic Welfare (Oxford: Clarendon Press, 1974).

5.   On   creative   destruction,   see   Joseph   A. Schumpeter, Capitalism, Socialism and Democracy, 5th edition (London: Unwin University Books, 1966) Part II, ch. VII.
6.   F.A. Hayek's classic article on the problem of knowledge is 'The Use of Knowledge in Society', American Economic Review, September 1945, pp. 519-30.
7.   See Robbins, op. cit., Parts II and III, for a lucid discussion   of   the   problem   of   partial   or   complete international planning.
8.   On the inter-war experience and the reasons for the emergence of an executive agreement after World War II, contrary to the intentions of important participants, see Tumlir, Protectionism: Trade Policy in Democratic Societies, op. cit., ch. 2.
It is important to recognize the widespread sentiment that   a   purely   unilateral   trade   policy   would   prove particularly undesirable in the United States, where such a policy would be decided in the legislature. Policy makers in the United States made the reciprocal approach, combined with non-discrimination, the centre-piece of their global trade policy. There were two main reasons. First, by making trade policy a matter of international negotiation the Administration could justify its request to Congress for authority to determine the shape of trade policy. Secondly, policy-makers in the United States believe, rightly, that an offer of access to the market of the United States would prove an effective means of bringing about trade liberalization worldwide.
9.   On 'selective incentives' to create a private interest in the provision of collective goods, see Mancur Olson, The Logic of Collective Action: Public Goods and the Theory of Groups (Cambridge, Massachusetts: Harvard University Press, 1977) p. 51.
10.   See International Trade 1983-84 (Geneva: GATT Secretariat, 1984) pp. 19-22. See also Gerard Curzon, Multilateral   Commercial   Diplomacy: the   General Agreement on Tariffs and Trade and its Impact on National Commercial Policies and Techniques (London: Michael Joseph, 1965) ch. 3 on 'the most favoured-nation clause'.
11.   The best account of the process of creating the international economic order after World War II is Richard N. Gardner, Sterling-Dollar Diplomacy: the Origins and Prospects of Our International Economic Order, 2nd edition (New York: McGraw-Hill, 1969). On the trade issue, see, in

particular, chs. 14 and 17. On the early development of the GATT, see Gerard Curzon, op. cit.
12.   See, for example, Cordell Hull, The Memoirs of Cordell Hull (London: Hodder and Stoughton, 1948).
13.   See Gardner, op. cit., p. xl.
14.   These terms have gained wide currency. See, for example, Rodney de C. Grey, 'A Note on US Trade Practices', in William R. Cline (ed.), Trade Policies in the 1980s (Washington: Institute for International Economics, 1983) ch. 8. See also J. Michael Finger, H. Keith Hall, and Douglas R. Nelson, 'The Political Economy of Administered Protection', American Economic Review, June 1982, pp. 452-66.
15.   That the countervailing duty provisions of American trade law are protectionist in effect is an important finding of Finger et al., loc. cit.
16.   The present discussion of the policies of the European Community is based in large measure on two previous papers by the author: Wolf, 'The European Community's Trade Policies', in Roy Jenkins (ed.), Britain and the EEC (London: Macmillan, 1983) ch. 9; and Wolf, 'Dividing the Sheep from the Goats: Protectionism, the European Community and the Third World', Irish Studies in International Affairs, Vol. 1, No. 1, 1984, pp. 63-78. Both these articles give extensive references to the literature.
17.   On the security objective and discrimination in the case of inter-war France, see Tumlir, Protectionism: Trade Policy in Democratic Societies, op. cit., pp. 22-25.
18.   On Lomé, see Wolf, 'Dividing the Sheep from the Goats', loc. cit., pp. 74-6. On the general subject of the European Community's Lomé Convention, see Christopher Stevens (ed.), EEC and the Third World: a survey 4 - Renegotiating Lomé (London: Hodder and Stoughton, for the Overseas Development Institute, London, and the Institute of Development Studies, University of Sussex, 1984) especially ch. 1. See also Philip Mishalani, Annette Robert, Christopher Stevens and Ann Weston, 'The Pyramid of Privilege', in Christopher Stevens (ed.), EEC and the Third World: a survey 1 (London: Hodder and Stoughton, for the Overseas Development Institute, London, and the Institute of Development Studies, University of Sussex, 1981) ch. 4.
19.   On the European Community's Global Mediterranean Policy, see Richard Pomfret, Mediterranean Policy of the European Community: Study of

Discriminatioan in Trade (London: Macmillan, for the Trade Policy Research Centre, 1986).

20. See ibid., p. 10.

21. See Wolf, 'The European Community's Trade Policy', loc. cit., pp. 164-70 for a brief description of some of these policies. On the general issue of this form of protection, see Brian Hindley and Eri Nicolaides, Taking the New Protectionism Seriously, Thames Essay No. 34 (London: Trade Policy Research Centre, 1983). On the MFA, see Donald B. Keesing and Wolf, Textile Quotas against Developing Countries, Thames Essay No. 23 (London, Trade Policy Research Centre, 1980). On the costs of voluntary export restraints for one member country of the European Community, the United Kingdom, see David Greenaway and Brian Hindley, What Britain Pays for Voluntary Export Restraints, Thames Essay No. 43 (London: Trade Policy Research Centre, 1985).

22. The distinction between redistribution of income among the citizenry at large via the mechanism of progressive taxation and the welfare state, on the one hand, and reassignment of income among organized interests, on the other hand, is made by Dan Usher in The Economic Prerequisite to Democracy (New York, Columbia Press, 1981) p. 29 as follows: 'A change in income is a redistribution if the gap between rich and poor is reduced but the ordering of incomes is preserved. A change is a reassignment if there is a reordering of people on the scale of rich and poor.' It is Professor Usher's principal point that a democratic state dedicated to reassignment of income will become like Hobbes' state of nature, characterized by bellum omnium contra omnes. Trade policy is a classic instrument of reassignment.

23. The argument in this section derives largely from Wolf, 'Two-Edged Sword: Demands of Developing Countries and the Trading System', in Jagdish N. Bhagwati and John Gerard Ruggie (eds), Power, Passions and Purpose: Prospects for North-South Negotiations (Cambridge, Massachusetts and London: MIT Press, 1984) and Robert E. Hudec, Participation of Developing Countries in the GATT Legal System (London: Trade Policy Research Centre, forthcoming).

24. The argument is made by Deepak Lal. See 'Nationalism, Socialism and Planning: Influential Ideas in the South', World Development, Vol. 13, No. 6, 1985, pp. 749-59.

25. See Hudec, op. cit.

26. For a careful evaluation of the American and European Community preference schemes, see Rolf J. Langhammer and André Sapir, Economic Impact of Tariff Preferences (London: Trade Policy Research Centre, forthcoming).

Chapter Three

THE EVOLVING PATTERN OF WORLD TRADE, EC TRADE POLICY AND EXPORTS FROM THE SOUTH

Jean Waelbroeck and Jacob Kol

1. INTRODUCTION

With the usual hesitations, the world has been moving to a new round of trade negotiations. There is nothing wrong in this caution. An unsuccessful attempt to get talks under way might however be worse for the future of world trade than the present somewhat uneasy truce. The key to successful negotiations is understanding by the parties of what they stand to gain from the negotiating process. For this purpose, a discussion of the basic evolution of the trade system may be useful.

Taking such a long view may be particularly useful with respect to North-South issues. Developing countries, which have been increasingly active in the GATT, will play a significant and perhaps fundamental role in the new trade talks, in continuation of a trend already apparent during the Kennedy Round. The basic evolution of thinking in the developing world, stressing the advantages of outward oriented strategies, will also lead them to play a larger role in these negotiations.

The paper will focus on North-South trading relations with the "Big Three" trading nations: the United States, Japan and the European Community. (1) The approach will be factual: what has been happening and why. A first section will review the overall evolution of the trade of these nations, covering both their trade with other developed countries and with the South. After a brief discussion of the extent to which the trade policy process in the Community is truly centralized, a third part of the paper will discuss the comparative advantages of developing countries and chances for their exports to the Community. The paper concentrates on trade in manufactures. Agricultural trade is covered in the paper by Wouter Tims in this volume, while data on trade in services is very poor. For manufactures two complementary data sets are used. The first comprises comparable data on production and trade of the main developed countries, and has been put together by the World Bank Group on Market Penetration for the years 1973-83. These data follow a classification based on the International Standard Industrial Classification (ISIC).

To attain more detail this set is complemented by United Nations data on trade according to the Standard International Trade Classification, covering the same period. This chapter is an abbreviated and modified version of a paper presented at the Workshop on "European Trade Policies and the South". The interested reader is referred to that paper and its update (Waelbroeck and Kol (1986)) for more detailed information.

2. THE TRADE STANCE OF THE 'BIG THREE' TRADING NATIONS

This chapter provides some background to the present position the 'Big Three' hold in production and trade of manufactures. In section 2.1 the developments in the market size of the 'Big Three' will be considered as well as their openness to imports. The EC, the USA and Japan are strikingly different regarding their geographical distribution of trade. This will be examined in section 2.2.

The main focus of this paper is on trade relations of the big three nations with the developing countries. These countries figure in section 2.3, which describes the various degrees of openness of the EC, USA and Japan towards manufactured exports from the South.

2.1 The EC, USA and Japan in trade and production of manufactures

Table 3.1 presents figures on production, trade and domestic consumption of manufactures by the big three trading nations. The data combine SITC trade figures with production figures according to the ISIC/IBRD classification, referred to in section 1. The benchmark year is 1983; more details, also for 1973, are found in Waelbroeck and Kol (1986).

With respect to <u>production</u>, it appears that the USA is the largest producer of manufactures. The lead over the EC is considerable. Japan is in third position (but decreased its distance to the EC considerably).

The figures for <u>exports and imports</u> of manufactures in Table 3.1 show a surplus for both the EC and Japan. Taken relative to total exports plus imports the surplus amounts to some 17 per cent for the EC. For Japan it is much larger: 50 per cent.

The EC is a large net exporter of metal products, though the surplus is no larger than Japan's. The chemical industry is the Community's other major net earner of foreign exchange. Net exports of steel (group 371) remain considerable. They have however ceased to have a rationale in terms of comparative advantage, and remain high only thanks to the extremely heavy subsidies which member country governments grant to Community producers and to the strict import restrictions which the European Commission administers. These exports are bound to dwindle. Will the EC allow itself to become one day a large net importer of steel, as the United States has done?

The USA had a large deficit in 1983. Even group 38, Metal products, showed a deficit then, being the only 2 digit item showing a surplus in 1973.

The European and Japanese surpluses would have been even larger if resource-intensive manufactures such as food and beverages (group 31) wood and wood products (33) and paper (34) would be excluded from the total. In 1983 the EC still is a net exporter of textiles (321), Japan preserves much of its trading strength, which it enjoyed at the time it was specialized in textile exports.

The figures for <u>domestic consumption</u> in Table 3.1 display almost the same pattern as the production data. That is, the USA is the largest consumer of manufactured goods, followed at an increasing distance by the EC, with Japan gaining rapidly on the latter. Compared with the production data, the figures on consumption reflect also of course the trade balance, discussed above.

Figures on <u>market penetration</u> are represented in the last column in Table 3.1. The market penetration rate is found by dividing total imports by domestic consumption; the figures are expressed in percentages.

Market penetration seen as an indicator for openness, the EC is clearly the most open of the three big trading

Table 3.1: Production, trade and market size of the EC, the USA and Japan for manufactures (in billions of US dollars) 1983

Product Group	EC					USA		
	P	M	E	C	MP(%)	P	M	E
31 Food Products (etc)	219.3	19.8	18.8	220.3	9.0	282.9	14.3	11.0
32 Textiles (etc)	76.6	19.1	16.5	79.2	24.1	116.7	18.6	3.6
321 Textile	41.3	7.0	8.4	39.8	17.5	65.1	3.3	2.4
322 Wearing Apparel	22.8	9.0	4.5	27.3	32.9	42.7	10.2	0.7
324 Footwear	7.7	1.6	2.0	7.3	21.7	5.0	3.7	0.2
33 Wood & Wood Prods.	34.5	6.8	1.7	39.6	17.3	53.5	6.4	1.4
34 Paper & Printing	69.8	10.2	4.5	75.5	13.5	172.4	6.7	5.5
35 Chemicals	282.7	33.3	47.3	268.7	12.4	426.5	29.4	25.1
353 Petroleum Refineries	97.6	14.8	8.2	104.2	14.2	175.2	14.1	4.2
354 Prods of Petr., Coal	7.8	1.0	2.1	6.7	14.6	9.7	0.4	0.9
356 Plastic Prods.	22.4	0.5	0.4	22.5	2.1	41.0	1.2	0.1
36 Non-Metallic Prods.	41.1	1.9	5.8	37.2	5.2	44.9	2.9	1.6
37 Basic Metal Prods.	97.5	14.5	19.3	92.8	15.6	98.6	15.6	4.0
371 Iron & Steel	71.5	5.2	13.4	63.2	8.2	54.9	7.9	1.6
372 Non-ferrous Metal	26.1	9.3	5.8	29.6	31.5	43.7	7.7	2.4
38 Metal Prods. & Mach.	414.8	65.9	121.2	359.5	18.3	723.1	91.0	84.1
382 Non-elec. Mach.	123.5	21.2	44.5	100.2	21.2	177.2	18.9	33.0
383 Elec. Machinery	79.5	13.2	17.0	75.7	17.5	143.7	17.9	14.0
384 Transport Equipment	135.9	19.6	40.6	114.9	17.1	246.9	43.6	24.6
39 Other Manufactures	10.6	5.9	7.1	9.5	62.7	21.5	5.9	2.0
3 All Manufactures	1247.0	177.5	242.1	1182.3	15.0	1940.1	190.8	138.4

Table 3.1 continued

Product Group	USA C	USA MP(%)	Japan P	Japan M	Japan E	Japan C	Japan MP(%)
31 Food Products (etc)	286.1	5.0	128.5	6.5	1.2	133.8	4.9
32 Textiles (etc)	131.7	14.2	49.4	3.7	6.4	46.7	8.0
321 Textile	66.0	5.0	33.0	1.8	5.4	29.4	6.0
322 Wearing Apparel	52.2	19.5	11.7	1.5	0.6	12.6	11.7
324 Footwear	8.5	43.3	2.1	0.2	0.0	2.3	9.9
33 Wood & Wood Prods.	58.5	11.0	36.0	1.2	0.2	37.0	3.2
34 Paper & Printing	173.5	3.8	54.1	1.6	1.1	54.6	3.0
35 Chemicals	430.8	6.8	194.3	10.3	11.2	193.5	5.3
353 Petroleum Refineries	185.1	7.6	61.7	2.8	0.2	64.3	4.3
354 Prods of Petr., Coal	9.3	4.8	8.2	0.3	0.6	7.9	3.9
356 Plastic Prods	42.1	2.8	30.1	0.1	0.2	30.1	0.3
36 Non-Metallic Prods.	46.2	6.3	37.0	0.4	2.2	35.2	1.3
37 Basic Metal Prods	110.2	14.2	68.4	5.8	14.7	59.4	9.7
371 Iron and Steel	61.2	12.9	54.1	1.4	13.1	42.4	3.3
372 Non-Ferrous Metal	49.0	15.8	14.3	4.4	1.6	17.0	25.7
38 Metal Prods. & Mach.	730.0	12.5	427.8	11.8	97.8	341.8	3.5
382 Non-Elec Machinery	163.1	11.6	93.5	3.3	22.7	74.1	4.4
383 Electrical Machinery	147.7	12.1	105.5	2.4	22.4	85.6	2.8
384 Transport Equipment	266.0	16.4	131.3	3.0	40.8	93.4	3.2
39 Other Manufactures	25.3	23.2	12.8	1.2	2.4	11.6	10.0
3 All Manufactures	1992.5	9.6	1008.2	42.6	137.2	913.6	4.7

P = production. M = imports. E = exports. C = P+M-E = apparent domestic consumption.
MP = M/C = market penetration (in percentages). Trade figures exclude intra-EC trade.

nations; its market penetration rate is 15 per cent in 1983. The USA is second with nearly 10 per cent in 1983. Both in the EC and in the USA overall market penetration for manufacturing increased by some 50 per cent from 1973 to 1983. For Japan, in third position, market penetration remained stable at nearly 5 per cent.

Has Japan earned as black a mark as is generally suggested? The imbalance in its trade in manufactures has often been quoted as proof that an occult system of protection exists in that country. The resulting resentment has contributed to the trade tensions of the decade, the corresponding suspicion will complicate trade talks.

However, economics tells us that there is no reason why trade should balance for one particular category of goods such as manufactures. Geography and comparative advantage are a first explanation. Japan is as far from major producers and users of manufactured goods as the Community is close to the EFTA countries. As a former NIC, its comparative advantage continues to overlap with that of the neighbouring newly industrialized countries of Asia (see also Yamazawa (1984)).

Another basic fact is Japan's lack of domestic natural resources, in particular of energy, coupled with its paradoxical specialization in energy intensive exports. The United States has been shielded from the oil shock by its large domestic energy production and the opening up of Alaska, the Community by the existence of large coal industries in the Federal Republic of Germany and Great Britain and the opening up of the North Sea. Japan had to pay all of the additional cost of the oil which it consumes by increased net exports of other goods.

What is however true is that when two countries trade together, the one which is in deficit has a bargaining edge, because it can credibly threaten to limit imports from its partner in the knowledge that the partner will not be able to inflict upon it equivalent harm by retaliating.

2.2 The geographical pattern of trade

The differences among the big three trading nations in openness to imports of manufactures reflect in part geography.

The Community is situated very close to major exporters and importers of manufactured products in the rest of Europe, which drives up the total trade figures.

These of course reflect policy as well as proximity: the trade agreements between the Community and European Free Trade Area countries have made all of Western Europe into a vast free trade area.

The geographical pattern of trade of the three big trading nations is considered in Table 3.2. Trade relations with four groups of developing countries are represented: East Asia, Latin America, Southern Europe and other LDCs. In addition to these four groups, trade with the European Centrally Planned Economies (CPEs) is represented. Details on country grouping are given in the Annex.

Table 3.2 shows that exports from <u>East Asia</u> predominantly are bought in the USA, followed at a distance by the EC and Japan. Imports into East Asia however mainly stem from Japan, with the USA and EC supplying much less. <u>Latin America</u> trades with the USA; the EC and Japan are partners of much less importance. Trade figures for <u>Southern Europe</u> indicate the EC as by far the most important partner in trade, followed at a distance by the USA and Japan. The <u>CPEs</u> display much the same pattern as Southern Europe.

These findings illustrate the polarization of trade according to proximity: Latin America trades predominantly with the USA; Southern Europe and the CPEs with the European Community; and the Eastern NICs and ASEAN with Japan.

The lower part of Table 3.2 shows, that the <u>USA</u> imports predominantly from East Asia followed by Latin America with Southern Europe and CPEs in last positions. North-American exports find their way first of all to Latin America with East Asia in second position but close to the Latin American share. <u>Japan</u> trades with East Asia. The other country groups are far behind.

Apart from the position of other LDCs, the most important destinations of exports from the <u>European Community</u> are Southern Europe and the CPEs. At the import side Southern Europe is important, the CPEs being replaced by East Asia as second import source.

The strong involvement of the United States in trade with the (East Asian) NICs is to be noted. That country has borne more than its share of the adjustment required by the latter's surge into world markets (see also Branson (1984)). It is only recently that East Asia gained a strong position on the EC market. But still EC trade relations are dominated by Southern Europe and by other LDCs among which the

Table 3.2: Geographical orientation of ltrade in manufactures of the big three trading nations

1983	EC (a) (in billions of US dollars)		USA		Japan	
	Imp.	Exp.	Imp.	Exp.	Imp.	Exp.
East Asia	12.0	12.1	32.6	14.7	5.3	29.7
Lat America	3.5	10.2	11.9	17.0	1.4	5.8
S. Europe	13.1	28.1	1.7	3.9	0.3	3.8
Other LDCs	8.3	33.7	4.3	5.3	1.8	14.8
All LDCs	26.5	69.7	48.9	39.1	8.5	52.3
CPEs	6.1	14.4	0.8	0.7	0.5	3.3
LDCs+CPEs +Entr	43.0	98.5	51.3	41.6	9.3	57.4
World	136.1	220.7	170.7	132.6	31.2	142.1

1983	EC (a) (in percentages of trade with LDCs+CPEs+Entrants)		USA		Japan	
	Imp.	Exp.	Imp.	Exp.	Imp.	Exp.
East Asia	28.0	12.3	63.4	35.4	56.8	51.8
Lat America	8.1	10.4	23.2	40.8	14.9	10.0
S. Europe	30.4	28.6	3.3	9.4	2.8	6.7
Other LDCs	19.4	34.2	8.3	12.6	19.6	25.8
All LDCs	61.6	70.8	95.3	93.9	91.4	91.1
CPEs	14.2	14.6	1.6	1.7	5.8	5.8
LDCs+CPEs +Entr	100.0	100.0	100.0	100.0	100.0	100.0
World	316.5	224.0	332.7	318.6	337.1	247.3

(a) EC (9) figures for World trade exclude intra-EC trade
Manufactures comprise SITC sections 5-8
Trade partners: (see also the Annex)

East Asia	= East Asian NICs + ASEAN countries
Lat America	= Latin America
South Europe	= Entrants + Mediterranean Agreement Countries
Other LDCs	
All LDCs	= East Asia + Latin America + Mediterranean Countries + Other LDCs
CPEs	= Centrally Planned Economies in Europe
LDCs + CPEs + Entr.	= All LDCs + CPEs + Entrants

Source: UN Trade Data

countries in Africa are found. Such an orientation is easy to understand in terms of geography and past colonial links. Because of it, the Community up to now has been somewhat sheltered from the export competition of the NICs.

2.3 Are exports from the South reaching market limits?

Figures for 1973 and 1983 on market penetration by manufactured imports from the developing countries into the EC, the USA and Japan are represented in Table 3.3. The striking finding is that these rates are still very low, except for textiles (group 32) and for miscellaneous manufactures (group 39). But also for these products as for the other groups, market penetration by developing countries is still much lower than penetration by imports from all sources, as reported in section 2.1.

This underlines calculations in for instance Balassa (1984), Schumacher (1984) and Kol and Mennes (1983) showing that imports from developing countries can only account to a very limited degree for the decline in industrial employment in industrial countries in the seventies. Next, there are export flows to consider in the reverse direction; details are given in Waelbroeck and Kol (1986) but overall a surplus in manufactured trade was shown to exist with the developing countries for the EC and Japan in section 2.2.

Returning to Table 3.3, the EC (figures excluding intra-EC trade) is still the most open of the big three to manufactured imports from developing countries. Furthermore the low levels of market penetration suggest considerable room for further expansion of the exports of developing countries if they can increase and diversify supply. (2)

It could be argued that the low level of market penetration rates by developing countries into the "big three" traders reflects undue aggregation of the data in the tables. Detailed data on the four and five digit ISIC are presented in Waelbroeck and Kol (1986) a summary of which is given in Table 3.4. The coverage of products with a market penetration of more than 10% (in 1983) is summarized per 2-digit group: in terms of numbers of 4 or 5 digit items in column 3 and in terms of total imports from developing countries per 2-digit group in column 4.

The earlier findings are confirmed: coverage is only high for the textiles group and for miscellaneous manufactures. There is ample room for export increases

Table 3.3: Market penetration in the EC, the USA and Japan by manufactured exports from developing countries

| Product Group | Market penetration in % of domestic market | | | | | |
| | 1973 | | | 1983 | | |
	EC	USA	Japan	EC	USA	Japan
31 Food Products (etc)	5.4	2.6	2.4	5.1	2.4	1.9
32 Textiles (etc)	5.5	3.7	5.8	13.0	10.9	5.0
321 Textiles	3.8	1.7	5.3	7.1	2.5	3.2
322 Wearing Apparel	8.6	5.9	8.0	21.2	17.2	9.0
324 Footwear	2.5	4.9	3.0	10.4	29.8	7.4
33 Wood & Wood prods	3.9	1.8	2.0	4.5	3.4	1.3
34 Paper & Printing	0.2	0.1	0.1	0.8	0.3	0.2
35 Chemicals	1.7	2.5	1.4	2.2	3.2	1.3
353 Petroleum Refineries	1.2	7.0	5.1	3.4	5.7	2.5
354 Prods of Petr. Coal	0.7	0.0	0.0	0.6	1.0	0.6
356 Plastic Prods	1.3	2.4	0.3	1.3	2.4	0.2
36 Non-metallic prods	0.2	0.4	0.3	0.8	1.5	0.3
37 Basic metal prods	4.5	1.5	2.3	3.7	3.7	4.5
371 Iron and Steel	0.7	0.7	0.3	0.8	2.7	2.2
372 Non-ferrous metal	13.3	2.9	7.5	9.9	4.8	10.2
38 Metal prods & mach	0.6	0.8	0.2	1.6	2.3	0.4
382 Non-elec mach	0.3	0.3	0.2	1.1	2.3	0.3
383 Electrical mach	0.9	3.1	0.5	2.5	5.4	0.7
384 Transport equip	0.6	0.2	0.1	1.4	0.7	0.1
39 Other Manufactures	5.7	4.9	4.9	17.5	11.1	4.6
3 All Manufactures	2.7	1.6	1.5	3.5	3.1	1.4

Trade figures exclude intra-EC trade

Market penetration: imports as percentage of apparent domestic consumption.

elsewhere. (3)

It has been said (Cline (1982)) that a market penetration of 15% 'would be likely to overburden the political-economic absorptive capacity in major industrial country markets by exceeding this threshold'. However 4 and 5 digit products show much higher market penetration ratio's (Waelbroeck and Kol (1986)) while also the role of import penetration in triggering off protective measures underlined in Cline (1984) is seriously questioned in other studies (see section 3 of this paper).

Of course, scope for diversification of LDCs manufactured exports is to be matched by comparative advantage (see section 4) and marketing possibilities (see section 3 on some aspects). Lastly, further industrialization in developing countries will evoke exports from the industrialized world (see Glismann and Spinanger (1982)).

3. THE COMMON TRADE POLICY AND OPENNESS OF INDIVIDUAL MEMBER COUNTRIES

3.1 The common trade policy

Does the EC offer to developing countries a unified market? Does the Community have a trade policy of its own? Given the threat of protection, it is important for developing countries to give thought to identifying the most effective negotiating strategy in dealing with the European Community.

In principle, what the EC offers to developing countries is indeed a common market. There is a common external tariff. Most of the overt national quantitative restrictions which existed in 1957 when the Rome Treaty was signed have been abolished. The European Commission represents member country governments in negotiations. To regard the Community as a single entity for purposes of trade negotiations would seem the right basis for policy thinking.

As it sought to open up its domestic market, the Community has become more aware of the multitude of invisible trade barriers that impede the flow of trade across borders. Health and safety regulations, norms, public procurement procedures and the sourcing policies of nationalized enterprises, these and other barriers have proved to be stubborn obstacles to the unification of the domestic market, which have proved extremely difficult to remove.

Table 3.4: Coverage of high market penetration products

Manufactured products at the 4- or 5-digit level (a) imported from LDCs with a market penetration of more than 10% in 1983 in the EC, the USA and Japan. Recorded per 2-digit group.

1 2-digit group	2 Number of 4- or 5-digit items per 2-digit group. (a)	3 Number of 4- or 5-digit items with market penetration of more than 10%. (a)			4 Import coverage of high market-penetration products as share of total imports from LDCs per 2-digit group. (b)		
		EC	USA	Japan	EC	USA	Japan
31 Food	16	3	2	1	0.69	0.56	0.12
32 Textiles	27	19	18	11	0.98	0.97	0.61
33 Wood	6	2	2	2	0.78	0.35	0.40
34 Paper	6	0	1	0	0.00	0.00	0.00
35 Chemicals	17	3	2	2	0.14	0.04	0.04
36 Non-metal Products	5	0	1	0	0.00	0.43	0.00
37 Basic Metals	4	1	3	1	0.83	0.58	0.63
38 Metal Products	40	7	10	1	0.36	0.47	0.08
39 Misc. Manuf.	8	6	8	1	0.94	1.00	1.00

(a) Classification by IBRD based on ISIC, allowing for 5-digit products. 4-digit items have been included only when no 5-digit products are classified.

(b) Imports of 4- and 5-digit products with a market penetration of more than 10% as a share of total LDC imports at the corresponding 2-digit level. Figures are rounded off.

69

More importantly from the point of view of international negotiations, it is important to understand that it is an inherent part of EC policy-making to leave to member countries a significant discretion to limit imports. The weakness of the Community decision mechanism accounts for this situation. Good examples are the Multifibre Arrangement and steel import quotas administered under article 58 of the Treaty. A few of the import quotas which existed before the Community was formed and which member countries continue to administer, are important, such as those for automobiles in Italy and for consumer electronics in Italy and France. Subsidies to producers are a very important form of "non-border protection"; except for agricultural products they are granted almost exclusively at the discretion of individual governments, though the Commission can and does try to limit them - to the extent that "political realities" make this feasible.

Why should this be wrong? The task of the Commission is to pool the bargaining powers of member countries in their common interest, and to see to it that any differences in import procedures do not trigger trade barriers between members as the more protectionist ones seek to keep out products diverted via their more liberal partners. Without some leeway, the policy process might well break down, or negotiations in the Council might lead to more protectionism overall than is implied by present arrangements.

3.2 Openness of individual member countries

The figures provided in Table 3.5 confirm that, 26 years after the Rome Treaty was signed, the various national markets in the Community are not yet equally open to developing countries. These differences reflect structural factors only to a limited extent. The main reason for the differences in openness appears to be the considerable residual control which governments continue to exercise over access to domestic markets.

That some of the differences are the result of structural factors is of course true. The Dutch and Belgian figures for imports of textiles and clothing are a clear example of this. Benelux is a single trading area from the point of view of the administration of the EC version of the Multifibre Arrangement, yet because of the greater strength

Table 3.5: Openness of EC countries to manufactured imports from developing countries

Market penetration (in percentages)

1983

Product Group	Belgium	BRD	France	Italy	Netherl.	UK
31 Food, Beverages	7.2	6.5	4.3	4.6	7.1	2.7
32 Textiles	9.2	18.6	10.7	5.7	27.7	11.4
35 Chemicals	2.5	1.3	2.0	5.4	1.8	1.3
372 Non-ferrous Metals	30.4	8.6	6.9	15.5	5.2	9.4
38 Metal Products	1.5	1.4	0.9	1.7	3.7	2.2
39 Other Manuf. Prods.	184.2 (a)	11.0	7.7	432.1 (a)	29.3	13.8
3 Total Manuf.	5.4	3.6	2.6	3.7	4.9	2.8

(a) Penetration rates for 'other manufactured products' reflect difficulties in exact correspondence of data on production and trade.

of the Belgian industry, developing countries have achieved much higher penetration of the Dutch than of the Belgian market.

Who the protectionist and non-protectionist members of the Community are is not difficult to find out: the EC Council alignment in debates of trade policy for manufactures (4) never varies. The Netherlands, the Federal Republic of Germany, and Denmark (not in Table 3.5 by lack of data) are for free trade, the United Kingdom, France, and Italy for a restrictive policy, with Belgium liking protection instinctively but held back by Benelux loyalties. These attitudes are remarkably immune to political shifts.

It had been feared that France would become even more protectionist when a popular front government was elected which advocated "reconquest of the domestic market"; this did not happen; the liberal convictions of Britain's Mrs. Thatcher should have tilted that country's attitude in favour of free trade; this turned out not to be true. Trade policy appears to reflect a quite stable modus vivendi between interest groups, the bureaucracy, and what in France is called the "political class" (see Messerlin (1987) on the French case in particular).

The match between openness and trade policy preference is quite apparent in the line "textiles, clothing, shoes" (group 32), which is influenced by key MFA decisions which individual governments continue to control, (5) and is also affected by the VER agreements for shoes which some governments have negotiated outside of the EC framework. France and Italy are among the most closed countries, while the Federal Republic is quite open. The Netherlands market is highly open.

The key to effectiveness in economic diplomacy is to apply pressure at the right time and to the right point. Perhaps the developing countries should take a pointer from US practice, and direct a greater share of their efforts at persuasion and retaliation to the individual member countries, whose governments control EC decisions through the Council. Perhaps the Commission would be relieved to get support for the usually liberal proposals which it usually brings before the Council in preparation for trade negotiations.

3.3 Protection and its "political economy"
Economists have been interested in recent years in

determining the causes of protection. Can "trigger points" be identified, indicating the levels of market penetration which bring about protectionist measures.

The topic goes beyond the confines of economics (6) and should be approached by means of both econometric and historical approaches, which should confirm and verify each other's intuitions and findings. The results of this work (7) provide coherent conclusions.

A first important finding is that the trigger point concept does not work: the level or change of market penetration (8) does not account satisfactorily for the observed level or change of protection, whether alone or in combination with other explanatory variables. It is necessary to look for deeper forces. What do seem to work best are indicators of the political power of interest groups, in particular the size and regional concentration of industries, which determine the numbers of votes which they are able to mobilize, and their ability to mobilize their political strength (see also recently Gerken et al. (1986) on steel in the BRD).

The human solidarity of voters appears to matter also, low wage industries appear to be more protection prone than others. It appears that protection does not help the industries that, in the GATT language, have experienced "injury": it is a benefit that can be extracted from the political process by those that are politically powerful, (9) or are able to inspire sympathy through the poor wages which they pay out. Last but not least, the regressions do not give very good results: it is necessary, as was said above, to look at deeper determinants of protection than the rate of market penetration. Econometrics cannot go deep enough to cover all of the political determinants of protection; there is an element of luck, of the political skill through which a lobby is able to extract benefits. Being small may be as valuable as being large. Small industries may, when political circumstances are favourable, extract astonishing windfalls. (10)

4. COMPARATIVE ADVANTAGE AND THE PROSPECTS OF SOUTH-EC TRADE

4.1 <u>Comparative advantages of developing countries: an overview</u>

The traditional comparative advantages of developing

countries have rested on a relative abundance of natural resources and unskilled labour. Both are the result of underdevelopment. As to resources, the populations of European stock which make up most of the developed world have grasped for more than their share of those which are available in the world but in relative terms - in proportion to GNP - resources are more abundant in the South. (11) It is thus normal that the largest group of the exports from developing countries to the Community has traditionally consisted of such products.

It is in the last twenty years especially that intensity in unskilled labour has come to the fore as the second major source of comparative advantages of the South. (12)

Factor abundance matters because of its impact on prices; the relation between these two variables is however not a straightforward one, there are significant "endogenous distortions" (13) that result from institutional factors. (14)

It is essential also to view comparative advantage in a dynamic context.

Balassa has stressed in a number of articles (15) that the rapid accumulation of physical and human capital in the more advanced NICs is changing in the same way, though less visibly the relative abundance of factors of production in these countries reducing their comparative advantage in exporting unskilled labour intensive goods. This has resulted in very sharp increases in real wage rates, which now exceed those in such a poor European country as Portugal. This is alleviating the pressure which these countries exerted in the past on the markets for typical developing country exports such as clothing and shoes, providing room for newcomers in these markets, (16) and reducing the difficulties experienced by developed country exporters of these products.

Technology, finally, is not static: there are factor reversals which change patterns of comparative advantages. Textiles has become more capital intensive than in earlier times thanks to modern techniques for process control, the skilled labour intensity of steel and glass making has become less marked than was formerly the case.

Again, there is a need to avoid an overly mechanical interpretation of events. This migration of production is accompanied by a host of minor innovations: in the Schumpeterian spirit these require entrepreneurship. (17) Westphal has stressed the role of industrial competence - the complex set of abilities that enable producers in a country to master complex production processes. (18)

4.2 Simply transformed primary products

Table 3.6: Developing country exports to the EC of barely transformed primary products

Product Group (b)	Imports into the EC (in thousands of US dollars)		Penetration rate (in percentages) (a)	
	1973	1983	1973	1983
3115 Oils and fats	1410	3314	18.6	24.6
3118 Sugar	476	668	12.2	7.7
32117 Fibres/Wool for textile use	173	308	17.4	63.8
3231 Tanneries, leather finishing	342	461	16.2	16.7
33111 Lumber etc. from sawmills	603	1013	11.1	17.3
33112 Veneer sheets, ply-wood etc.	253	398	11.2	17.1
3511 Basic industr. chemicals	236	1023	1.4	2.4
353 Petroleum ref.	214	2398	0.7	2.3
3720 Non-ferrous basic metals	2367	2768	12.0	9.4
3901 Jewelry	134	731	51.8	56.4
Total	6207	13080		

(a) Share of imports in EC apparent domestic consumption.
(b) ISIC classification; 5 digits according to World Bank classification.

Even within manufactures (SITC groups 5-9; ISIC group 3), there are many products that are in reality primary products, exported after simple processing which in most cases adds little value to the goods. Such products are manufactures only statistically (this of course does not mean that their export is less worthwhile than that of "true manufactured goods"). Table 3.6 provides data on these exports.

Disregarding refined petroleum for the moment, the import figures in Table 3.6 are dominated by oils and fats (code 3115), lumber (33111), basic chemicals (3511) and non-ferrous basic metals (3720). In terms of market penetration also fibres/wool (32117) and veneer (33112) are important.

Basic chemicals are included in the table because what developing countries tend to sell consists largely of crude, barely elaborated products; sales have tended to grow quite quickly, and there exists a potential for quite a lot more growth if developing countries are quick to seize market opportunities, considering also the very low market penetration of 2.4 in 1983.

Refined petroleum should be set apart. Here the extremely quick growth of exports is to a large extent a price phenomenon. The efforts of oil exporting countries to refine their own oil were another contributing factor. Removing oil from the total focuses attention on the products which are of interest mainly to oil importing developing countries. When this is done, the proportion of these products in total manufactured exports from developing countries to the EC changes from 52 per cent in 1973 to 38 per cent in 1983, a substantial drop. Resource based manufactures have thus accounted for a steadily falling fraction of the South's exports of manufactured goods to the Community. (19)

4.3 Unskilled labour-intensive products

4.3.1 **Textiles, clothing, shoes.** As two other chapters in this volume, namely those by Hamilton and by Koekkoek and Mennes, deal with textiles and clothing, this section contains a brief summary only of the corresponding sections in the background paper (Waelbroeck and Kol (1986)).

The textiles, clothing and shoes industries have undergone a dramatic structural change. In some decades, they switched from being producers of goods that were little traded across continents to a situation where markets are very open to such trade.

Especially progress in transport and communications accounts for this evolution. Modern airlines make close buyer-seller contacts possible almost independently of distance, whereas air freight makes possible almost instant delivery of goods that have proved popular.

It is a striking result of this evolution that international trade in textiles and clothing has increased by and large as fast as the total amount of world trade in spite of the unfavourable evolution of protection, also in developing countries. (20)

Table 3.7 sets out the shares of textiles and clothing in exports of groups of developing countries that have attained different stages of development during the 1973-83 decade. (21)

The figures in Table 3.7 reveal that textiles and clothing have become sharply less important for the most advanced of the NICs, those in East Asia and the upper income countries of Latin America. There is a fall in the share of these products even for the EC entrants, in spite of the preferential treatment which they have enjoyed in the Community. (22) An opposite evolution is apparent in the less industrially advanced new NICs, (23) the Mediterranean agreement countries, the Lomé/ACP countries and in China. There has been a clear change of the international division of labour for textiles and clothing products.

With respect to shoes, the European Community is quite open to imports. Britain and France have negotiated voluntary export restraint agreements with some developing country suppliers, but these are not very useful given the ease of sourcing via other EC countries. Furthermore, the shoe industry is not a politically powerful one. (24)

For textiles and clothing EC producers are protected by a very complicated multitiered system. Non-tariff protection is likewise complex. E.g. imports of manufactures from the Lomé countries are in principle free, but under the safeguard clause of the agreements the Community was swift to move against Mauritius when that country, with Hong Kong capital, set out to export tiny quantities to the EC market: this puzzling decision may have been meant more as a warning to other Lomé countries and to Hong Kong capitalists than because the Community perceived a real threat.

The Community's agreements with Mediterranean countries are not as watertight as those concluded under the MFA. And Turkey - a prospective entrant - has quite successfully refused to sign any general agreement, and gone on to build up exports using every trick in the rule book, and some which the book does not describe. A good deal of cheating goes on of course, only a small fraction of which is probably detected.

So far, the lobbies have always been stronger than the governments' - that make up the EC councils - intentions to arrive at a more flexible MFA. Yet there are reasons to propose a more flexible import policy.

Structural change is a first reason. (25) The textiles and clothing industry is markedly smaller today than when protection began.

Table 3.7: Shares of textile and clothing products in imports of manufactured goods of the big three trading nations from selected groups of developing countries

	EC		USA		Japan		Big 3	
	1973	1983	1973	1983	1973	1983	1973	1983
East Asian NICs	0.53	0.33	0.29	0.25	0.49	0.30	0.40	0.27
New NICs	0.09	0.27	0.17	0.19	0.13	0.09	0.13	0.21
Entrants (No LDCs)	0.25	0.23	0.13	0.06	0.17	0.04	0.22	0.20
Mediterr. Agr. Cs	0.57	0.63	0.56	0.32	0.23	0.07	0.56	0.61
Upper Income Lat. Am.	0.25	0.18	0.13	0.05	0.15	0.04	0.16	0.07
Lomé/ACP	0.01	0.07	0.06	0.11	0.00	0.01	0.02	0.08
India	0.39	0.49	0.70	0.36	0.34	0.20	0.49	0.41
China	0.38	0.49	0.29	0.63	0.52	0.58	0.45	0.57
Other LDCs	0.38	0.34	0.37	0.32	0.37	0.19	0.38	0.32
LDCs total	0.32	0.33	0.26	0.22	0.35	0.26	0.30	0.26

Large parts of the textile industry in industrialized countries are now capable of confronting successfully the competition of low wage producers. The Swiss case is a first example. That country does not limit imports of textiles from low wage countries, yet it is even now a net exporter of textiles. And the Federal Republic of Germany is by now the largest textiles exporter in the world.

There is yet another, more global test of the competitive strength of EC textiles producers. An interesting way of viewing the MFA is to regard it as a kind of customs union that shelters the developed market economies behind a common wall of protection from an "open" market elsewhere, where tariff walls may be very high but are not discriminatory. (26)

Trade theory leads us to expect that such a union should affect trade in well defined ways. If the discriminatory protection is effective, exports of the customs union producers to third countries should drop if protection increases, as import barriers raise prices on the protected market above the world level; union producers should obtain a rising share of the union's previous imports as trade diversion occurs.

MFA protection was tightened a great deal during the 1970s. Yet Table 3.8 does not reveal the strong changes in the orientation of trade flows that would be expected. There was swift growth of imports from low wage countries into the Community, but also of exports to the latter. This confirms that a large number of Community producers remain able to compete on world markets for many products.

4.3.2 **Miscellaneous light manufactures.** Under any realistic assessment, even if the fourth MFA would turn out to be less restrictive than the third, protection will continue to contain developing countries exports of textiles and clothing, and possibly also of shoes. (27) These countries will have to identify other products, the markets of which remain open.

Table 3.9 provides figures that are relevant. The goods listed are light industrial products, the exports of which were significant in 1983.

What is striking, is the wide range of items listed in the table, from brooms and brushes to computers. Exports of each type of such goods are not large, but the aggregate

Table 3.8: EC trade in MFA goods

(in millions of US-dollars)

Textiles	1973 Exp.	1973 Imp.	1973 Trade Balance	1983 Exp.	1983 Imp.	1983 Trade Balance
Developed	2514	1314	1199	3772	2697	1074
Developing	2500	2005	494	4533	4139	393
Total	5015	3320	1694	8305	6836	1468

Clothing	Exp.	Imp.	Trade Balance	Exp.	Imp.	Trade Balance
Developed	1053	348	705	3032	884	2148
Developing	424	2121	-1696	1414	8032	-6617
Total	1478	2469	-991	4447	8917	-4469

volume is impressive: more than 5 billion dollars, and a rising percentage (42 in 1983) of total textile and clothing LDCs exports to the EC. In quite a few instances, exports were negligible fifteen years ago: these exports were "invented" quite recently, as entrepreneurs identified items that could be produced at low cost, given the cost structure of developing countries.

In some cases, the innovators were multinationals, who saw a chance to shift to low wage countries unskilled labour-intensive stages of the production processes. Examples are computers and television sets (in the more advanced NICs there are also local companies producing television sets and other consumer electronics items, and even (copied) micro computers). In the majority of cases, however, it is local entrepreneurs who, in the Schumpeterian way, identified products and the combinations of factors of production that were new and profitable.

For a few products, the rate of market penetration has become rather high, and exports could encounter absorption limits and possibly new protection barriers (preserves, furs, cutlery, radios and television equipment, watches and clocks, sporting goods, umbrellas for instance). If, as econometric work on the political economy of protection suggests (see section 3.3), minor industrial sectors find it more difficult than large ones to get tight protection from policy-makers, there would be reason for optimism about the continued openness of these markets (28).

The list should however mainly be looked on as an indication of the type of products for which developing countries have potentially a comparative advantage. Many of these exports were only recently "invented"; there will be more such discoveries. Industrial competence has been a limiting factor but its acquisition is a cumulative process: the range of goods which developing countries are able to produce efficiently becomes ever broader, and this also will help the process of diversification of exports.

4.4 **New breakthroughs in the troubled "new mature" industries?**

In this section, we will examine prospects for breakthroughs in three sectors where developing countries have registered successes in recent years and where a decisive breakthrough could yield very large amounts of foreign exchange: shipbuilding, steel, and automobiles.

Table 3.9: Developing country exports to the EC of miscellaneous light manufactures.

Product Group (b)		EC imports (in mln. US$) 1973	1983	Market penetration (in %) (a) 1983
3113	Fruits and vegetables pres.	260	660	7.7
3114	Fish and products pres.	78	298	9.7
3119	Cocoa, chocolate & sugar	117	254	2.5
3232	Fur dressing and dyeing	36	38	36.3
3319	Wood and cork products n.e.c. (c)	30	95	6.2
3320	Furniture (non metal)	43	93	0.5
34202	Books, newspapers, cards etc.	24	117	1.6
3551	Tires and tubes	10	120	2.0
3559	Rubber products n.e.c.	21	94	1.4
356	Plastic products n.e.c.	127	281	1.2
3610	China and earthware	13	140	2.8
38111	Cutlery	14	65	23.2
38112	Hand tools & general hardware	26	186	7.9
38192	Metal containers	54	210	3.1
38251	Typewriters, calculators etc	25	257	10.3
38252	Computers	48	243	3.5
3829	Machinery (non electr.) n.e.c.	53	350	0.8
38321	Radio & TV components	135	110	4.4
3833	Electrical appliances	10	78	1.0
3839	Electrical apparatus n.e.c.	30	208	1.7
38523	Photographic & cinematographic eq.	35	72	5.6

Table 3.9 continued

Product Group (b)		EC imports (in mln. US$)		Market penetration (in %) (a)
		1973	1983	1983
3853	Watches and clocks	13	310	20.1
3902	Musical instruments	7	40	6.8
3903	Sporting goods	22	168	15.4
39092	Toys, ornaments	84	455	32.3
39094	Brooms and brushes	2	29	17.6
39095	Pipes, lighters, umbrellas	53	167	50.6
Total		1370	5134	

(a) Market penetration in percentage of apparent domestic consumption
(b) ISIC-classification; 5 digits according to World Bank classification
(c) n.e.c. = not elsewhere classified

These "new mature industries" have several characteristics in common. Poor demand prospects is one (29). Maturity in terms of the product cycle is a second. A third characteristic is <u>size</u>. All three industries are large. This makes them tempting targets for planners concerned with achieving big results from a given effort in mastering imported technology.

The fourth is an intensity in <u>management skills</u>, which quite a few of the more advanced NICs have acquired by now. A number of the NICs appear to share Japan's comparative advantage in securing the labour peace that is so important to success in "union intensive" industrial activities.

Table 3.10 contains import figures for the three big trading nations of cars, ships and steel from the South, of which the meaningful exporters of the three categories of goods are included. The substantial rises in US steel imports, and in the Community's imports of automobiles, are worth singling out. It is hard to forecast the evolution of steel imports; these will be strongly affected by the politics of steel in the United States, and also in the Community, the NICs main competitor on the US market. For automobiles, almost all of the EC imports originate from the new entrants. The "ships and boats" totals do not provide a full picture of the market available in the big three, as it does not include sales to flags of convenience fleets.

Steel

For steel, the situation will remain as it is for some years on the EC market. Union power in the Community has had a disastrous effect on the steel industry by delaying adjustment of the labour force and of capacity, but this has not been beneficial to importers as the worker interest groups have also used their political power to close borders to imports. Protection under article 58 of the Rome Treaty is far more effective than that provided by the Multifibre Arrangement.

It is unlikely that the frontiers of the EC will open up to steel imports, but the world market is a very large one: world steel apparent consumption amounted to 705 millions of tons, where exports (excluding intra EC trade) were somewhat over 20% (GATT (1984)) (30). That the progress of the NICs on the world market will be very fast is however doubtful.

Judging by the figures quoted by Crandall (1981) about productivity in different countries and costs of construction of steel mills in the United States and in the East Asian NICs, production in the latter area using newly built capacity is no cheaper than production with an existing plant in Europe, where capital is a sunk cost. If the Community's programme of rationalization progresses as much as is feasible, the existing tariff of 5 to 7% should in fact eventually be enough to assure the long run survival of most of the existing plants.

Shipbuilding

For shipbuilding the war is over. The EC industry is dying rapidly.

Protection in the Community is of little avail to Europe's shipyards. Shipping is a world industry, tariffs would not be effective. Half of world tonnage is in the flags of convenience fleets or in the hands of countries such as Greece which do not have a large shipbuilding sector to protect. And EC shipyards, which in some recent instances have quoted prices that were three times as high as the Korean ones, can be kept going only by subsidies that are so prohibitive that governments are - however reluctantly - closing one unit after another. The industry, which is much smaller than steel, does not indeed have the political weight required to win the very heavy protection which it would need to survive. The rates of subsidization indeed make no sense. EC regulations allow 30% of the prices of ships to be covered by subsidies, in an industry where value added in shipyards is 40% of the cost of production (31).

Future progress of the NICs will depend on gaining ground from the more efficient Japanese shipyards. Thus far South Korea, Taiwan and Brazil have managed to enter the list of eight top producers (at place 2, 4 and 6 respectively) in 1982, a list on which they did not figure at all in 1973. There is scope for further gains, but it should not be exaggerated.

Automobiles

For automobiles also, prospects depend on a complex interplay between trade unions, multinationals, and the governments of both developed and developing countries. The world market is extremely large - over 100 billions in

Table 3.10: Imports of cars, ships and steel by the big three trading nations

(Millions of US$ and annual growth rates in percentages)

		East Asian NICs			EC Entrants		
		1973	1983	Growth	1973	1983	Growth
EC	Passenger Cars	0	24	–	118	1614	29.8
USA	Passenger Cars	0	17	–	0	1	–
Japan	Passenger Cars	0	0	–	0	0	–
EC	Ships and boats	8	219	39.2	19	12	-3.7
USA	Ships and boats	25	324	29.2	1	7	23.1
Japan	Ships and boats	3	54	33.8	0	0	–
EC	Steel	35	33	-0.6	237	728	11.8
USA	Steel	91	646	21.7	29	251	24.1
Japan	Steel	11	581	48.7	1	25	38.5

Table 3.10: continued

(Millions of US$ and annual growth rates in percentages)

		Upper Income Latin Am.			Total	
		1973	1983	Growth	1973	1983	Growth
EC	Passenger Cars	1	171	67.2	119	1809	31.2
USA	Passenger Cars	20	13	-4.2	20	31	4.5
Japan	Passenger Cars	0	0	-	0	0	-
EC	Ships and boats	0	22	-	27	253	25.1
USA	Ships and boats	1	13	29.2	27	345	29.0
Japan	Ships and boats	0	0	-	3	54	33.8
EC	Steel	22	112	17.7	294	874	11.5
USA	Steel	91	724	23.1	211	1623	22.6
Japan	Steel	20	190	25.3	32	798	38.0

1980 - and a breakthrough in automobile exports by developing countries would provide them with enormous amounts of foreign exchange.

The EC common tariff on automobiles is 10.9% (compared to e.g. 3% for the USA) and is of the same order of magnitude as for textiles in the Community. This is a substantial barrier in view of the fact that the cost advantage which a few developing countries enjoy is far smaller than that which exists e.g. for clothing.

The EC benefits from free entry into EFTA countries and also from the protection in those countries. But the EC has lost considerably on third markets (32).

On markets that are accessible to them, therefore, developing countries finally will have to cope with the formidable competition from Japan. There is ample reason not to be oversanguine therefore (33).

Should exports from developing countries not grow impressively, production might grow.

Total production of automobiles in the developing world is estimated to have reached 8.9 million cars in 1985, in comparison with 11.7 millions in Europe, 9.3 and 7.6 in the USA and Japan (34).

Production numbers may give a misleading impression of the export potential, however. Most is high cost output, extensive rationalization would be needed to make some of this capacity internationally competitive. This will not be easy.

5. CONCLUSION

The paper has started by painting a broad picture of the recent history of foreign trade in the "big three" trading nations: the USA, Japan and the EC. The United States and the Community appear to be rather open to trade, the EC being somewhat more open to manufactured imports from developing countries.

The precedent set by Japan is of interest to the East Asian NICs which have followed its lead in building up large export surpluses with the main developed countries, a development that makes them vulnerable to trade discrimination.

Study of the EC market suggests that member countries retain much tighter control over their domestic markets than usually thought. This suggests that influencing member country governments should be accorded more attention in the trade diplomacy of developing countries, in addition to maintaining the indispensable links with the European Community authorities in Brussels. The United States has used systematically such "ad hominem" tactics to defend its interests. Such an approach might be specially fruitful, given that, by the time that the Commission comes to the bargaining table, it has usually been assigned so tight a negotiating brief that it is hardly able to take account of unexpected negotiating opportunities that might come up, and to seek the deal that is truly advantageous to all concerned.

The paper subsequently reviewed the comparative advantage of developing countries. The commodity composition of developing country exports of manufactures to the Community confirms that the primary components of their comparative advantage are the natural resource and unskilled labour contents of the exported goods. Setting apart refined oil, the share of natural resource intensive goods in these countries' exports of manufactures has been falling. A very large share of other exports consists of unskilled labour intensive goods.

The latter goods have been hit by protection, but the European Community market continues to be very open.

For miscellaneous light manufactures, developing countries have shown much inventiveness in spotting opportunities to produce and to export goods which they are able to sell cheaply. The list of such products is widening quite rapidly. There is a great deal of room for increase of exports of manufactures from South to North, if developing countries remain flexible enough to shift to new products as some existing markets close up.

The last topic discussed in the paper is somewhat speculative. What opportunities will arise in the troubled and politically sensitive "new mature industries": steel, shipbuilding and automobiles? These industries are handicapped both in the Community and in the United States by adversary relations between employers and very powerful trade unions, which keep costs a good deal higher than they should be: an "endogeneous trade distortion" which is valuable to competitors. The more advanced of the NICs have shown themselves to be able to master the relevant technology for the first two and are trying to do the same for automobile technology. A breakthrough for these goods is unlikely, because of both the competitiveness of Japanese producers, and the protection which these industries are able to obtain. On the other hand the markets for those goods are so large that, even though market shares remain low, exports of these goods could make quite a large contribution to the foreign exchange receipts of the South.

But what is to be expected is a broadly based increase of developing countries exports, rather than a surge into these industries.

Notes

The authors wish to acknowledge useful comments on an earlier version of the present paper by Martin Wolf and the other participants of the seminar on European Trade Policies and the South held September 1985 in The Hague. The usual provisos apply.

1.   Called a "nation" here and in what follows for ease of language.
2.   Some figures have to be looked at carefully. "Other manufactures" contain diamonds; transit trade in diamonds is hard to separate from imports for further processing. Refined petroleum has a large weight in group 35.
3.   Even the high import coverage of 0.83 for basic metals in the EC does not contradict this, while it indicates that the other products (3 out of 4) have very low imports into the EC.
4.   The alignment is different for other types of trade. Virtuous free trading Germany, for example, merits a smatter of black marks for its stubborn hostility to freer trade in agricultural products and services.
5.   In particular on "basket exit": subjecting imports of new products into a country to MFA controls, and the authorization of offshore processing contracts allowing producers to process abroad a part of their output.
6.   Hence the term 'political economy of protection' has been used to describe the work.
7.   For econometric studies of the determinants of protectionism in Europe, see the papers by Cable and Rebelo (1980); Glismann and Weiss (1980); Grilli and La Noce (1983); Koekkoek, Kol and Mennes (1981); Lundberg (1981); Messerlin (1982); and Tharakan (1980).
8.   Most studies in footnote 7 focus on tariff protection mainly. Cline (1984) reports on 'trigger point'

analysis as well and finds that import penetration is near to significant a variable in explaining non-tariff barriers for the country group USA, Canada and the UK.
9.   Compare for instance the sectors of clothing and footwear in this respect (see section 4.3).
10.   In British Columbia - in a country which has an extraordinary comparative advantage in basic agricultural exports - the liquor board system has enabled wine producers to get an 80% rate of nominal protection although much of the wine is produced with imported grapes; in addition the industry (which is in the electoral precinct of the provincial Prime Minister) obtained adjustment subsidies amounting to 600,000 dollars for each of the few hundreds of workers employed).
11.   See Leamer's (1984) interesting attempt to quantify the natural resource availabilities of different groups of countries.
12.   Econometric studies suggest on the other hand that, physical capital intensity does not have a clearcut impact on the competitivity of the South. Perhaps, capital is mobile enough to equalize returns across countries. Weiss (1983) has reviewed German work on this topic, while Ohlsson (1982) has made an interesting discussion of the evolution of comparative advantage of Sweden.
13.   Bhagwati (1971).
14.   In Italy and Japan, for instance, labour market distortions drive up the wages of workers in large enterprises, making these countries less competitive than they would otherwise be in producing goods that compete with developing country exports.
15.   E.g. Balassa (1979).
16.   Mohs (1985) in this respect argues that chances for exports from the Second Generation of NICs (SGNs) are bleaker than for their predecessors in earlier days, not only because the latter still are competitors to some extent but also because traditionally labour-intensive industries in developed countries have, meanwhile, successfully restructured themselves.
17.   Members of the neo-classical school would add that the role of human capital is also important in facilitating the acquisition of new know-how by top staff and workers in new enterprises.
18.   It was at one time popular to view such industries as steel as leading sectors. In contrast to disappointing experiences elsewhere, the success in these areas of such

countries as Korea and Taiwan suggests that it would have been more appropriate to view successful steel making as an excellent indicator of a country's ability to run complex industrial operations.

19.   Figures for USA and Japan (shown in Waelbroeck and Kol (1986)) confirm the important position of basic chemicals and non-ferrous basic metals, with also a very low market penetration for basic chemicals, giving scope for additional exports to Japan and the USA too.   Also the relative decline of primary based manufactured exports is confirmed.

20.   The average tariff on textiles and clothing is for example in the range of 50-60% for such strong exporting countries as Columbia, Taiwan, and Sri Lanka; in weaker exporting countries, such as Pakistan and India the average is close to 135% and 95% respectively. The share of textiles in world manufactured trade was 6.7% in 1973 and dropped to 4.8% in 1983; for clothing this share increased somewhat from 3.6 to 3.9.

21.   Balassa's (1979) concept of "stages of comparative advantage", according to which countries that start on the road to development begin by exporting simple unskilled labour-intensive goods and shift later on to products that embody more human and physical capital, implies a process through which these countries relinquish in favour of later starting countries the markets where they scored early successes as exporters of manufactures.

22.   The figures do reflect this preference however; the decline in the importance of textiles and clothing products is less marked for EC imports from these countries than for those of the other big three.

23.   E.g. the very interesting article on the Sri Lanka breakthrough (Textile Asia (1984)).

24.   In addition, it does not truly require protection thanks to the remarkable efficiency of Italian shoe producers and within a short while of Portugese competitors. The rise in wages in Korea and Taiwan, the main developing country exporters of shoes, mean that wage costs outweigh those in Portugal and may come close to those in Italy.

25.   Furthermore, wages in the textile NICs have risen dramatically: the wage rate in Korea, thirty five years ago a country as poor as India, exceeded that in Portugal by 50% in 1983. Low wage Portugal and Greece - before it joined the Community - did not feel it necessary to protect its

producers against competition from low wage exporting countries. These countries and Spain are ready to grab markets that a stricter MFA would deny to outsiders.

26. Of course, a special case is Japan, that does not make use of its MFA rights, but has been 'called' like a developing country to restrict its exports to the USA. Switzerland offers another special case.

27. This would be the case even with the liberalization advocated above, which basically implies elimination of the "water" in the agreement, i.e. the protection that shields producers who can fend for themselves.

28. In the EC only France, for obscure reasons, bothers to protect these tiny sub-sectors. Access to other EC markets is quite free (and smuggling into France easy).

29. Total world new orders for ships in millions of gross registered tons fell from 73.6 in 1973 to 19.5 in 1983. It is unlikely that this will return to earlier levels. The drop in demand for steel has been substantial in developed countries, reflecting both the impact of the recession on investment and a structural shift to designs that use less steel and more of other materials. The automobile industry experienced market saturation decades ago in the United States, and is reaching a similar stage in Europe. The industries are also reaching the stage of the product cycle where technology has stabilized, and can be bought more easily than was formerly the case, making entry by new producers easier.

30. A part of the Community's trade with the rest of Europe consists in an exchange of steel of different types, an indispensable type of trade in a sector with indivisibilities that make large scale production necessary to efficient use of available equipment. Such exports are not likely to dwindle.

31. Various tricks are in fact sometimes used to give even higher subsidies.

32. In volumes, GATT (1985) reports that the EC share of imports of North America and Oceania (including Australia and New Zealand) dropped from 68% and 58% respectively in 1970 to only 21% and 12% in 1980. Japan took over, three-doubling their shares in import volumes on these markets to above 75% in 1980. Jones (1983) indicates that productivity in terms of motor vehicles produced per employee was in Japan 2 to 4 times as high as in the major EC producing countries in 1978, having been at a

comparable level in 1965.

33. The DRI World Auto's Forecast Report registrates for Brazil and Korea exports of 139 and 16 thousand units in 1983 and estimates this to become 255 and 206 thousand respectively in 1990. This to be compared e.g. with present exports of Japan amounting to 3806 thousand units in 1983.

34. These developments illustrate the process of outsourcing. Brazil and Mexico have become large producers in 1983 of engines for GM, Ford and VW (Jones (1983)). Furthermore, South Korean firms recently engaged in joint ventures with large car producers: Daewoo with GM, Samsung with Chrysler, Kia with Ford etc. (see also Westphal et al. (1984)).

References

Balassa, B. (1979), 'A Stages Approach to Comparative Advantage', in I. Adelman (ed.), Economic Growth and Resources, volume 4, National and International Issues, Macmillan, London

Balassa, B. (1984), Trends in International Trade in Manufactured Goods and Structural Change in the Industrial Countries, World Bank Staff Working Paper, No. 611, January

Bhagwati, J. (1971), 'The Generalized Theory of Distortions and Trade', in Bhagwati J., R.A. Mundell, and J. Vanek (eds), Trade, The Balance of Payments, and Growth, Papers in Honour of Charles P.K. Kindleberger, North Holland, Amsterdam

Branson, W.H. (1984), 'Trade and Structural Interdependence between the USA and the NICs', in C. Bradford (ed.), The Global Implications of the Trade Patterns between the USA and the NICs, Chicago University Press

Cable, V. and I. Rebelo (1980), Britain's Pattern of Specialization in Manufactured Goods with Developing Countries and Trade Protection, World Bank Staff Working Paper, No. 425

Cline, William R. (1982), 'Can the East Asian Model of Development Be Generalized?' World Development, Vol. 10, No. 2, pp. 81-90

Cline, William R. (1984), Exports of Manufactures from Developing Countries, The Brookings Institution, Washington D.C.

Crandall, Robert W. (1981), The US Steel Industry in

Recurrent Crisis, The Brookings Institution, Washington D.C.

GATT, (1984), International Trade 1983/84, GATT, Geneva

GATT, (1985), International Trade 1984/85, GATT, Geneva

Gerken, Egbert, Martin Gross and Ulrich Lachler (1986), 'The causes and consequences of steel subsidization in Germany', European Economic Review, Vol. 30, No. 4, August 1986, pp. 773-804

Glismann, H.H. and F.D. Weiss (1980), On the Political Economy of Protection in Germany, World Bank Staff Working Paper, No. 427

Glismann, Hans-Heinrich and Dean Spinanger (1982), 'Employment and Income Effects of Re-locating Textile Industries', The World Economy, Vol. 5, No. 1, March 1982, pp. 105-109

Grilli, E. and M. La Noce (1983), The Political Economy of Protection in Italy, World Bank Staff Working Paper, No. 567

Hamilton, C. (1987), 'Follies of Policies for Textile Imports in Western Europe', This volume

Jones, Daniel T. (1983) 'Motor Cars: A Maturing Industry?' in G. Shepherd et al. (eds), European Industries, Frances Pinter, London

Koekkoek, K.A., J. Kol and L.B.M. Mennes (1981), On Protectionism in the Netherlands, World Bank Staff Working Paper, No. 493

Koekkoek, K.A. and L.B.M. Mennes (1987), 'Some potential effects of liberalizing the MFA', This volume

Kol, J. and L.B.M. Mennes (1983), 'Trade and Industrial Employment', in Istvan Dobozi and Peter Mandi (eds), Emerging Development Patterns: European Contributions, EADI, Budapest, 1983

Leamer, E.E. (1984) Sources of International Comparative Advantage, The MIT Press, Cambridge, USA

Lundberg, L. (1981), Patterns of Trade Barriers in Sweden, World Bank Staff Working Paper, No. 424

Messerlin, P.A. (1982), 'Groupes de Pression et Choix Protectionnistes', in J.L. Reiffers (ed.), Economie et Finance Internationales, Dunod, Paris

Messerlin, Patrick A. (1987), 'Does French Protection Discriminate against LDCs?' This volume

Mohs, Ralf M. (1985), 'Can the Second Generation Succeed?', Intereconomics, January/February 1985, pp. 21-26

Ohlsson L. (1982), Sweden's Trade with Developing Countries: Comparative Advantage and Barriers to

Adjustment, World Bank Staff Working Paper

Schumacher, D. (1984), 'North-South Trade and shifts in employment,' International Labour Review, Vol. 123, No. 3, pp. 333-348

Textile Asia, 'Island of Hope', June 1984

Tharakan, P.K.M. (1980), The Political Economy of Protection in Belgium, World Bank Staff Working Paper, No. 431

Waelbroeck, Jean and Jacob Kol (1986), EC Trade Policy, The Evolving Pattern of World Trade, and the South, Erasmus University, Rotterdam

Weiss, F.D. (1983), The Structure of Germany's International Competitiveness, World Bank Staff Working Paper, No. 571

Westphal, L.E., L. Kim, and C.J. Dahlman (1984), Reflections on Korea's Acquisition of Technological Capability, Discussion Paper, Development Research Department, Economics Research Staff, World Bank, April

Yamazawa, I. (1984), 'Japan and the Asian Neighbours in a Dynamic Perspective', in C. Bradford (ed.), The Global Implications of the Trade Patterns of East and Southeast Asia, Chicago University Press

Annex: Country Classification

1
East Asian NICs

Hong Kong
Korea Rep.
Singapore (ASEAN)
Taiwan

4 countries

2
New NICs

Chile
Indonesia (ASEAN)
Jordan
Macau
Malaysia (ASEAN)
Mauritius
Peru
Philippines (ASEAN)
Sri Lanka
Thailand (ASEAN)

10 countries

3
East Asia

East Asian NICs (group 1)
ASEAN (part of grps 1,2)

4
Upper Income Lat Am

Argentina
Brazil
Mexico
Uruguay

4 countries

5
Latin America

Upp Inc Lat Am
(group 4)
other Latin
American
countries

6
Mediterranean Agr Ctrs

Algeria
Cyprus
Egypt
Malta
Morocco
Tunisia
Turkey

7 countries

Annex: continued

7
<u>Lomé/ACP</u>
61 countries having
signed Lomé
convention II
(Oct. 31 1979)

8
<u>India</u>

9
<u>China</u>

10
<u>Other LDCs</u>
<u>83 countries (World</u>
<u>Bank Classification)</u>

11

All LDCs

Group 1   East Asian NICs
Group 2   New NICs
Group 5   Latin America
Group 6   Mediterr Agr Ctrs
Group 7   Lomé/ACP
Group 8   India
Group 9   China
Group 10   Other LDCs

12
Entrants
(no LDCs)

Greece
Portugal
Spain

3 countries

13
Centrally planned
economies

Albania
Bulgaria
Czechoslovakia
German Dem Rep
Hungary
Poland
Romania
USSR

8 countries

Chapter Four

THE SECTOR-COUNTRY INCIDENCE OF ANTI-DUMPING AND COUNTERVAILING DUTY CASES IN THE EUROPEAN COMMUNITIES

P.K.M. Tharakan

1. INTRODUCTION

The present paper focuses attention on the sector and country incidence of the anti-dumping and countervailing duty (AD/CVD) cases in the European Communities (EC) for the period 1980-1984. It presents, probably for the first time, detailed estimates of such incidence, using data compiled on a case by case basis and put together from a very fine level of disaggregation. (1)

The plan of the paper is as follows: in section 2, a very brief overview of the import restrictions in the European Communities is provided to set the place of the AD/CVD mechanism within the constellation of such restrictive measures. Subsequently, in section 3, some features of the AD/CVD procedures and practices in the European Communities are briefly sketched. An overview of the import-incidence of the AD/CVD cases in the EC is provided in section 4. Section 5 contains the analysis of the country incidence of the AD/CVD cases and section 6 that of the sector incidence. The quantitative investigation reported in the last mentioned three sections (sections 4, 5 and 6) basically concentrates on the question of the amount of imports subjected to the AD/CVD cases in the European Communities. More specifically, it examines: (a) the prevalence (sector and country wise) of AD/CVD actions on EC's imports, (b) its frequency and changes over the period covered and (c) whether the imports from the developing countries are particularly affected by the AD/CVD actions. Although the empirical thrust of the analysis is based on the trade data compiled specifically for this study, information obtained by the analysis of the relevant case law and through discussions with practising lawyers and administrators at the Commission of the European Communities is used to complement, qualify or illustrate the patterns which the empirical data suggest and where possible, to draw reasonable inferences. These inferences and the main conclusions are summed up in the last section.

2. IMPORT RESTRICTIONS IN THE EUROPEAN COMMUNITIES: A BRIEF OVERVIEW

The arsenal of import restricting measures at the disposal of the European Communities consists of, in addition to tariffs, a number of non-tariff measures (NTBs). A selective list of such measures includes escape clause provisions, complaints against foreign government actions, anti-dumping and countervailing measures, various types of import licensing procedures, "voluntary" restraint arrangements, the Multifibre Arrangement, minimum price systems and various surveillance measures. This list does not necessarily include the separate measures which the member states might deploy (2) or the use of restrictive business practices such as market sharing, price fixing, collusive tendering, prohibitions on exports and tied purchasing designed to preserve existing trade flows and prevent or discourage new entrants. Neither does it include the so-called "new commercial policy instrument" established by Regulation 2641/84 adopted by the Council of the European Communities in September 1984 and which, in contrast to the anti-dumping countervailing duty or safeguard measures (which aim at avoiding or limiting injury caused to domestic industry by imports) enables the EC to respond to "unfair" trade practices attributable to third countries which adversely affects its exports (see Steenbergen (1985)).

A systematic quantification of the impact of the incidence of the various import restricting measures deployed by the European Communities is, of course, beyond the scope of this paper. A recent study (Nogués, Olechowski and Winters (1985)) which has examined the extent of NTBs to sixteen industrial countries' visible imports show that 22.3 per cent of the "own imports" of the EC were covered by such measures in the year 1983. (3) The corresponding figure for USA was 43.0% and Japan 11.9%. (4) One of the reasons behind this significant recourse to NTBs is probably the perception by a number of governments that tariffs, the traditional protectionist tool, have been negotiated down to levels at which they do not provide sufficient insulation for domestic industries. One estimate (UNCTAD (1982)) (5) puts the trade-weighted actual tariff rates for EC imports from the world at 2.1 per cent while the corresponding figure for the US is 4.3 per cent and for Japan 7.0 per cent. (6)

A common characteristic shared by a number of NTBs is that they tend to fall outside the traditional rules of the game based on principles of multilateralism and non-discrimination. But some non-tariff measures are less system-constrained than others. Thus, for example, protective measures taken by resorting to escape clause provisions under article XIX of GATT must normally be applied generally and may result in retaliatory action, taken in accordance with the provisions of GATT, by other signatories that have been adversely affected. But the anti-dumping and countervailing measures resorted to under articles VI, XVI and XXIII can be far more selective and discriminatory in character. Hence the temptation to use, in practice, the procedures foreseen under articles VI, XVI and XXIII as a substitute for measures under article XIX of GATT. This, plus the fact that the procedure for escape clause actions can be initiated only by the member states while the anti-dumping and anti-subsidy cases can be filed by member states or private parties has led to the situation that during the period 1980-1984, there were about 200 AD/CVD cases involving the imposition of definitive duties or the acceptance of price undertakings while there were just 3 cases of recourse to escape clause provisions. (7)

Although precise comparisons are difficult due to the inevitable differences in the methods of calculations, classification used, etc., the ratio of imports covered by the AD/CVD measures to the total imports is apparently far less important in the case of the European Communities than that of the USA. According to the study of Nogués, Olechowski and Winters (1985), the "monitoring measures" of which the AD/CVD cases form one of the components, covered 7.8 per cent of the total imports of the EC in 1983 compared to 34.9 per cent in the case of the United States. While the imports under AD/CVD cases are not separately given in that particular study, our own calculations, presented in more detail elsewhere in this paper, show that imports under such cases covered 0.262 per cent of the total imports of the EC in that year. In contrast Finger's (1981) estimates (pertaining to the second half of 1970s) showed that about 1/6th of all US imports were covered by the AD/CVD cases. Although the import coverage of EC's AD/CVD cases are thus much smaller than that of the US it still merits closer scrutiny. For one thing, own import coverage ratios underestimate the real incidence of trade barriers, particularly in the case of AD/CVD actions. (8) Secondly, the general characteristics of the AD/CVD system already referred to and some of the particularities of the variant operated by the European Communities (which we shall presently examine) make it a potentially important trade-impeding instrument.

3. SOME FEATURES OF THE AD/CVD PROCEDURES AND PRACTICES IN THE EUROPEAN COMMUNITIES

Detailed information on the mechanism and procedures concerning the AD/CVD system of the European Communities are available elsewhere (see Cunnane and Stanbrook (1983), Tharakan (1985)) and hence we shall limit our analysis in this section to two of its particularities namely: (a) the discretionary powers of the administrators and (b) the popularity of price-undertakings. Both of these elements can, in principle, impart a bias to the pattern of the sector and country incidence of AD/CVD actions and hence are briefly described here.

(a) **The discretionary powers of the administrators**
In terms of Article VI of GATT, Article 2(1) of the Agreement on the Implementation of the Article VI of GATT and Article 2(2) of Regulation (EEC) 3017/79, "a product is considered to be dumped if its export price is less than its normal value". The most usual method of the determination of the normal value is by reference to the price paid or payable on the domestic market of the country of origin or export. But, for various reasons, this approach may not be always operational. (9) In such cases, "normal values" of the "like product" will have to be established on the basis of the export sales to third countries or of "constructed value". The American law lays down a minimum of 10% for overheads and 8% for profits in determining the constructed value while in the case of the Community what is stipulated is to apply a "reasonable

margin" of overheads and profit. In practice, the level of profits taken into account by the Commission has varied considerably from case to case. Only 1 per cent of profit was considered reasonable in the case of chemical fertilizers from the USA, (10) while in the 1985 case on electronic typewriters from Japan, 32.39% profit on turnover was considered reasonable. In the latter case, the rate of 32.39% profit was applied even to those exporters for whom no individual profit margin could be determined owing to lack of sales on their domestic market. (11)

In the construction of "normal value" in the case of state-trading countries, which is usually a complicated process, the discretion available to the administrators in the European Communities is substantial. The currencies of such countries are very often non-convertible. Costs and prices are determined by the state authorities as a function of the overall economic plan. In such cases, the Commission determines normal value on the basis of either export or domestic prices in a market economy third country or constructed value in a market economy third country. But the Community law lays down no specific guidelines for the choice of an analogue country. In practice, the market economy countries chosen for comparison have varied from Austria, Spain (before it joined the EC) and the Scandinavian countries. (12) Further, the constructing of prices for comparison in such cases obviously depends on the willingness of outside producers to open their books to EC investigators. Such "cooperation" could turn out to have some "boomerang" effects. (13)

Since a product is considered to be dumped if its export price is less than its normal value, the Commission has to, in addition to the construction of the normal value, also estimate the "normal export price". The Regulation defines "export price" as the price actually paid or payable for the product sold for export to the Community. In order to construct an export price, the Commission establishes the price at which the imported product is first resold to an independent buyer and then reduces this price by the amount of costs incurred between importation and resale. The Regulation lays down that in addition to the costs incurred, allowance must be made for "a reasonable profit", but no basis is provided for constructing what could be considered as "reasonable profit". In some cases, the approach adopted by the Commission was to take the average of the profit realized by the importers of the product in question in the

Table 4.1: Anti-dumping and Anti-subsidy Investigations in the European Communities in the period from 1st January 1980 to 31st December 1984

No.	Category	1980	1981	1982	1983	1984 Provisional
1	Investigations initiated during the period (a)	25	48	58	38	43
2	Investigations concluded by the imposition of definitive duties	8	10	7	20	9
3	Investigations concluded by the acceptance of price-undertaking	46	7	35	27	29
4	Investigations concluded by the determination either of no dumping, no subsidization or no injury	9	13	9	8	12
5	Provisional duties imposed during the period	7	10	18	22	14

Table 4.1: continued

(a) The number of cases initiated will only rarely be equal to the cases terminated in the same year, as the latter cases will generally be initiated earlier.

Sources: Commission of the European Communities, First Annual Report of the Commission of the European Communities on the Community's Anti-Dumping and Anti-subsidy Activities, submitted to the Council and the European Parliament by the Commission, COM (83) 519 final/2, Brussels, September 28, 1983 (mimeo).
Commission of the European Communities, Second Annual Report of the Commission of the European Communities to the European Communities on the Community's Anti-dumping and Anti-subsidy Activities, COM (84) 721 final, Brussels, December 17, 1984 (mimeo).
Various issues of the Official Journal of the European Communities, 1984

EC. In other cases, it has taken the average profit made by the importing company on all its operations. In the 1985 case concerning electronic typewriters from Japan, in the construction of export prices, the Commission estimated first a rate of profit on the sales of the producing firm to its affiliate in the E.C. and secondly on the sales of the affiliate to the independent buyer in the European Communities.

The treatment of countervailable subsidies in the EC Regulation No. 2176/84 is rather precise and an attempt is made to lay down some ground-rules for the definition and calculation of a subsidy and an illustrative list of export subsidies is provided as an annex to the Regulations. In general, a countervailable subsidy must involve a charge on the public account in the subsidizing country and confer a benefit on an industry. In the case of domestic subsidies - as distinct from export subsidies - two additional conditions, namely an adverse effect on conditions of normal competition and sector specificity of subsidies must be fulfilled before they risk countervailability. In general, the Commission tends to initiate very few subsidy investigations. For example, out of the 38 anti-dumping and countervailing duty cases initiated by the Commission in 1983, only 2 pertained to subsidies. One of the reasons for this apparent prudence could be that given the record of the Community's member states on subsidies, they are conscious of their vulnerability on this point and tend to avoid actions which could lead to retaliation.

(b) The frequency of price undertakings

The AD/CVD proceedings initiated in the European Communities might lead, after due investigation to a rejection of the claim if it is found that the conditions requiring anti-dumping measures are not met; or to acceptance of undertakings from the foreign exporters or to the imposition of provisional or definitive anti-dumping or countervailing duties. The practice by which the Commission terminates proceedings with the acceptance of undertakings concerning the price and/or the volume exported to the Community given by the exporters and in subsidy cases guaranteed by the government of the exporting country, is different from that which is followed by other major trading nations. Table 4.1 gives an overview of the frequency of the AD/CVD measures initiated and terminated in the European Communities during the period 1980-1984. As can be seen from the table, there was an increase in the anti-dumping and anti-subsidy investigations initiated between 1980 and 1982. The number of investigations concluded by the imposition of definitive duty also showed an upward trend during the years for which definitive data are available (1980-1983). An even more steady increase was seen for the number of cases in which provisional duties were imposed during 1980-1983. This is probably also due to the Community's recently adopted approach that once a preliminary determination has been made that dumping or subsidization has caused injury to a Community industry, provisional duties are to be imposed unless the exporter offers a satisfactory price-undertaking. (14)

The frequency with which the Commission has concluded AD/CVD investigations by the acceptance of a price-undertaking by the exporter has varied from year to year. But, as is evident from Table 4.1, it has remained an important means of concluding such investigations in the EC. For example, during the period 1980-1984, the number of investigations concluded by the acceptance of price-undertaking accounted for nearly 58 per cent of the total number of investigations concluded during 1980-1984. (15) During 1981, the corresponding figure was less than 25% and in 1983 it was just below 50%. But in 1980 and 1982 the number of investigations concluded by a price-undertaking accounted for 73% and 68.6% respectively of the total number of investigations concluded during those two years.

The rationale given for the adoption of price-undertakings as a means for concluding AD/CVD investigations is that it provides for the exploration of the possibility of a "constructive remedy" before imposing anti-dumping duties. Article 13 of the Anti-dumping code specifically encourages such undertakings where the exporters are from the developing countries. But those who are familiar with the actual working of the AD/CVD system in the European Communities suggest more mundane reasons for the high frequency of price-undertakings. (16) The exporters who are subjected to AD/CVD investigations prefer terminating the cases with a price-undertaking, once it is clear that duties will be imposed. Price increases, as distinct from the payment of AD/CVD duties mean that the exporters can pocket the difference instead of paying it into the coffers of the governments of the importing countries.

Their price advantage would be of course blunted, but they can, as some Japanese exporters are believed to have done, invest the additional profits thus accrued in research and development to introduce products which are technologically superior and could compete with EC producers in third markets or Europe itself. (17) The complainants do not generally object to terminating the cases with a price-undertaking by the exporter, because first of all their primary objective of raising the price of their rivals' product is achieved and secondly because they do not usually want to push the matters to the point of imposition of definitive duty as this might provoke retaliation against their exports to their competitors' countries. It is likely that the Commission itself perceives the price-undertakings as a rather gentlemanly way of settling the issue and minimizing the risk of economic and/or political retaliation. But when the Commission is actively involved in pursuing AD/CVD actions against a particular country which it considers to be circumventing the barriers through the acceptance of price-undertakings and subsequent shift to a similar, yet differentiated competitive product, it might reject the offer of price-undertakings. (18)

The termination of an AD/CVD case by the acceptance of a price-undertaking by the exporter concerned still leaves the possibility to reactivate the case if "circumstances change". For example, in October 1983, the Commission had accepted a price-undertaking concerning the imports of copper sulphate from Czechoslovakia. But in 1984, in the light of the increase in the price of the raw material, increase in the imports of copper sulphate from Czechoslovakia, etc. the Commission reopened the case, dumping was found to exist and Czechoslovakia offered another price-undertaking which was accepted by the Commission. (19)

Quoting Van Bael (1978), Nelson (1981) argues that the Commission's apparent policy of favouring the enforcement of the anti-dumping and anti-subsidy regulation by the conclusion of price-undertakings may be explained by the fact that by doing so, the Commission avoids having to go to the Council of Ministers (which tends to stress the national interests of the member states) for approval of its actions (pp. 31-32). But the undertakings are now accepted by the Commission only after a formal decision has been reached that dumping or subsidization has taken place and caused injury to the Community industry. And during the course of such proceedings, the member states can have their say, particularly in the Advisory Committee.

4. IMPORTS UNDER THE AD/CVD CASES IN THE EUROPEAN COMMUNITIES

An overview of the imports under the AD/CVD cases in the European Communities is given in Table 4.2. The value figures contained in the table were obtained by grouping together data on imports collected on a case by case basis, at the most detailed level of aggregation available. (20) A brief analysis of the overall figures thus obtained is in order before examining the more detailed country and sector breakdown provided in the subsequent sections.

As Table 4.2 clearly shows, there has been an increase in the value of the imports subjected to AD/CVD investigations in the European Communities in recent years. In 1980, imports worth about 376 million ECU were covered by the AD/CVD cases initiated. By 1983, the corresponding figure stood at more than 1.7 billion ECU. Even if we use 1981 as the base year in order to avoid the distortion caused by the non-inclusion of the figures pertaining to Greece in 1980, the imports affected by the AD/CVD cases had increased by more than 3.5 times by 1983. Such imports as percentage of total imports into European Communities increased steadily from 0.072 per cent in 1980 to 0.262 per cent in 1983. During the period 1980-1983, about 0.173 per cent of the imports into the European Communities came under AD/CVD investigations. The imports from LDCs similarly affected as percentage of total imports from the LDCs into the European Communities were somewhat higher at 0.209%.

The imports under AD/CVD cases terminated by the acceptance of price-undertakings showed a less consistent pattern. Such imports amounted to 408 million ECU in 1980. It declined sharply in 1981 and by 1983 had reached a figure (244 million ECU) which was still much smaller than that for 1980. During the period 1980-1983, the value of the imports covered by such undertakings accounted for 0.040 per cent of the total imports into the European Communities. The corresponding figure for the LDCs was almost identical at 0.039 per cent.

The imports under AD/CVD cases concluded by the

Table 4.2: Imports under the Anti-dumping and Countervailing Duty (AD/CVD) Cases in the European Communities 1980-1983. An Overview

No.	Category	1980		1981		1982	
		Value in million ECU	Per cent of total imports	Value in million ECU	Per cent of total imports	Value in million ECU	Per cent of total imports
1	Imports under AD/CVD cases initiated	376	0.072	497	0.086	1535	0.243
2	Imports under AD/CVD cases terminated by the acceptance of price-undertakings	408	0.079	159	0.027	143	0.023
3	Imports under AD/CVD cases terminated by the imposition of definitive duties	70	0.014	204	0.035	242	0.038

Table 4.2: continued

| No. | Category | 1983 | | 1980–1983 | | Imports from the LDCs affected as % of total imports from LDCs |
		Value in million ECU	Per cent of total imports	Value in million ECU	Per cent of total imports	
1	Imports under AD/CVD cases initiated	1742	0.262	4150	0.173	0.209
2	Imports under AD/CVD cases terminated by the acceptance of price-undertakings	244	0.037	954	0.040	0.039
3	Imports under AD/CVD cases terminated by the imposition of definitive duties	114	0.017	630	0.026	0.013

Note: The value figures are rounded to the nearest million and the percentage figures are rounded to the nearest decimal.

Sources: The value figures were obtained from data on imports collected on a case by case basis at the finest level of disaggregation available. For details concerning the data sources see Tharakan (1986).

imposition of definitive duties rose from about 70 million ECU in 1980 to about 242 million ECU in 1982, but then declined sharply in 1983 to 114 million ECU.

During the period 1980-1983, 0.026 per cent of the total imports were affected by the cases concluded by the imposition of definitive duties. The corresponding figure for the LDCs was about half of that (0.013%).

If the more recent developments (pertaining to the years 1985 and 1986) reported in sub-section 6.d of this paper are any guide, the imports affected by the AD/CVD cases initiated and terminated by the imposition of definitive duties are likely to maintain their upward trend.

In concluding this section, a few words of comparison between our estimates and those of UNCTAD (1984) which were basically limited to 1980 and 1981 (and give only aggregate figures) are in order. Unfortunately, because of the differences in the system of aggregation and coverage used, no direct comparison between the two estimates is possible. But if we limit ourselves to the total of the two categories (21) included in both studies, it can be seen that the UNCTAD estimates of the value of the imports into the EC affected are less than our estimates by 167 million ECU in 1980 and 131.3 million ECU in 1981. But as the UNCTAD (1984) document itself suggests, because of the method it made use of, its computations are likely to have led to an underestimate. The most important difference with our estimates is in the coverage. The UNCTAD (1984) study used a sample which covered "75 to 95 per cent of products and countries involved in all investigations". (22) We covered all cases.

5. COUNTRY INCIDENCE OF AD/CVD CASES IN THE EUROPEAN COMMUNITIES

In view of the extensive nature of the data presented here on the country incidence of AD/CVD cases (and on sector incidence in the ensuing section) the following streamlining procedures are adopted for our analysis. Only the tables containing information on AD/CVD cases initiated are presented in the text. The tables pertaining to the AD/CVD cases terminated by price-undertakings and imposition of definitive duties are presented in Tharakan (1986), but the main elements of the information given there are analysed in the text. To limit the inevitable tedium resulting from the reference to numerous figures, only those instances where the imports affected amount to at least 1 per cent of the imports, from the countries concerned or where imports were affected in a number of years are mentioned in the analysis. In order to illustrate the nature of some of the cases represented by these figures, some of the details are explained in a selected number of instances, particularly where less developed countries were involved.

(a) **Country incidence of AD/CVD cases initiated**

As the figures given in the last column of Table 4.3 show, if we consider the period 1980-1983 together, only in the case of 5 countries the imports under AD/CVD cases initiated in the European Communities amounted to more than 1 per cent of the total imports from the countries concerned into the EC.

These countries were: Argentina (6.157%), the German Democratic Republic (1.451%), Japan (1.706%), Norway (1.343%) and Surinam (6.788%). Yugoslavia came close to being in this group with 0.959%. In the case of Surinam, the high percentage of imports coming under AD/CVD cases initiated was due to just one case (concerning Unwrought aluminium) in one year (1983). In the case of Argentina also, the high percentage is basically the result of one case (concerning soya bean oil cake) initiated in 1983. That particular case was a countervailing duty case filed by the "Fédération de l'Industrie de l'Huilerie" (FEDIOC) which claimed that the Argentinian government provided subsidies and preferential rates for the financing of exports and reimbursed direct taxes.

The analysis of the figures pertaining to individual years reveal the following points: In the case of 8 countries, AD/CVD cases were initiated in every year during the period 1980-1984. (23) These countries were Brazil, Canada, China, Hungary, Japan, Spain, USA and USSR. Only the German Democratic Republic had more than 1 per cent of its exports to the European Communities affected by AD/CVD cases in more than one year during the period 1980-1983.

Over the period considered here, there has been an increase in the number of countries whose exports to EC were affected at least up to 1 per cent by the AD/CVD cases initiated. In 1980, only the Dominican Republic fell in this category. This was due to just one case concerning the

Table 4.3: Country Incidence of the Antidumping and Countervailing Duty Cases (AD/CVD) Initiated in the European Communities (January 1980 – December 1984)

Eurostat-Nomenclature Country

Imports under the Antidumping and Countervailing Duty Cases Initiated

	Country	1980 Per cent of total imports	1981 Per cent of total imports	1982 Per cent of total imports	1983 Per cent of total imports	1984(a) Per cent of total imports	1980-1983 Value (in '000 ECU)	1980-1983 Per cent of total imports
528	Argentina	0.000	0.000	0.383	22.214	10.730	460173	6.157
800	Australia	0.000	0.000	0.412	0.000	0.000	12178	0.109
038	Austria	0.000	0.000	0.042	0.000	0.000	3605	0.011
508	Brazil	0.181	0.959	2.147	0.001	16.825	189257	0.851
068	Bulgaria	0.000	0.048	0.000	0.000	0.132	269	0.013
404	Canada	0.038	1.195	0.508	0.028	0.078	117193	0.456
720	China	0.192	0.156	0.435	0.067	0.067	19074	0.208
062	Czechoslo-vakia	0.000	0.000	1.099	0.388	0.226	51743	0.780
456	Dominican Republic	3.708	0.000	0.000	0.249	0.000	2041	0.870
220	Egypt	0.000	0.000	0.000	2.546	0.000	75574	0.700
032	Finland	0.000	0.000	0.000	0.000	0.000		

Table 4.3: continued

Imports under the Antidumping and Countervailing Duty Cases Initiated

Eurostat-Nomenclature	Country	1980 Per cent of total imports	1981 Per cent of total imports	1982 Per cent of total imports	1983 Per cent of total imports	1984(a) Per cent of total imports	1980–1983 Value (in '000 ECU)	1980–1983 Per cent of total imports
052	German Democratic Republic	0.000	3.389	1.989	0.249	0.131	68469	1.451
064	Hungary	0.093	2.090	0.141	0.010	0.018	35585	0.169
024	Iceland	0.000	0.000	0.164	0.000	0.000	437	0.037
624	Israel	0.000	0.000	0.014	0.000	0.000	245	0.003
732	Japan	0.100	0.032	5.411	0.762	1.504	1142571	1.706
728	South Korea	0.000	1.295	0.000	0.000	0.000	30279	0.317
724	North Korea	0.000	0.000	0.647	0.000	0.000	1055	0.187
701	Malaysia	0.056	0.000	0.000	0.000	0.000	991	0.013
028	Norway	0.000	0.000	0.745	3.601	0.208	587929	1.343
060	Poland	0.000	0.840	0.320	0.100	0.084	26935	0.287
066	Romania	0.000	1.266	0.107	0.328	0.058	31004	0.435
706	Singapore	0.520	0.000	0.000	0.448	0.506	17538	0.278
390	South Africa	0.000	0.000	0.133	0.304	0.013	29168	0.107
042	Spain	0.227	0.028	0.320	0.944	0.227	163881	0.425

Table 4.3: continued

Eurostat-Nomenclature	Country	Imports under the Antidumping and Countervailing Duty Cases Initiated						
		1980 Per cent of total imports	1981 Per cent of total imports	1982 Per cent of total imports	1983 Per cent of total imports	1984(a) Per cent of total imports	1980-1983 Value (in '000 ECU)	1980-1983 Per cent of total imports
492	Surinam	0.000	0.000	0.000	22.863	0.000	49533	6.788
030	Sweden	0.050	0.000	0.033	0.000	0.048	10007	0.019
736	Taiwan	0.000	0.000	0.000	1.139	0.000	34499	0.334
680	Thailand	0.000	0.000	0.000	0.000	0.048	0	0.000
052	Turkey	0.000	0.000	0.472	0.452	0.000	16855	0.282
400	USA	0.696	0.340	0.158	C.010	0.063	562105	0.281
056	USSR	0.091	0.047	0.278	0.176	0.027	279357	0.468
484	Venezuela	0.000	0.000	0.879	0.000	0.000	21584	0.214
048	Yugoslavia	0.000	0.660	0.373	2.160	0.076	101159	0.959
382	Zimbabwe	0.000	0.000	2.143	0.000	0.000	7836	0.640

(a) The figures for 1984 should be considered as provisional, for reasons explained in Tharakan (1986)

Sources: Commission of the European Communities, Official Journal, C and L series, various issues, Brussels. EUROSTAT, Analytical Tables of Foreign Trade, NIMEXE Series, Volumes A to Z, various issues, Luxembourg. For details see Tharakan (1986).

product Furfal and involved about 2 million ECU. By 1981, imports under AD/CVD cases initiated affected more than 1 per cent of the total imports into the EC, of 5 countries, namely: Canada, the German Democratic Republic, Hungary, South Korea and Romania. In all these instances, except the one concerning South Korea, more than one case was involved. For South Korea, the case concerned monochrome portable television sets and the complaint was based on a comparison between the domestic prices in South Korea and that country's export prices in the European Communities. In the following year (1982) also there were 5 countries for which the imports affected by the AD/CVD investigations amounted to more than 1 per cent of the total imports and the countries concerned were: Brazil, Czechoslovakia, German Democratic Republic, Japan and Zimbabwe. In the case of Zimbabwe, only one case was involved and the product concerned was Ferro-Chromium the imports of which into the EC from Zimbabwe amounted to about 7.8 million ECU in 1982.

In 1983, there were 6 instances in which imports under AD/CVD cases initiated amounted to more than 1 per cent of the total imports. The countries concerned were: Argentina, Egypt, Norway, Surinam, Taiwan and Yugoslavia. For Argentina and Surinam, the imports affected as percentage of total imports from those countries to the EC in 1983 reached high figures: 22.214% and 22.863% respectively. The cases involved in these two instances as well as that of Norway have been already referred to while analysing the figures for 1980-1983 as a whole. In the cases of Taiwan and Egypt only one product each were involved. For Taiwan, the product concerned was Exterior-panel doors and the complainants claimed that the imports from Taiwan had gained important market shares, particularly in the UK and the Netherlands. Since the domestic market of Taiwan was considered to be too small, the "constructed price" in Taiwan was compared with the export price to the European Communities. In the case of Egypt, the product concerned was Unwrought aluminium and the complaint was based on a comparison of "constructed prices" for Egypt with the import prices into the European Communities. In the case of Yugoslavia, the following three products were involved: Artificial corundum, Unwrought aluminium and Caravans for camping.

(b) **Country-incidence of AD/CVD cases terminated by the acceptance of price-undertakings**

A detailed analysis of the country-incidence of AD/CVD cases terminated by price undertakings in the European Communities is given in Tharakan (1986). Summarizing, if we consider the data for the period 1980-1983 as a whole, for two countries the imports coming under this category of cases amounted to more than 1 per cent of the total imports coming into the EC from those countries. These countries were Czechoslovakia and the German Democratic Republic.

The figures pertaining to the individual years reflect - imperfectly of course - the fluctuating pattern of the frequency of these cases noted in sub-section 3.b on the basis of the number of cases. In 1980, the cases concluded by the acceptance of price-undertakings accounted for more than 1 per cent of the imports coming to the EC from Czechoslovakia (9.428%), the German Democratic Republic (2.433%), Hungary (1.775%) and Poland (1.148%). In 1981 only in the case of Brazil (1.235%) did the corresponding figure reach this benchmark. In 1982, imports under AD/CVD cases concluded by the acceptance of price-undertakings reached more than 1 per cent of the imports into the EC from the German Democratic Republic (3.325%) and Hungary (1.474%). In 1983, this was the case for Czechoslovakia (1.230%), the German Democratic Republic (1.173%) and Zimbabwe (2.888%).

For some countries, the termination of AD/CVD cases by the acceptance of price-undertakings has been a regular feature during the years considered here. Thus, Japan, Poland, Romania and the USSR concluded price-undertakings with the European Communities in every one of the five years during the period 1980-1984. In the case of three centrally planned economies, namely Czechoslovakia, the German Democratic Republic and Hungary the imports under price-undertakings amounted to more than 1 per cent in more than one year during the period 1980-1983. Romania came close to being in this category. In general the impression that emerges is that in terms of frequency and incidence, the centrally planned economies had greater recourse to this way of terminating AD/CVD cases than other countries during the period considered here.

(c) **Country-incidence of AD/CVD cases terminated by the imposition of definitive duties**

For the period 1980-1983 as a whole, only in the case of Turkey did the imports under the AD/CVD cases terminated by the imposition of definitive duties amount to more than 1 per cent of the total imports from a particular country into the European Communities. This was due to one decision affecting one industry in 1982. The product concerned was cotton yarn (24) and this decision resulted from a case that was initiated in 1979. (25)

If we consider the data for individual years separately, only in the case of Turkey pertaining to the decision in 1982 mentioned above did the imports affected account for more than 1 per cent of the total imports from any given country into the E.C. No country had definitive AD/CVD duties imposed on its exports to the European Communities during every one of the years during the period 1980-1984. But in the cases of the German Democratic Republic, USSR and USA, in four out of the five years concerned, there was the occurrence of the imposition of definitive duties. Brazil had definitive AD/CVD duties imposed on its exports to the European Communities in 1982 and 1983. The imports concerned in 1982 were Steel sheets and in 1983 Steel coils for re-rolling. The last mentioned product was also adversely affected by the imposition of definitive duties in 1983 in the cases of two other developing countries: Argentina and Venezuela. Singapore and Yugoslavia were the two other developing countries whose exports were subjected to the imposition of definitive anti-dumping duties during the period considered here. In the case of Singapore, the product concerned was "certain types of ball bearings" and in the case of Yugoslavia it was copper sulphate which was subjected to the imposition of definitive anti-dumping duties.

6. SECTOR-INCIDENCE OF AD/CVD CASES IN THE EUROPEAN COMMUNITIES

In choosing the level of aggregation at which the detailed NIMEXE 6 digit data were to be regrouped, we have opted for the Customs Cooperation Council Nomenclature (CCCN) 2 digit chapter headings. Choice of a more detailed level of aggregation such as NIMEXE 4 digit would have rendered the comprehensive presentation and analysis of the extensive data collected practically impossible within the restricted confines of an article. Nevertheless this high level of aggregation should be kept in mind while referring to yardsticks of convenience such as 1 per cent of imports.

(a) Sector-incidence of AD/CVD cases initiated

The sector incidence of the AD/CVD cases initiated in the European Communities during the period 1980-1984 is shown in Table 4.4. If we take the period 1980-1983 as a whole, in the case of 4 sectors, the imports of products subjected to AD/CVD cases amounted to more than 1 per cent of the total imports into the European Communities in the sectors concerned. These were: CCCN 23 Residues and waste from the food industries, prepared animal fodder (1.785%); CCCN 75 Nickel and articles thereof (1.882%); CCCN 76 Aluminium and articles thereof (3.444%); and CCCN 92 Musical instruments, sound recorders or reproducers, television image and sound recorders or reproducers, parts and accessories of such articles (5.083%).

Consideration of the figures pertaining to individual years show a certain amount of shift in the pattern of high sector incidence. In the year 1980 four sectors had more than 1 per cent of their imports into the E.C. subjected to the initiation of AD/CVD cases. They were: CCCN 29 Organic Chemicals (1.659%), CCCN 31 Fertilizers (2.819%), CCCN 35 Albuminoidal substances, glues and enzymes (1.112%) and CCCN 51 Man-made fibres (continuous) (2.453%). In the case of Organic chemicals 5 NIMEXE six digit products imported from different sources were involved. But in the case of Fertilizers there was only one case against imports from USA amounting to about 53.5 million ECU which accounted for the "high" percentage of imports affected. In the case of Albuminoidal substances etc. also only one case involving Gelatine imported from Sweden was involved. In the case of Man-made fibres (continuous), the products subjected to the AD/CVD cases were Polyester yarn and Textured polyester fabrics, both imported from USA.

In 1981, the sectors which had more than 1 per cent of their imports adversely affected by the initiation of AD/CVD cases were entirely different from those thus affected during the previous year and consisted of: CCCN 44 Wood and articles of wood, wood charcoal (2.054%); CCCN 62 Other made up textile articles (1.908%); and

CCCN 64 Footwear, gaiters and the like, parts of such articles (1.187%). In the case of Wood and articles of wood, there were two products at NIMEXE six digit level involved. These were Fibre-building board imported from Bulgaria and Hungary, and plywood imported from Canada and USA. The "high" percentage of imports adversely affected in the sector of other made up textile articles has been due to one case concerning Polyester/cotton bed linen from the US. An anti-subsidy case on the imports of women's shoes from Brazil accounted for the import incidence shown in the case of the Footwear group of products. This particular complaint was based on a claim that the Brazilian authorities had installed a direct export subsidy of 15% in the case of that country's exports of women's shoes.

In the year 1982, for CCCN 73 Iron and steel and articles thereof and CCCN 92 Musical instruments, sound recorders or reproducers, television image and sound recorders or reproducers, parts and accessories of such articles, the imports covered by the AD/CVD cases accounted for more than 1 per cent of the total imports into the E.C. in those sectors. In the case of sector CCCN 73 there were 15 different cases involving a number of products and concerning countries as varied as Sweden and Zimbabwe. Brazil had anti-dumping <u>and</u> anti-subsidy investigations initiated against its exports of steel plates and steel sheets to the European Communities. Similarly Spain had cases initiated against it on both counts in the case of steel broad-flanged beams. In the case of sector CCCN 92, the imports adversely affected amounted to 19.172% of the imports coming into the EC in that sector. The product concerned in this case was video tape recorders from Japan and the imports of that particular product in 1982 amounted to 943 million ECU or 74.68% of the total imports of video tape recorders into the European Communities in that year!

In 1983 the imports adversely affected surpassed the benchmark 1 per cent in the case of the following 5 sectors: CCCN 23 Residues and waste from the food industries, prepared animal fodder; CCCN 37 Photographic and cinematographic goods; CCCN 69 Ceramic products; CCCN 75 Nickel and articles thereof; and CCCN 76 Aluminium and articles thereof. In the case of CCCN 23 one case - concerning soya bean oil cake from Argentina which we referred to while analysing the country incidence - accounted for the high percentage. For the sector CCCN 37

Table 4.4: Sector Incidence of Antidumping and Countervailing Duty (AD/CVD) Cases Initiated in the European Communities (January 1980 - December 1984)

| CCCN (1) Description of the Sector | Imports under the Antidumping and Countervailing Duty Cases Initiated | | | | | | |
	1980 Per cent of total imports in the sector	1981 Per cent of total imports in the sector	1982 Per cent of total imports in the sector	1983 Per cent of total imports in the sector	1984 Per cent of total imports in the sector	1980-1983 Value (in '000 ECU)	1980-1983 Per cent of total imports in the sector
11 Products of the milling industry; malt and starches; gluten; insulin	0.505	0.000	0.000	0.000	0.000	2309	0.126
20 Preparations of vegetables, fruit or other parts of plants	0.000	0.000	0.759	0.000	0.000	23538	0.203
23 Residues and waste from the food industries; prepared animal fodder	0.000	0.000	0.000	5.760	17.280	453034	1.785

Table 4.4: continued

CCCN (1) Description of the Sector	Imports under the Antidumping and Countervailing Duty Cases Initiated						
	1980 Per cent of total imports in the sector	1981 Per cent of total imports in the sector	1982 Per cent of total imports in the sector	1983 Per cent of total imports in the sector	1984 Per cent of total imports in the sector	1980-1983 Value (in '000 ECU)	1980-1983 Per cent of total imports in the sector
25 Salt; sulphur; earths and stone; plastering materials, lime and cement	0.000	0.000	0.253	0.000	0.000	9384	0.064
28 Inorganic chemicals, organic and inorganic compounds of precious metals, of rare earth metals, of radio active elements and of isotopes	0.000	0.035	0.302	0.161	0.750	32756	0.129
29 Organic chemicals	1.659	0.357	0.397	0.048	0.097	313156	0.535
31 Fertilizers	2.819	0.000	0.000	0.000	0.000	53494	0.583

Table 4.4: continued

Imports under the Antidumping and Countervailing Duty Cases Initiated

CCCN (1) Description of the Sector	1980 Per cent of total imports in the sector	1981 Per cent of total imports in the sector	1982 Per cent of total imports in the sector	1983 Per cent of total imports in the sector	1984 Per cent of total imports in the sector	1980-1983 Value (in '000 ECU)	1980-1983 Per cent of total imports in the sector
35 Albuminoidal substances; glues; enzymes	1.112	0.000	0.000	0.000	0.000	5638	0.225
37 Photographic and cinematographic goods	0.000	0.000	0.000	2.649	0.000	79347	0.755
39 Artificial resins and plastic materials; cellulose esters and ethers; articles thereof	0.000	0.415	0.646	0.000	0.028	158319	0.263
44 Wood and articles of wood; wood charcoal	0.035	2.054	0.184	0.340	0.000	238486	0.633

Table 4.4: continued

Imports under the Antidumping and Countervailing Duty Cases Initiated

CCCN (1) Description of the Sector	1980 Per cent of total imports in the sector	1981 Per cent of total imports in the sector	1982 Per cent of total imports in the sector	1983 Per cent of total imports in the sector	1984 Per cent of total imports in the sector	1980-1983 Value (in '000 ECU)	1980-1983 Per cent of total imports in the sector
48 Paper and paperboard; articles of paper pulp, of paper or of paperboard	0.004	0.000	0.000	0.000	0.102	338	0.001
51 Man-made fibres (continuous)	2.453	0.000	0.000	0.000	0.000	61499	0.536
56 Man-made fibres (discontinuous)	0.000	0.000	0.000	0.216	0.126	9249	0.061
62 Other made up textile articles	0.000	1.908	0.000	0.000	0.000	24703	0.471

Table 4.4: continued

CCCN (1) Description of the Sector	1980 Per cent of total imports in the sector	1981 Per cent of total imports in the sector	1982 Per cent of total imports in the sector	1983 Per cent of total imports in the sector	1984 Per cent of total imports in the sector	1980-1983 Value (in '000 ECU)	1980-1983 Per cent of total imports in the sector
64 Footwear, gaiters and the like; parts of such articles	0.000	1.187	0.000	0.000	0.000	50071	0.274
68 Articles of stone, of plaster, of cement, of asbestos, of mica and of similar materials	0.000	0.000	0.000	0.000	0.297	0	0.000
69 Ceramic products	0.000	0.000	0.000	2.020	0.000	50845	0.515
70 Glass and glassware	0.000	0.000	0.230	0.360	0.023	19795	0.163

Imports under the Antidumping and Countervailing Duty Cases Initiated

Table 4.4: continued

CCCN (1) Description of the Sector	1980 Per cent of total imports in the sector	1981 Per cent of total imports in the sector	1982 Per cent of total imports in the sector	1983 Per cent of total imports in the sector	1984 Per cent of total imports in the sector	1980–1983 Value (in '000 ECU)	1980–1983 Per cent of total imports in the sector
73 Iron and steel and articles thereof	0.024	0.023	1.237	0.318	0.007	416341	0.418
75 Nickel and articles thereof	0.000	0.000	0.000	8.419	0.000	80390	1.882
76 Aluminium and articles thereof	0.000	0.000	0.114	11.450	0.000	839135	3.444
81 Other base metals employed in metallurgy and articles thereof	0.000	0.000	0.000	0.000	9.664	0	0.000

Imports under the Antidumping and Countervailing Duty Cases Initiated

Table 4.4: continued

CCCN (1) Description of the Sector	Imports under the Antidumping and Countervailing Duty Cases Initiated						
	1980 Per cent of total imports in the sector	1981 Per cent of total imports in the sector	1982 Per cent of total imports in the sector	1983 Per cent of total imports in the sector	1984 Per cent of total imports in the sector	1980-1983 Value (in '000 ECU)	1980-1983 Per cent of total imports in the sector
82 Tools, implements, cutlery, spoons and forks, of base metal; parts thereof	0.000	0.000	0.000	0.013	0.000	345	0.004
84 Boilers, machinery and mechanical appliances; parts thereof	0.094	0.109	0.046	0.140	0.474	202601	0.097
85 Electrical machinery and equipment, parts thereof	0.000	0.173	0.000	0.000	0.000	43440	0.041

Table 4.4: continued

Imports under the Antidumping and Countervailing Duty Cases Initiated

CCCN (1) Description of the Sector	1980 Per cent of total imports in the sector	1981 Per cent of total imports in the sector	1982 Per cent of total imports in the sector	1983 Per cent of total imports in the sector	1984 Per cent of total imports in the sector	1980–1983 Value (in '000 ECU)	1980–1983 Per cent of total imports in the sector
87 Vehicles, other than railway or tramway rolling-stock, and parts thereof	0.000	0.000	0.000	0.006	0.000	2573	0.002
97 Toys, games and sports requisites; parts thereof	0.000	0.000	0.000	0.000	0.147	0	0.000
90 Optical, photographic, cinematographic, measuring, checking, precision, medical and surgical instruments and apparatus; parts thereof	0.000	0.011	0.000	0.000	0.000	1299	0.003

Table 4.4: continued

CCCN (1) Description of the Sector	Imports under the Antidumping and Countervailing Duty Cases Initiated						
	1980 Per cent of total imports in the sector	1981 Per cent of total imports in the sector	1982 Per cent of total imports in the sector	1983 Per cent of total imports in the sector	1984 Per cent of total imports in the sector	1980-1983 Value (in '000 ECU)	1980-1983 Per cent of total imports in the sector
91 Clocks and watches and parts thereof	0.685	0.000	0.000	0.000	0.000	9844	0.164
92 Musical instruments; sound recorders or reproducers; television image and sound record- ers or reproducers; parts and access- ories of such articles	0.000	0.537	19.172	0.000	0.000	968200	5.083

(1) CCCN: Customs Cooperation Council Nomenclature

Note: The figures for 1984 should be considered as provisional for reasons explained in Tharakan (1986).

Sources: Commission of the European Communities, Official Journal, C and L series, various issues, Brussels. EUROSTAT, Analytical Tables of Foreign Trade, NIMEXE Series, Volumes A to Z, various issues, Luxembourg. For details see Tharakan (1986).

also just one case concerning the imports of Sensitized paper for colour photographs from Japan led to the percentage mentioned above. In the case of CCCN 76, imports coming from Egypt, Surinam and Yugoslavia as well as Norway and USSR were involved.

Although there were thus clear shifts in the sectors whose imports were rather significantly and adversely affected by AD/CVD proceedings, some sectors showed high frequency of such cases over the period considered. In every one of the five years during the period 1980-1984 imports in sectors CCCN 29 Organic chemicals, CCCN 73 Iron and steel and articles thereof and CCCN 84 Boilers, machinery and mechanical appliances and parts thereof, were subjected to AD/CVD cases. Imports in CCCN 28 Inorganic chemicals etc. and CCCN 44 Wood and articles of wood were similarly affected in four out of the five years considered here.

(b) **Sector incidence of the AD/CVD cases terminated by the acceptance of price-undertakings**

In none of the sectors did imports under the price-undertakings reach 1 per cent of the imports into the EC, if we consider the data for the period 1980-1983 together. But in 1980, CCCN 44 Wood and articles of wood, wood charcoal (1.017%) and in 1981, CCCN 64 Footwear, gaiters and the like, parts of such articles (1.463%) reached this benchmark. Provisional data for 1984 show that in the case of CCCN 37 Photographic and cinematographic goods also a rather high proportion of imports (2.649%) came under the AD/CVD cases terminated by price-undertakings. We have referred to this case in the context of the initiation of AD/CVD proceedings in 1983. (26)

The frequency of price undertakings was highest in CCCN 73 Iron and steel and articles thereof as such undertakings were reached in every one of the years during 1980-1984. In the case of two other sectors, price-undertakings were reached in 4 out of the 5 years considered here: CCCN 29 Organic chemicals and CCCN 44 Wood and articles of wood.

(c) **Sector incidence of AC/CVD cases terminated by the imposition of definitive duties**

Only in the case of one sector, namely CCCN 55 Cotton did the AD/CVD cases terminated by the imposition of definitive duties amount to more than 1 per cent of the total imports in a sector if we consider the period 1980-1983 as a whole. This was due to the imposition of definitive anti-dumping duties on the imports of cotton yarn from Turkey which we have already mentioned in section 5 while analysing the country incidence.

If we consider individual years separately, the following observations can be made. In 1980, only one sector i.e. CCCN 51 Man-made fibres (continuous) had more than 1 per cent of its imports adversely affected by the imposition of definitive duties. The specific product concerned was Polyester yarn imported from the United States. In the year 1981, two sectors - CCCN 29 Organic chemicals (1.045%) and CCCN 31 Fertilizers (1.711%) - were in this category. In the case of Organic chemicals, three specific products were involved: Paraxylene, Styrene Monomer and Vinyl Acetate Monomer. The imports came mainly from the United States. The case involving Fertilizers also involved the United States. The case dealing with cotton (3.892%) in 1982 has been already referred to. In 1983 and 1984, there were no sectors which had more than 1 per cent of its imports adversely affected by the imposition of definitive duties.

Concerning the frequency of the incidence, it should be noted that there were no sectors which came under the imposition of definitive duties in every one of the 5 years considered here. But two sectors had their products adversely affected by the imposition of definitive duties during four of the five years taken into account here. These were: CCCN 29 Organic chemicals and CCCN 73 Iron and steel and articles thereof.

(d) **Some recent developments**

As the foregoing detailed analysis of the sector and country incidence of AD/CVD cases take into account data up to 1984 only, we shall very briefly mention some of the more recent developments to complete the picture. In 1985 and 1986, the AD/CVD investigations and decisions with respect to imports from Japan intensified. In March 1985, the Commission imposed a provisional tariff of 26.6 per cent on Hydraulic excavators exported to the EC by Komatsu of Japan. The complaint which led to this decision was initiated by European producers such as Britain's J.C. Bamford and W. Germany's Orenstein and Koppel and

Liebherr who were joined by Caterpillar Tractor of US who in fact has half of its sales outside the US Komatsu's offer for a price-undertaking was refused by the Commission and the duty was made definitive in July 1985. In order to circumvent the barrier Komatsu then started exploring the possibility of building a plant in Europe for building construction equipment. (27)

Another recent AD/CVD decision against Japanese imports that attracted considerable attention, concerned electronic typewriters. We have briefly referred to this case in section 3 while explaining the discretion available to the E.C. officials in determining reasonable rates of profits. The definitive duties of about 21-35 per cent which were imposed in June 1985 concerned a number of Japanese electronic typewriter exporters such as Brother, Canon, Silver Seiko, Tokyo Electric and Towa Sankiden. In October 1985 the decision was extended to include also the exports by Nakajima All, although the last mentioned company pointed out that one of the European companies launching the anti-dumping complaint - believed to be Olivetti of Italy - is a substantial importer of Nakajima All typewriters for sale under its own brand name and hence the claim of injury to the European industry is hardly credible. After the decision was made definitive, one of the Japanese companies concerned (the Brother manufacturing group) at least was reported to be building up the volume and range of electronic typewriter production at its newly established factory in Wales and in the meantime looking to develop its exports of computer printers, microwave ovens and sewing machines to the European market to make up for the impetus lost. (28)

In probably the biggest anti-dumping suit ever brought before the E.C. Commission, Rank Xerox and four other European photocopiers filed complaints against a number of Japanese firms such as Canon, Rioh, Toshiba, Minolta and others claiming that the Japanese are charging less in Europe than they do at home for the same products with the extra domestic revenue subsidizing overseas sales. Imports worth about $1 billion are involved and according to reports, the Commission was expected to find dumping margins of up to 40 per cent. (29) This complicated case with high stakes may turn out to be significant in many respects. The Japanese producers who rely on exports to absorb about 85 per cent of the copiers they make have unleashed a flurry of defensive activity by starting or expanding photocopier production in Europe. Minolta has acquired a 75% stake in Develop which is a party to the anti-dumping complaint! Canon plans to add and Rioh and Toshiba to begin copier production in Europe. Claiming that most of these plants will be used for assembling imported parts rather than for producing copiers from scratch, Rank Xerox is reported to be ready to file an anti-dumping complaint against the imports of photocopier parts.

7. SUMMARY AND CONCLUSIONS

The substantial amount of empirical and institutional information presented in the preceding sections lend themselves to certain inferences which we note at some length here in addition to summarizing the essential points reviewed so far.

The use of anti-dumping and countervailing measures which are less system-constrained than some other non-tariff measures such as recourse to escape clause provisions, has increased in the European Communities in recent years. The AD/CVD mechanism of the European Communities has certain particularities which, in principle, can render a bias in the country and sector incidence of such actions. One of these particularities is the greater discretionary powers which the EC administrators have, compared to their American counterparts, specifically in the determination of "reasonable" profit margins in constructing "normal" values and "normal" export prices. More important is the fact that the AD/CVD mechanism in the EC provides for the termination of the proceedings also by the acceptance of undertakings offered by the exporters. Substantial use of this mechanism has been made by the Commission during the period covered by this study. This high frequency of the price-undertakings is probably because the exporters find the arrangement profitable while the Commission and the complainants usually see it as a less harmful way to end the proceedings. Notwithstanding a certain flexibility provided by the mechanism of undertakings for treating particular cases, it can also lead to an increased emphasis on bilateralism. This hazard becomes specially pronounced if the AD/CVD mechanism is used to force exporters to enter into "Voluntary" Export Restraints.

Given the hitherto lack of sound empirical evidence concerning the import incidence of AD/CVD actions in the

European Communities, we have attempted to present, in some detail, the data we have compiled on this question. The major elements emerging from these data can be summarized and interpreted as follows:

The AD/CVD cases initiated in the EC covered a steadily increasing amount of imports during the period 1980-1983 for which there are definitive data available. The indications are that this trend continued in the subsequent years also. The imports thus affected as a percentage of the total imports coming into the EC also steadily increased during the period considered. Nevertheless, the import incidence of AD/CVD cases in the EC is apparently much smaller than that of USA. The value and the share of the imports under the AD/CVD cases terminated by the price-undertakings fluctuated. So did the value and the share of the imports under the AD/CVD cases terminated by the imposition of definitive duties.

The share of the imports of the LDCs against which AD/CVD cases were initiated in the total imports into the EC from them was somewhat higher (0.209% in comparison to 0.173%) than the corresponding figure concerning imports under all AD/CVD cases as a share of the total imports. The share of the imports for which AD/CVD cases were terminated by the acceptance of price-undertakings and by the imposition of definitive duties respectively were, in the case of LDCs less than that of all the imports affected by those two categories of cases in the total imports. Thus it cannot be argued that on the whole, the AD/CVD cases of the E.C. have had, during the period considered here, a clearly accentuated incidence on the imports from the developing countries. But this is only part of the story. In addition to the undeniable existence of such accentuated incidence in the case of particular developing countries, the LDCs as a whole face special difficulties in coping with AD/CVD procedures and practices. These have been presented in detail elsewhere (see UNCTAD (1984)) and hence require only a fleeting reference here. New entrants such as some of the developing countries into the international trade in manufactures may be easily perceived as carrying out dumping while the lower prices they offer might be simply due to their comparative advantage. One of the most detrimental affects of the AD/CVD procedures is the uncertainty and expenses they generate for the exporters, even if the complaints are finally rejected. Frequent investigations can constitute a harassment of the exporters involved and provides a mechanism which the protectionist lobbies can resort to. While these last mentioned considerations apply to AD/CVD cases against imports from all sources, the LDCs are less well equipped to cope with these difficulties. According to one source, (30) the cost of a fairly routine AD/CVD proceeding in the US can easily exceed $100,000. European sources suggest that the cost of such proceedings in the EC may not be much different. (31)

Detailed analysis of the country-incidence of the AD/CVD cases in the European Communities suggest certain patterns. Over the period considered here, there has been an increase in the number of countries whose exports to the EC were affected at least up to one per cent by the AD/CVD cases initiated. During particular years, certain developing countries had an important percentage of their total exports to the EC subjected to AD/CVD investigations. But in most of these cases such high percentages resulted from one case concerning one product, while in the case of market economy industrialised countries, the high percentages resulted from a number of cases involving different products.

As far as the AD/CVD cases terminated by the price-undertakings are concerned, both in terms of frequency and incidence, the centrally planned economies had greater recourse to this way of concluding such cases than other countries. Japan, and to a lesser extent, the U.S.A. also showed high frequency of undertakings. The frequency of definitive duties imposed was high for the German Democratic Republic, USA and the USSR.

The sector-incidence of the AD/CVD cases initiated in the European Communities has shown some fluctuations over the different years considered here. Nevertheless, over the period 1980-1984, high frequency of the initiation of such cases was seen in sectors such as Organic chemicals, Iron and steel and articles thereof, Boilers machinery and mechanical appliances, Inorganic chemicals and Wood and articles of wood. Three of the above mentioned sectors, namely Iron and steel and articles thereof, Organic chemicals and Wood and articles of wood also had a high frequency of price-undertakings. Such high frequency in the case of the imposition of definitive duties was evident again for Organic chemicals and Iron and steel and articles thereof. Note that in the above mentioned sectors (as well as in certain other sectors enumerated in the text) the imports covered by the AD/CVD cases amounted to a relatively "high" percentage of the total imports in those sectors in particular years.

While sectors such as Chemicals and Iron and steel are not usually associated with the comparative advantage of the LDCs, the imports of certain sub-categories of products from those sectors coming from the developing countries (for example, steel plates from Brazil) were involved in these AD/CVD actions. Note also that the basic price system for steel which was in operation in the EC till 1982, apparently contributed to the high frequency of AD/CVD actions in that sector. The most recent trends suggest that the thrust of the European Community's AD/CVD actions has been increasingly focusing on products such as electronic typewriters, photocopiers, etc. coming from Japan.

Notes
I am thankful to J.M. Finger for detailed comments on an earlier version of this paper, J. Bourgeois for explanations about the functioning of the Anti-dumping and Counter-vailing mechanism of the European Communities, L. Blieschies, H. Stardecker and R. Wright for suggesting sources or providing relevant documentation and maitre J. Steenbergen for patient clarifications about the growing case law in this field. None of them of course bear any responsibility for the results of the research I have reported here or the inferences I have drawn from my findings.

1.   Data on all cases were collected at NIMEXE 6 digit level and then aggregated to CCCN 2 digit chapter headings level and country totals. For details concerning the procedure use, see Tharakan (1986).

2.   Although the Treaty of Rome confers powers on common commercial policy to the Community, the EC has retained the practice of authorizing member states to keep certain national commercial policy measures mainly in cases where the policy or economic interests of the member states are too divergent to establish uniform Community rules, or where third countries are unwilling to enter into trade agreements with the European Community or for political or economic reasons.

3.   Nogués, Olechowski and Winters (1985) p.43.

4.   Ibid.

5. pp. 7-8.
6. The same source (UNCTAD 1982) estimates the actual trade-weighted tariffs on imports from the developing countries at 1.0 per cent in the EC, 3.0 per cent in USA and 4.2. per cent in Japan. The corresponding rates, exclusive of raw material products were 3.0 per cent, 6.7 per cent and 8.7 per cent respectively.
7. The data on AD/CVD case decisions are from the various issues of the <u>Official Journal of the European Communities</u>. The information on the number escape clause cases was provided by the Anti-dumping Unit of the Commission of the European Communities.
8. An important weakness of the "own imports coverage ratio" is that the more restrictive instruments tend to receive lower weight than less restrictive ones, because they reduce imports by more. Neither can it of course capture the uncertainty effect created by the initiation of AD/CVD actions, even if such cases are finally rejected by the Commission or the Courts.
9. For example, there may be no sales of a "like product" in the domestic market, the sales carried out may not be in the "ordinary course of trade", it may be between related companies or the sales in the domestic market of the exporting country may be made at a loss.
10. O.J.L. no. 39, 12.2.1981, p. 35.
11. O.J.L. no. 163/I, 22.6.1985.
12. See Buchan (1986).
13. Although this author could not trace such an occurrence in the EC cases, the reported experience of Finnish steel producers should cause some concern to those third country producers trying to decide whether to open their books to the EC investigators or not. The Finnish steel producers, in what has been termed "a fit of cooperation" opened their books to the US Commerce Department Officials measuring dumping margins of Romanian steel plates in 1982. An unexpected by-product of this cooperation was that the Finnish steel producers were hit by an anti-dumping petition themselves in 1984 on the basis of the same information!
14. Commission of the European Communities (1983), p.3.
15. AD/CVD investigations terminated by the imposition of definitive duties, by the acceptance of price-undertakings or by the decision that no dumping, subsidization or injury has occurred are considered here as

investigations concluded. If we take into account the period 1980-1983 for which definitive data are available, the number of price-undertakings marks out practically at the same level (5.78%) as the figure for the period 1980-1984.

16. For the points contained in the ensuing part of this paragraph, I am thankful to the explanations provided by Maitre Steenbergen.

17. See, for example the case concerning the Brother manufacturing group reported in sub-section 6.d of this paper.

18. A recent example of an offer for price-undertaking being rejected by the Commission was the case concerning hydraulic excavators exported by Japan's Komatsu. See sub-section 6.d of this study. The officials at the Anti-dumping Unit of the Commission also state that they are finding out that the price-undertakings are increasingly difficult to implement. Nevertheless, they insist that there has been no change in the policy concerning price-undertakings.

19. See OJL, 22.8.1984.

20. The reader is referred to Tharakan (1986) for the data sources, the method of calculations used, and the caveats in interpreting the results.

21. "Duty levied" plus "undertakings" in the UNCTAD study compared to "cases terminated by the imposition of definitive studies" plus "cases terminated by the acceptance of price-undertakings".

22. UNCTAD (1984), p.11.

23. In analysing the frequency of AD/CVD cases, the year 1984 is also taken into account as the exactness of the value figures are less important in this particular context.

24. This product group consists of several product items at NIMEXE six digit level, made up mainly of Bleached Cotton Yarn. The text of the decision (ref. OJL 3.4.1982) does not specify if the imposition of duties was limited to any particular product sub-group. Hence there is the possibility that the incidence is overestimated in this particular case.

25. Hence it does not appear among the cases initiated during the period 1980-1983 taken into account in Table 4.3.

26. This price-undertaking concerning the imports of sensitized paper for colour photographs from Japan was reached in 1984. Since the data used here refer to imports of 1983, the figures given here are not exact.

27.   Financial Times, 3.9.1985. According to the most recent reports available (see Financial Times, 2.7.1986), Komatsu is due to begin assembling excavators and wheel loaders near Newcastle (where it has set up a plant after EC's anti-dumping decision against it) in early 1987. An ironic twist to this development is the fact that out of the £12.5 million cost of Komatsu's Newcastle plant, about £2.65 million (or about 21.2%) was met by cash subsidies provided by the regional development funds and other selective financial assistance agencies in the United Kingdom! Recall that the original dumping margin found against Komatsu in 1985 was 26.6%. Note also that the import content of the output of the Newcastle plant will be 40%, although this is "expected to decline" in the coming years.

28.   Financial Times 8.10.1985.

29.   Financial Times 2.6.1986. EC sources have refused to confirm this report.

30.   UNCTAD (1984).

31.   But the same sources also point out that as far as lawyers' fees are concerned there is considerable variation between various EC countries. It seems that the range could be between 1 to 5. A recent, complex anti-dumping case handled by a British law firm is reported to have cost $200,000 in legal fees alone. It appears that the same case, if handled by law firms in some of the Continental countries would have cost only around $40,000. Although the procedure involves costs to both parties, it is more expensive to be a defendant than a complainant, especially in instances where the European Commission is actively pursuing such cases. The complainant can limit himself mainly to the costs of the research and legal fees, while the defendant has to incur larger legal expenses particularly for spending considerable time with the Commission Officials during the investigations and has to, in most cases, avail himself of the services of an independent auditor because the very fact that the case is filed, raises doubts about the objectivity of the reports of the defendant's auditors. Lobbying activity - and hence lobbying costs - are apparently much less in the EC than in the United States. Most of it is directed at the representatives of the member states. It was not possible to obtain specific figures concerning this activity.

References

Buchan, D. (1986) EEC takes Three-step Approach to Unfair Trade, Financial Times, February 13, p.4.

Commission of the European Communities (1983), First Annual Report of the Commission of the European Communities on the Community's Anti-Dumping and Anti-Subsidy Activities, Brussels, September 28th, COM (83), 519 final/2.

Commission of the European Communities (1984), Second Annual Report of the Commission of the European Communities to the European Communities on the Community's Anti-Dumping and Anti-Subsidy Activities, Brussels, December 17th, COM (84) 721 final.

Commission of the European Communities, Official Journal, C and L series, various issues during the period 1980-1985, Brussels.

Cunnane, J. and C. Stanbrook (1983), Dumping and Subsidies: the Law and Procedures governing the Imposition of Anti-Dumping and Counter-vailing Duties in the European Community, European Business Publications, London and Brussels.

EUROSTAT, Analytical Tables of Foreign Trade Import, NIMEXE series, volumes A to Z for the years 1980 to 1983, Luxembourg.

Financial Times (1985, 1986) various issues (see footnotes), London.

Finger, J.M. (1981), 'The Industry-Country Incidence of "Less than Fair Value" Cases in US Import Trade', Quarterly Review of Economics and Business, vol. 21. no. 2 (Summer), pp. 259-277.

Nelson D.R. (1981), The Political Structure of the New Protectionism, World Bank Staff Working Paper 471, Washington DC (mimeo).

Nogués, J.J., A. Olechowski and L.A. Winters (1985), The Extent of Non-Tariff Barriers to Industrial Countries' Imports, World Bank Discussion Paper, Report No. DRD 115, Washington D.C.

Steenbergen, J. (1985), Ondernemingen en handelspolitieke instrumenten: bescherming van export, Tijdschrift voor Europees en Economisch Recht, vol. 33, no. 10, pp. 624-636.

Tharakan, P.K.M. (1985), Administered Protection in the European Community, (mimeo).

Tharakan, P.K.M. (1986), Anti Dumping and Countervailing

Duty Cases in the European Community, (mimeo).
UNCTAD (1982), Protectionism and Structural Adjustment, Protectionism and Structural Adjustment in the World Economy: TD/B/888, Geneva.
UNCTAD (1984), Protectionism and Structural Adjustment: Anti-Dumping and Countervailing Duty Practices: Note by the UNCTAD Secretariat TD/B/979, 20 January, Geneva.
Van Bael, I. (1978), 'The EEC Anti-Dumping Rules: A Practical Approach', International Lawyer, vol. 12, pp. 523-545.

Part Two

SECTOR STUDIES

Chapter Five

EC AGRICULTURAL POLICIES AND THE DEVELOPING COUNTRIES

Wouter Tims

1. POLICIES AND DEVELOPMENTS IN THE EUROPEAN COMMUNITIES' AGRICULTURE

1.1 The common agricultural policy

Compared to the United States, agriculture in the European Communities (EC) has some distinct characteristics which go some way in explaining differences in agricultural policies. In 1980, total land used for agricultural purposes in the EC was less than one quarter as compared to the US, whereas the economically active population in EC agriculture was almost four times the number in the US (see Table 5.1).

Table 5.1: Agricultural land use and agriculturally active population in the EC and the US, 1980

	EC-10	U.S.
Land use (mln ha):		
arable land	49.0	188.8
permanently cropped land	5.8	1.9
permanent pasture	46.4	237.5
Total	101.2	428.2
Economically active population in agriculture ('000)	8,400	2,229
Agricultural land per economically active (ha/person)	12.5	192.0

Source: FAO Production Yearbook 1983.

For those employed in EC agriculture to achieve the same income as their counterparts in the US, they would need to be about 15 times as productive per hectare. In 1980 one could in fact consider parity between EC and US farmers to be a realistic objective as per capita GDP in the EC - at prevailing exchange rates - was within eight per cent of the level in the US, and parity between agricultural and non-agricultural incomes was an avowed objective for both. Farmers in the US came close to parity, in fact on average earning 90 per cent of non-farm average incomes. In the EC the gap was expectedly larger: on average farmers earn 45 per cent of what non-farm agriculturally active persons earn. In both cases this includes an element of support to farm incomes, without which farm incomes would be lower; one estimate (Buckwell et al. (1982)) suggests that farmers in the EC gained about one third of their total income from subsidies and through effects of price policies; another for the US (World Bank (1982)) suggests a similar 40 per cent. Even so, there is a very substantial difference in the income generated per hectare either including or excluding subsidies. Comparatively speaking EC agriculture is dominated by family farms which use a small area very intensively for relatively high-value products.

Against this background the objectives of the EC concerning agriculture are to be understood, as those are formulated in article 39 of the Treaty of Rome:

i   to increase agricultural productivity by developing technical progress and by ensuring the rational development of agricultural production and the optimum utilization of the factors of production, particularly labour;
ii to ensure thereby a fair standard of living for the agricultural population, particularly by increasing the individual earnings of persons engaged in agriculture;
iii to stabilize agricultural markets;
iv to guarantee regular supplies of food to consumers;
v   to ensure supplies at reasonable prices to consumers.

The purposes of the Common Agricultural Policy (CAP) in terms of increased agricultural production are not only to be understood as a means to enhance agricultural incomes but also as an expression of the desire to reduce the dependence of the EC-countries on food imports. These constituted a significant part of consumption in the EC at the time when the CAP was formulated.

Between 1960 and 1964 the CAP was given its shape and content which remained in effect to the present day. Its cornerstone is a market and price policy for the most important agricultural products, executed by the European Orientation and Guarantee Fund for Agriculture (EOGFA, or FEOGA as a acronym of its French equivalent) and supplemented by a common policy for structural adjustments in agriculture. The choice was thus made for a common EC market organization to replace the various existing national organizations. Structural policies were not well defined and limited to coordination and joint financing of national policies, aimed in particular at regions expected to be hurt in terms of agricultural incomes by the establishment of common markets and prices. National agricultural policies did, in addition, continue to be carried out.

Market organization is based on three principles: the unified character of EC-markets, community preference and financial solidarity. (1) Common markets were created by replacing national market organizations and creating a single one at the community level, the equalization of national producer prices and the removal of internal trade barriers between community member countries. The community preference took the shape of providing a margin of advantage to internal trade over trade with third countries, through the establishment of a common external tariff. Financial solidarity found its expression through the joint financing of the budgetary consequences of market and price policies by way of FEOGA.

Common market and price policies are detailed in a number of basic regulations for individual products and some more general administrative regulations for their implementation. Annual price fixing, the use of special exchange rates and the like are the subject of regular executive regulations. Each market regulation contains basically two distinct instruments, both used to guarantee farmers in the EC a product price which is fixed in advance. One instrument is the intervention price which rules the internal market, being the price at which farmers can sell their output to intervention bureaux of the EC. The other is the somewhat higher entry price for imports from non-EC sources, which is obtained by taxing away the difference between the lowest observed offer price in the main port of entry and the intervention price. This levy is variable as it can be adjusted on a daily basis to offset price movements in international markets.

The system does not provide uniform and guaranteed prices to all farmers in the EC: the entry and intervention prices are minimum levels and actual prices received by farmers depend on the market situation and on their location. The price policies do, however, limit variations in actual prices considerably and make prices more predictable for farmers.

A complementary instrument that has become increasingly important is the export restitution. As the EC over the years increased its food self-sufficiency and for some products became a net exporter, these restitutions which cover the difference between the internal intervention and the world market price have claimed an increasing part of the budget for market and price policies. If the influence of EC exports on world market prices is small, then the major part of export restitutions serves to support internal prices; with a large share in world markets, these expenditures probably depress world market prices (Meester en Oskam (1983)). In a few cases international agreements prohibit the use of border measures to support internal prices; the EC has in those cases resorted to direct production support either by supplementing market prices, subsidizing production per hectare cultivated or subsidizing product processing.

Market organization does not cover all agricultural products of the EC; it was expected that a focus on major products would raise the general price (and income) levels in agriculture and carry prices of products not covered also upward. Whether this occurs in fact will depend on the role of international markets and of the EC in those markets. About 10 per cent of the value of agricultural production is not covered by market organization.

The other 90 per cent can be split into two groups: those with strong market organization (60 per cent) and with light market organization (30 per cent). It is called strong when there is a full set of permanent and obligatory support measures including intervention and entry prices and/or production subventions. Light intervention implies that support measures are applied only in some periods or under prescribed circumstances, or that border protection is the only instrument used. Strong organization is the case for cereals, dairy products, beef, sugar, wine and olive oil. It is classified as light for pork, poultry, eggs, fruits and vegetables. Some of the latter (pork, poultry and eggs in particular) are designed to compensate for the effects of the cereals price regime on these production sectors. Price fluctuations in the markets with light intervention are relatively large as compared to those with strong measures.

A number of additional measures were taken in the course of the years, some of which to ease the national price implications of floating or pegged exchange rates, others to cope with overproduction. Common prices are fixed in European Currency Units (ECU) and exchange rate adjustments between European currencies thus lead to price changes for agricultural products measured in national currencies. To smooth these price changes, separate ('green') exchange rates were introduced to translate common prices from ECU's into national currencies and their differences - as compared to prices at official exchange rates - are offset by border payments on all agricultural trade, called monetary compensation amounts. As a consequence, prices in the member countries are no longer the same. In fact, it has given the member countries more scope for setting their own domestic prices.

Other additional measures were the co-responsibility levy on milk, guarantee ceilings for several products and the super-levy on milk. Slaughter-premiums for cows, stubbing premiums to remove orchards and vineyards and premiums for not delivering milk at intervention bureaux are also designed to reduce overproduction. Sugar is the only product for which there was a production quota system from the start of the CAP.

Although not all barriers to free trade within the EC have been removed, it is fair to say that the objective of free movement of agricultural products has largely been met. The still existing marketing boards in the UK are amongst the few examples of national regulation still in existence. Also, there are barriers because of divergent legislation concerning animal and plant diseases which are still in the process of being harmonized. For reasons of quality control, trade tends to be hampered for some products, particularly in the case of processed food. Gradually progress towards common rules and guidelines is being made.

This does not necessarily imply that a common market has been established with the same conditions governing market participation for all agricultural producers. There remain large differences between countries, and therefore between farmers, in terms of tax regimes, social security systems and their costs, the provision of infrastructure services and the general support facilities provided through government budgets. Tax differentials which are sometimes cited as affecting competition may in fact bite less if higher taxes go together with free access to (agricultural) education, extension services and the results from a broad range of agricultural research activities.

There are no reliable estimates available concerning the expenditures incurred by national member governments for agricultural purposes. The EC Commission inventorizes these expenditures but did not, until recently, publish them. The only published estimate of direct and indirect support (excluding tax advantages and social security provisions) suggests an amount in 1980 of ECU 9.5 billion (Agra Europe, 26-4-85), which is slightly less than the FEOGA expenditures in that year on account of EC market and price policies (ECU 11.3 billion). Some of these national measures are the subject, from time to time, of contention between member states and of submission to the European Court for adjudication. As the burdens and the benefits of the CAP are not satisfactorily distributed in the opinion of several member states, these national expenditures become even more contentious.

1.2 Agricultural development under the CAP

In virtually all developed countries there is a strong upward trend of agricultural supply. At the same time demand is sluggish due to low population growth and market saturation. The growth of supply has taken place notwithstanding stable or even declining use of agricultural land and translates therefore in a strong upward trend in yields per unit of land. As the input of labour has shown a steady decline, labour productivity has risen rather sharply over time.

Technological progress has been the main driving force behind agricultural production growth. In the case of the EC the growth of production according to the Commission's annual report on agriculture (1985a, 1985b) was about 2 per cent per year over the period 1974-1983. (2) Thiede (1984) comes on the basis of grain equivalents to about 2.4 per cent annually for the same period. Demand measured in the same terms increased over the same period by 0.9 per cent per year.

These production and demand trends occurred during a period of declining relative agricultural prices, by about 2-2.5 per cent per year. Assuming a price elasticity of supply around 0.5 (which is at the lower end of available estimates), one may conclude that production would have increased by 3.5-4.0 per cent per year if there had been no downward trend of prices and by even more if a higher supply price elasticity is assumed. At the same time, with a price elasticity of demand around -0.4, stable prices would have implied no growth of consumption. Together, these trends under conditions of unchanged relative prices would have accelerated the tendencies towards self-sufficiency and surplus production.

With the ratio of output to input prices declining as it did over the past ten years, agricultural incomes could roughly be maintained at constant parity with incomes outside agriculture: total income changed little in real terms but the steady reduction of the active labour force in agriculture resulted in an increase of agricultural income per economically active which stayed more or less in line with real income trends outside the agricultural sector. This performance with respect to agricultural ιincomes had its price as the production trends behind these income trends also caused increasing disequilibria in major internal markets of agricultural products, expressed by rapidly increasing intervention stocks, mounting costs of those and of export restitutions and increasing tensions with other exporters over world market shares and price effects. However, a lower rate of production growth would have required an even steeper relative price decline, resulting in no real income growth per economically active in agriculture or even some real decline, further widening the substantial disparity with non-agricultural incomes. All of this serves to emphasize the fact that one instrument - price policy - is not adequate to achieve simultaneously two objectives, i.e. market equilibrium as well as income parity.

At the time of its establishment, the EC was a net importing region for almost all agricultural commodities except potatoes and pork. The original six member countries were self-sufficient in sugar but the three members who joined in 1973 were not and made the Community into a net-importer during the middle-seventies. In the early eighties the EC had exceeded self-sufficiency for all agricultural commodities except fruits, vegetable oils and fats (from domestically produced oilseeds) and, if cereals are not taken as a group, corn as well. But self-sufficiency ratios should be interpreted with care as they depend on the method of surplus disposal. If exported, the surpluses are reflected by ratios exceeding unity; however, if surpluses are disposed of internally - usually with large subsidies - domestic absorption is increased and the ratio lowered towards unity. Export (with restitution) has been the rule for almost all products with market organization; domestic disposal (subsidized) was used for dairy products (for feed use), wine (for alcohol production) and more recently for wheat (soft wheat for feed use). Corrections to self-sufficiency ratios are not easily made as one should be able to estimate the extent to which subsidized disposal displaced regular market sales. In the case of the wheat disposal programme there is some evidence that it replaces previously used barley which gets exported. This lowers the apparent self-sufficiency ratio in wheat but increases it for barley - but has no effect on the overall ratio for cereals.

In the short run, oversupply can be managed by increasing intervention stocks, but this is not a good solution if there are persistent and even growing imbalances. Stocking also tends to be expensive in case refrigeration is needed, and some products cannot be considered suitable any longer for human consumption after some time. By the end of 1983, wheat stocks amounted to 17 per cent of annual internal consumption and increased further in 1984 with a bumper harvest; guaranteed prices are now restricted to a quantity of cereals about 80 per cent of peak (Meester and Strijker (1984), and Commission (1985b) production. Butter stocks, at almost 60 per cent of internal consumption, are being disposed of both internally and externally with large subsidies but nevertheless keep growing. For skimmed milkpowder, stocks were half of internal consumption, but only 10 per cent if disposal consumption takes place at market prices and the remainder is subsidized; exports declined continuously after 1979. The small stock of beef at 6 per cent of internal consumption is less worrisome as intervention is being reduced and prices allowed to decline to achieve better market balance.

The most significant adjustments took place in foreign trade of the EC. Imports of agricultural products which are also produced in the EC declined, exports increased in some cases very rapidly. Products for which the EC still was a net importer in 1974 are exported on a substantial scale in the first half of the eighties. Table 5.2 provides data for some of the most important products: it shows that such switches are particularly large for cereals, wine and sugar. Exports of dairy products more than doubled and imports of meat, pork and poultry disappeared.

Table 5.2: Agricultural trade of the EC-9*, 1974 and 1982 (in mln metric tons)

	Imports		Exports		Net Exports	
	1974	1982	1974	1982	1974	1982
Cereals	24.4	15.1	12.2	23.1	-12.2	8.0
Sugar	2.0	1.6	1.9	5.9	-0.2	4.3
Dairy products	0.4	0.4	1.8	3.8	1.4	3.4
Wine (mln hl)	7.2	6.0	3.2	10.9	-4.0	4.9
Meat, pork, poultry	1.5	1.4	0.8	1.4	-0.7	-
Vegetable oils, fats**	4.2	5.0	0.6	1.0	-3.6	-4.0

* Excluding Greece
** Including imported oilseeds

For tropical agricultural products and materials for animal feeds there was an offsetting increase of imports in the EC over the same period. Calculated in terms of grain-equivalents, these imports did not increase sufficiently (Thiede (1984)) to compensate for the declining net-imports of those agricultural products which are also produced within the EC. In those terms Thiede estimates a decline of net imports from 51 million tons in 1973 to 17 million tons in 1982, measured in terms of grain equivalents.

The decline of net imports and increasing net exports which reflect the move towards - or even past - self-sufficiency did have a major impact on the financing of the CAP. The basic principle that the policy should be self-financing was in practice never attained as already in the early days, when the Community was a large net-importer of agricultural products, income from border levies did not cover the costs of subsidized dairy exports. Even for grains and sugar the costs tended to exceed revenues in virtually all years. Since then, the costs have continued to increase and without additional measures to stem the tide of ever growing expenditures, this trend is expected to continue.

The trade developments also affect relations with other

trading countries. The EC has become a smaller market for competing agricultural products and a larger competitor to other exporters. For some commodities the EC has become the dominant exporter with significant impact on world prices. As a consequence, the marginal subsidy costs for those commodities are very high because of the declining world market price accompanying an additional unit of exports, raising the subsidy costs on total exports of that commodity. It also makes the EC more vulnerable to counteraction by other competing countries through subsidization of exports. The competition with subsidized exports of wheat and dairy products between the EC and the US in third markets provides an example of the costs which competitors can inflict on each other and on their taxpayers. Even more serious are the negative effects on third country producers, notwithstanding simultaneous gains to consumers in importing third countries.

The agricultural policies of the EC have created increasing frictions and tension, in turn necessitating a search for alternative policies or changes in the present approach which can lead to a more stable situation. The speed by which new technologies raise agricultural production is at the heart of the problems; the fact that this driving force was unleashed by favourable producer price policies does not imply that they can be reigned in or reversed by changes in producer prices. This applies in particular as downward price adjustments, if ever introduced, will be implemented by small annual steps which affect returns in agriculture only marginally.

The recently issued 'Greenbook' of the European Commission is an effort to come to grips with the financial and trade problems of the Community, at the same time ensuring an acceptable income to EC-farmers. It signifies the start of an internal discussion which must lead to specific measures to be taken in the years ahead. These must deal first of all with the curbing of production, reducing the costs of interventions and of export subsidies. Most likely, these measures will be a mix of price reductions, quota restrictions to price guarantees, superlevies or co-responsibility levies on excess production and other restrictions to intervention. Hardly any thought is given to a liberalization of agricultural prices and trade as it is feared to be strongly detrimental to farmers' incomes.

2. SPECIFICATION OF THE MODEL SYSTEM

2.1 Countries and commodities

The analysis of trade policy alternatives presented here is based on an empirically estimated system of models. This system consists of 20 detailed models built for policy analysis at the national or country-group level, comprising countries which represent approximately 80 per cent of world agricultural production, trade, land availability and population. The remaining countries are grouped together in 14 regional models, each of a simpler format than the 20 detailed ones. Within the latter category not all models are structured alike, some being more detailed than others, particularly in terms of the policy analysis they permit. The purpose of the model system is to study the effect on the domestic food situation in given countries of alternative policy measures as taken by their own governments, by the governments of other countries and by international organizations which operate under specified international agreements. The system of linked national models is called the Basic Linked System (BLS); it is largely constructed and maintained by staff of the Food and Agriculture Programme (FAP) at the International Institute for Applied Systems Analysis (IIASA) which is the centre of a network of collaborating institutions worldwide.

The countries covered are listed in Table 5.3. It shows that most models are of a common structure or close to that. Only three models - for the United States, India and countries participating in the Council for Mutual Economic Assistance (CMEA) deviate significantly. Considerable work continues on at least ten of the country models, detailing those further and adding new modules while at the same time updating them. Some ready models have not as yet been linked either because of the need to adapt them to the common structure or - for Bangladesh and Thailand - these models are very detailed. Though national models may have greater commodity detail, the international exchange between the national models takes place at the level of ten commodities shown in Table 5.4. The BLS is a simulation model solved in yearly time steps.

Table 5.3: Models in the BLS (as of December 15, 1983)

	Country	Type of Model
	Egypt	*
a	Kenya	x
	Nigeria	*
	China	+
	India	0
a	Indonesia	*
	Pakistan	*
	Thailand	x
	Turkey	*
	Argentina	*
a	Brazil	*
	Mexico	*
	Australia	*
a	Japan	*
	New Zealand	*
a	Canada	*
a	USA	0
	Austria	*
a	EC	*
	CMEA	++

Legend:
*   Models with the standard common structure
x   Models with the structure close to the standard structure
0   Detailed models with country-specific structures
++   Models with special structures
a   Detailed models under development

Note:
(i)   In addition to the above, the following detailed models are under development: USSR, CSSR, Bulgaria
(ii)   Detailed models of the following countries are available but not yet linked: Sweden, Finland, Thailand, Bangladesh, Hungary, Poland.

Table 5.4: The commodity list as used in international trade

Wheat	(1000 mt)
Rice	(1000 mt milled)
Coarse grains	(1000 mt)
Bovine & ovine meats	(1000 mt of carcass weight)
Dairy products	(1000 mt of fresh milk equivalents)
Other animal products	(1000 mt of protein equivalents)
Protein feeds	(1000 mt of protein equivalents)
Other food	(Millions of 1970 US$)
Nonfood agriculture	(Millions of 1970 US$)
Nonagriculture	(Millions of 1970 US$)

mt = metric tons

2.2 The nature of the BLS

The basic approach in modelling has been to concentrate on policy analysis in a realistic manner and therefore to try to ask the question who does what. This meant that the system had to account for specific policy instruments and the responses of the various actors in the system. As a consequence of this, it distinguishes various actors, including the government, and their behaviour is integrated through the classical accounting identities of quantities and financial flows. Thus one essentially winds up getting a general equilibrium framework, for each of the models at the national level and for the system at the international level.

The major features of the approach are that it is a quantitative approach, based on empirical estimates, that it includes behaviour responses, that it is a general equilibrium framework, that it is comprehensive in the sense that it includes the whole economy, and the whole world, and that there are no unaccounted supply sources or demand sinks. The last feature implies that all the feedback effects come home to roost, and there are no free lunches in this system. Moreover, it distinguishes nations and within nations various economic agents. It recognizes that in the system national governments are important actors with a wide range of permitted policies like taxes, transfers, tariffs, quotas and rationing, partial or total.

Though prices are important in the models, it is not necessary in this system or in the approach that governments only select price as their adjusting instrument. Governments may decide to fix prices and let other things adjust. The models are real models. There is no money in them, as a store of value. So essentially the models determine real prices. Also there is no demand for money or foreign exchange, and the models are independent of exchange rates.

The solution of the system gives not only a global agricultural balance sheet of commodity flows, but also how they come about to what they are, and under the influence of which policies. Not only does the system simulate international trade flows, but it identifies also the mechanisms by which the domestic supply and demand forces determine exports and imports. The solutions give the impact on the domestic food situation of a country's own government's policies as well as through the policies of other governments.

Again to emphasize what the basic linked system is, and what it is not, its main feature is that it is a policy analysis tool: it is a powerful analytical instrument to explore and to understand the impact of alternative policies. It is not, and one cannot emphasize this enough, a forecasting tool. Policy impacts are considered to be more robust than absolute magnitudes that come out.

2.3 A typical national policy model of the FAP

The basic elements of the model system of the FAP are the national policy models. A national model has to reflect the specific problems of interest to that particular nation. Thus the national models differ in their structure and in their descriptions of government policies. The model system of the FAP permits linking of such diverse models but requires that the models meet a few conditions. They have to have a common sector classification at the international trade level, nine agricultural and one non-agricultural sector, and some fairly reasonable additional technical requirements. For example, net exports have to be independent of the absolute level of world prices and should be continuous functions of them. Even though the national models differ from each other, the broad structure is common to most models. Food supply and demand may be distinguished by various income groups. The information flow in a typical model is shown in Figure 5.1.

Past prices and government policies affect production

decisions. The domestic production in the n sectors of the economy - y_1, y_2, ..., y_n - accrues to each of the sectoral groups - represented by the superscript j. Thus for group j, its share of the national product is given by the vector y_1^j, y_2^j, y_3^j, ..., y_n^j. The income this share amounts to is determined by the price that these products command. For example, if farmers would have grown two million tons of wheat and one million tons of rice, they would have an income of twice the price of a million tons of wheat plus the price of a million tons of rice, minus the cost of producing wheat and rice. The matrix y_i^j thus describes the initial entitlements of the different products for the various groups. Government policies may redistribute these entitlements to y_i^j.

Given these entitlements and world prices, the j=1, ..., J groups trade among themselves under the influence of government policies, which include national market policies, (price, buffer stock, trade) public finance policies, (balance of payments, public demand, direct tax) and international market and finance policies (agreements on price, buffer stock, trade, financing). The resulting exchange equilibrium determines the domestic prices, net exports, tax rates, and the consumption patterns of different income groups whose demand behaviour is characterized by a linear expenditure system, and which clear the markets and meet the balance of trade constraint. Within the broad schematic outline of a national model described above, the methodological approaches do differ from model to model. The approaches used for each of these elements can be briefly characterized as follows.

Supply responses

Three alternative approaches are used in various models:

- Econometric estimations of acreage response and yield functions. In these relative profitabilities and critical inputs and factors are included as explanatory variables. This is the approach followed in the models of India and the USA.
- China and the CMEA-countries are represented by models which assure internal consistency with regard to the basically prescribed trade pattern.
- A non-linear programming model to allocate land, factors and inputs to different crops based on estimated

Figure 5.1: Information flow in a typical national model

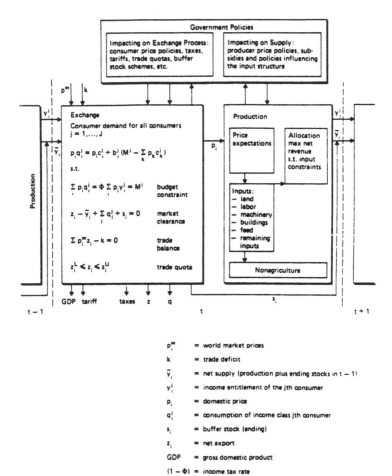

$$p_i^w \quad = \text{world market prices}$$

$$k \quad = \text{trade deficit}$$

$$\bar{y}_i \quad = \text{net supply (production plus ending stocks in } t-1)$$

$$y_i^j \quad = \text{income entitlement of the jth consumer}$$

$$p_i \quad = \text{domestic price}$$

$$q_i^j \quad = \text{consumption of income class jth consumer}$$

$$s_i \quad = \text{buffer stock (ending)}$$

$$z_i \quad = \text{net export}$$

$$\text{GDP} \quad = \text{gross domestic product}$$

$$(1 - \Phi) \quad = \text{income tax rate}$$

production functions is used in the models of the basic linked system for all other countries, including the EC.

Income generation

In some of the models of developing countries, different classes are identified based on the distribution of assets such as land, drought animals, equipment, etc., and the product is distributed across these classes as income entitlements as shares of labour, land, capital, etc. In some others, production itself is identified by different size classes. In the developed country models, as impact of income distribution is not significant on food consumption, only one class is distinguished.

Demand behaviour

The demand behaviour is described through estimated linear expenditure systems. For developing countries, whenever the number of income groups in the model exceeds one, a separate demand system is estimated for each class from time series or household expenditure surveys.

Government policy

Government policy in each national model can be described by a hierarchical set of adjustment rules for policy targets such as domestic price targets, trade quotas, stock targets and bounds, tax rate bounds, etc. However, to minimize the problem of exploding numbers of variants in the BLS, price transmission functions are used to characterize government policy. These functions relate current and past relative world market prices and self-sufficiency to the domestic relative target price.

2.4 The international linkage

The net exports of all the countries are thus calculated for a given set of world prices, and market clearance is checked for each commodity. The world prices are revised and the new domestic equilibria giving new net exports are calculated once again for all countries. This process is repeated until the world markets are cleared in all commodities, at each stage of the iteration the domestic markets are in equilibrium. The procedure is shown schematically in Figure 5.2. It may be noted that any international agency - such as a buffer stock agency - can be represented as a country, and the effectiveness of its policies can be evaluated within a framework in which country policies react to the policies of the agency.

Since these steps are taken period by period, this amounts to a dynamic simulation for a 5 to 15 year period to predict the consequences of various policies, not only for individual countries but also for the entire system.

Figure 5.2: International linkage

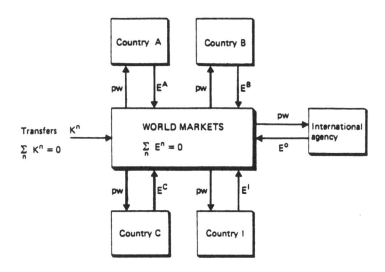

2.5 Validation and tuning

In validating and tuning the models emphasis is placed on the fact that the BLS is a medium term policy analysis model and not a short-term forecasting one. It does not incorporate short-term variations such as due to weather nor any speculative behaviour resulting from such variations. For policy analysis the BLS must track the central tendencies correctly.

The model system was 'validated' in three phases.

In the first phase individual national models were tested in a stand-alone mode (i.e. unlinked to other models) with given world prices over the historical period 1970 to 1976. For each of some 90 endogenous state variables which each model generated, values were regressed against the observed values.

In the second phase the country models were run up to the year 2000, again in stand-alone mode with given world prices.

In the last phase of the validation process a series of 'linked runs' with full interaction between the individual national models within the global exchange system were carried out.

The objective in phases 2 and 3 was to test whether the models behave reasonably. Since this is a very subjective notion, specifications and parameters were changed in individual models only when warranted and in case of extreme results. A result of this process is to generate certain base runs.

2.6 Exogenous and endogenous variables in the BLS

A number of important variables remain exogenous. The more important of these are listed in summary form below:

- **Population** and its growth is taken from the latest UN and ILO sources median projections, but for some individual countries, e.g. India, these have been adjusted by the latest local information/projections. Similarly, the participation rate in the total labour force is defined exogenously, but the allocation of the labour force between agriculture and the rest of the economy is endogenized.
- **Land** available for cultivation is exogenous and its value is taken predominantly from FAO sources and from specific local estimates. This also includes the development of land over time. But when pressure on land becomes strong relative to the past, additional land may be brought into cultivation.
- **Trade deficits** are specified exogenously in most scenarios as fixed shares of the GDP. They are fixed at the average shares as they existed in the 1970-76 period.
- **Rates of total investment** as a share of the GDP are

163

estimated from the historical period and after a period of adjustment in the early 80s they are kept constant. Some exceptions exist to this, e.g. India, where the investment rate changes over time and is exogenously specified. A number of important exogenous assumptions are made for the **'Rest of the World'**, i.e. the residual countries grouped into 14 regional models instead of being individually modelled in the system. These include growth rates for both agricultural and non-agricultural production and for demand based on the FAO-study "Agriculture: Toward 2000". Price elasticities are included on both the demand and supply sides, to allow for adjustments when relative world market prices vary.

3.   AGRICULTURAL TRADE POLICY ANALYSIS

3.1 The analytical framework
For a satisfactory analysis of the various issues related to the question of agricultural trade policy one needs a framework that accounts for a number of important interrelationships and feedbacks. Obviously it is necessary to evaluate the transformation possibilities in production amongst different agricultural commodities due to changes in relative prices, the impact on farm incomes, as well as the substitutions that consumers make.

Since traded quantities are the differences between domestic supply and demands, they are usually much smaller than domestic supply or demand. Changes in demand due to changes in income, assuming domestic supply is fixed, get fully reflected in traded quantities. Thus, even small income effects can lead to large changes in traded quantities.

And, of course, it is well known that the impact of changes in own prices on net export can be of either sign. The analytical implication of this is that the interaction between prices, supply, income, demand and trade have to be all considered. In order to fully account for these interactions, it is useful to consider a closed system where there are no unaccounted supply sources or demand sinks which can mask some feedbacks. In other words, a general equilibrium framework is indicated.

Trade policies are but a part of a government's

economic policies. For analysing consequences of substantial shifts in trade policies, such as implied by trade liberalization in most countries, one needs to account for the changes in the government's other policies. The macro-economic effects of such policy changes can have a significant impact on trade patterns as well as on income distributions.

For example, if tariffs were a major source of government revenues, trade liberalization not compensated by external aid or transfers would lead to higher taxes or lower government revenues, public consumption and/or public investment. Even when the lost tariff revenue is regained through changes in other taxes, the incidence of these taxes may fall on groups other than those which did bear the tariff.

Even small changes in policy such as changing over from tariff to an equivalent quota may affect income distributions. Unless the government auctions the quota, which governments seldom do, the tariff revenue which accrued to the government earlier now accrues to whom the quota is allotted.

Partial analysis based on consideration of nominal rates of protection or even effective rates of protection can be misleading. In fact it has been shown (Ramaswami and Srinivasan (1971), Jones (1971) and Bhagwati and Srinivasan (1973)) that except under restrictive assumptions, the relative values of effective rates of protection indices of two sectors cannot be relied upon to indicate even the directions in which factor reallocation, and hence supply changes, will take place when rates of protection are changed.

Thus a general equilibrium framework which incorporates the relevant government policy instruments and the behavioural responses of various economic agents - producers and consumers - to the changes in such policies is needed. But it is not enough just to account for the behavioural responses of economic agents within the country to changes in government policies - consideration of responses of other governments is also necessary. Particularly for major traders, the reactions of other nations to changes in their own policies can be very significant for analysis of trade policies. Even countries who at present follow policies of self-sufficiency and hence are not active in world trade, may become so once the trade environment changes.

One could argue that if the net export functions from the rest of the world are known for a country, one can do policy analysis using only the national model. For a number of policies such stand-alone analyses based on a national model may be adequate. However, net export functions are not easily available. Moreover, shifts in such functions consequent to the responses of other governments to major policy changes by one government would be difficult to account for in an analysis with a single country model. Thus the need is for a system of general equilibrium type national policy models linked together through trade and transfers. The Basic Linked System (BLS) of national policy analysis models of FAP is such a system.

3.2 The reference scenario

For evaluating the effect of a policy change, a reference scenario is required. It is designed to constitute the baseline projection and tries as much as possible to simulate the course of events under conditions of business-as-usual. In practice this is not an easy thing to do, as the initial situation of the base year and the trends of the past which are reflected in the parameters of the model system, carry with them the seeds of future developments which may necessitate adjustments of policies. It would be logically impossible, therefore, to construct a reference scenario that would be free from all policy adjustments, as these come about endogenously in response to changes in world market prices and are dictated by the permissible current account balance.

As the model system has only a rather limited set of exogenous variables, of which some are invariant (like population growth) the extent of potential manipulation is limited once one accepts the national models as fair representations of each country. Therefore the reference run can be described as the nearest possible course of development when past behavioural responses are projected in the future and policy changes remain limited to passive adjustment. This reference run serves as the 'neutral' point of departure from which policy scenarios take off as variants, with the impact of a policy being seen as the deviation of that policy run from the reference scenario. One should still bear in mind that the active policy change imposed in each variant is to be compared to the passive policy changes which are already included in the reference scenario, and that the comparison of outcomes needs to take account of this characteristic of the reference scenario.

The main outcomes of the reference scenario are shown in Table 5.5 below, together with the exogenous population projections. For comparison the past data for the period 1970-80 are also presented.

The global GDP rate of growth initially recovers in the 1980s from the average actually obtained in the preceding decades; after 1990 the growth rate gradually falls further. This development can largely be traced to the OECD-countries and to some extent also the CMEA country group. The economic performance of the developing countries is better, showing stable growth of around 5.4 per cent per annum; as their population growth rate declines, per capita income growth accelerates somewhat over time. This base-line growth rate for developing countries compares reasonably well with projections made by several international organizations in recent years. For the OECD-countries they are, in the same comparison, towards the lower end of most other projections.

Table 5.5: Growth rates (annual) of some indicators in reference run RO

	1970-80	1980-1990	1990-2000
Population			
World	1.9	1.8	1.7
OECD	0.8	0.8	0.7
DC's*	2.5	2.5	2.3
CMEA	0.9	0.8	0.7
GDP per capita			
World	3.1	2.7	2.2
OECD	2.3	2.3	2.0
DC's*	3.8	2.9	3.1
CMEA	4.8	3.9	3.2
GDP-Agriculture			
World	1.1	2.2	2.3
OECD	1.2	1.2	0.9
DC's*	2.6	3.0	2.9
CMEA	-0.9	2.4	2.8

* Developing countries, excluding China.

One of the central features of the model system is its capability to generate the prospective course of world market prices. Their role in the model can be described both as a major indicator of the results obtained in an overall sense, and as a generator of the changes that take place at the country level and in groups of countries. In the reference scenario these world market price changes are significant (measured in comparison to non-agricultural prices) and give a first impression of the direction of changes in world agriculture. They are presented in Table 5.6, below.

Table 5.6: Changes in world market prices of agricultural products relative to non-agricultural prices over the period 1980-2000 according to the reference scenario (in %).

	Price change in period:			Annual % price change
Commodity	1980-1990	1990-2000	1980-2000	1980-2000
Wheat	2	-10	-8	-0.4
Rice	-4	5	1	0.1
Coarse grains	1	-11	-10	-0.5
Bovine, ovine meat	28	20	53	2.2
Dairy products	23	11	37	1.6
Other animal products	5	1	6	0.3
Protein feed	2	-4	-2	-0.1
Other food	1	4	5	0.2
Non-food agr. products	20	4	25	1.1
Total agriculture*	5	3	9	0.4

* Weighted by using global base-year production levels.

The terms of trade of agricultural products apparently move slightly in favour of agriculture, but at a diminishing rate over time. For historical years there has been some controversy about the direction of these price trends, but this future course is not, on the whole, unlike the trends which prevailed over the past 10-15 years. Although for the various commodity groups shown in Table 5.6, the direction of change of relative prices in the reference scenario is not always in line with past trends, the similarities are rather strong for the major commodities. Cereals - except rice which is hardly traded internationally - continue their long-term decline of relative world market prices whereas those for animal products - notably dairy and red meat - rise substantially.

Both for dairy products and for bovine and ovine meat, the strong increases are related to high income elasticities of demand and to the fact that a number of countries in the course of these years will be passing through a stage of their development during which consumers diversify their food demand towards animal products at the expense of directly consumed cereals. On the supply side production costs go up as the scope for expanding roughage production is limited and additional supplies of meat and dairy require more use of other animal feeds. Other animal products (pork, poultry and eggs) are already largely produced on the basis of feedgrains and oilseed meals; the decline of feedgrains prices, particularly after 1990, contains therefore the price change of other animal products to a moderately upward move. Also, developing countries still have considerable scope for improving productivity in this sector with modest investments.

The strong relative price increase for non-food agricultural products is a significant benefit to developing countries as the main exporters of fibres, hides and skins and tobacco which comprise this group. It appears that this price movement stems from strong demand increases in the socialist countries of Europe and in the developing countries which, due to rapid growth of the modern sectors, require substantially expanding raw materials imports.

In some cases these price changes are related to the changes in government policies. As was stated before, these are of a passive character but are of course determined by particular objectives which are assumed to be operational in the various countries. For example, in the EC and in several other developed market economies the assumption is made that past trends in the parity ratio between agricultural and non-agricultural incomes will be maintained. Thus, upward changes in the parity ratio to the advantage of agricultural producers, are for example assumed to continue in the EC and in Canada. There is supposed to be little change one way or the other in Japan and in most developing countries.

Table 5.7: Income parity ratios, productivity and protection in the reference run for three countries, 1980-2000

	EC	Japan	Argentina
Income parity ratio':			
1961"	.47	.26	.67
1980	.61	.28	.81
2000	.71	.30	1.10
% change p/a, 1980-2000	+0.70	+0.40	+1.80
Labour productivity''' % change per annum	+0.50	+0.10	+1.10
Relative change of agric. prices % per annum 1980-2000	+0.20	+0.30	+0.70
Change (% p/a) in weighted'''' world prices	+0.20	+0.10	+1.10

Nominal tariff equivalents''''' in % of world market prices:	EC 1980	EC 2000	Japan 1980	Japan 2000	Argentina 1980	Argentina 2000
Wheat	84	112	35	31	-21	-20
Rice	65	61	253	254	7	11
Coarse grains	42	37	42	39	-20	-11
Bovine, ovine meat	61	12	52	56	-27	-28
Dairy products	70	34	106	69	-17	-18
Other animal products	26	24	43	27	-22	-16
Protein feeds	35	36	134	127	0	2
Other food	5	12	44	37	-32	-28
Non-food agriculture	26	28	98	74	-5	-10

'   Agricultural GDP per worker/non-agricultural GDP per worker at current prices.
"   FAP data base
'''   Ratio GDP per worker in agriculture to GDP per worker in non-agriculture at constant (base year) prices
''''   Weighted by base year production
'''''   Difference between border prices and domestic consumer raw material prices, including domestic transportation cost of the traded commodities.

Higher parity ratios are in most countries justifiable because of a more rapid increase of productivity per worker in agriculture as compared to non-agriculture. To the extent that parity improvement exceeds relative growth of labour productivity, agricultural prices must, also in a relative sense, adjust upward. This required price increase, compared to the properly weighted world market price, determines what change is needed in nominal protection rates in order to obtain the desired parity ratio. In Table 5.7 the relevant indicators are brought together for three selected countries, i.e. the EC, Japan and Argentina, in order to demonstrate these relationships. One should, however, be careful when interpreting these data in terms of causalities, as the character of the model does not permit the tracing of those in a recursive manner, as the model is truly simultaneous.

The decline of nominal tariff equivalents, particularly for dairy products and for bovine and ovine meat imply that higher world market prices are not passed on to consumers but compensated through lesser protection; producer prices in these countries also rise less than would be the case if protection were maintained. There is a trade-off here, as alternatively these countries could maintain protection levels and raise the income parity ratio faster, at the expense of domestic consumers. The assumption that income parity trends of past years will continue to apply result, however, in some decline of nominal protection. (3) As a consequence, the reference scenario shows hardly any increase in the production of bovine and ovine meat in the EC, whereas consumption increases quite rapidly, so that the EC absorbs some 25 per cent of additional world trade in bovine and ovine meat. Brazil, which maintains the (small but negative) rate of protection of this commodity and passes through a phase of rapidly rising demand for meat, notwithstanding higher prices absorbs more than 40 per cent of additional supplies in the world market. Among the main exporters, only Argentina and Canada appear to respond to higher world market prices.

The policy adjustments which express themselves through changes in nominal tariff equivalents in turn affect domestic producer and consumer prices, leading to subsequent adjustments in production, consumption and trade; this is what the example of bovine and ovine meat demonstrates. With this in mind, we can now turn to these internal changes by countries and by commodity groups as these appear in the reference scenario. These are presented

Table 5.8: Agricultural production growth, 1980-2000, in the reference scenario (in % per year)

Commodity	World	North Am. Oceania	Major country groups: W. Europe Japan	CMEA countries	China	Devel. countries
Wheat	1.94	2.8	1.1	0.8	1.1	3.3
Rice	2.12	3.4	0.7	2.1	0.6	2.9
Coarse grains	1.77	2.4	1.4	0.6	1.5	2.1
Bovine, ovine meat	1.54	0.9	1.0	0.9	1.4	2.8
Dairy products	1.57	1.5	0.9	0.9	3.8	3.1
Other anim. prod.	2.26	1.1	2.1	-0.3	2.9	3.9
Protein feed	1.94	1.7	1.6	1.3	1.8	2.8
Other food	2.08	1.4	0.9	0.4	1.7	3.1
Non-food agr. prod.	2.33	1.3	0.7	3.0	3.2	2.3
Total, agric.	1.82*	1.7	1.1	0.7	1.9	3.2
Ibid, 1970-1980	2.43	2.7	2.1	2.3	2.4	2.8

*Weighted at 1970-prices

for the major country groups in Table 5.8.

The projections of the reference run suggest slower growth of agricultural production volumes than in the past, which is to some extent to be expected when overall economic growth in the world economy is low. A more important reason appears to be that there is a significantly slower rate of agricultural growth in all countries at higher income levels which have low population growth and already high levels of food intake. In the developing countries - but not in China - there is, however, a slight acceleration of agricultural growth. In the case of China and the CMEA countries it should be remembered that the models are not fully integrated in the system and therefore the projections are, more than for the other countries, based on exogenous assumptions.

Domestic demand and production increase in most cases at comparable rates in each country group; as a consequence the changes in trade patterns are modest, and largely continue along the same lines as in the past. North America and Oceania remain the main suppliers of all cereals to the rest of the world and the most important suppliers of almost all other agricultural commodities. The other OECD countries remain a major supplier of dairy products, small exporters of wheat and increasingly dependent on imports of virtually all other agricultural products. Notwithstanding the rapid growth of agricultural production in the developing countries (excluding China) their imports rise very substantially when taken together as a group. Table 5.9 shows the trade balances by commodities and country groups.

The very substantial increase of net imports of coarse grains in the developing countries, notwithstanding their own production increases, indicates the demand for meat and dairy products in these countries which requires large quantities of feedgrains. It should also be noted that North America (and mainly, as we will see, the United States) expands dairy exports threefold whereas EC dairy exports stagnate and are in the end only half as large as North American supplies to the world market.

Table 5.10 summarizes the effects of changes in net agricultural trade by country groups in terms of their trade balances and the terms of trade.

As already suggested by the net exports shown earlier according to commodities, North America and Oceania continue to supply an increasing part of agricultural world

Table 5.9: Agricultural trade balances, 1980-2000, in the reference scenario (in volume terms)

Commodity	Unit	Year	Major country groups				
			N. Am. Oceania	W. Europe Japan	CMEA countries	China	Dev. countries
Wheat	Mln MT	1980	61.2	2.4	-19.7	-7.3	-28.3
		2000	106.0	3.4	-19.2	-13.7	-62.9
Rice	Mln MT milled	1980	2.9	-2.1	-0.7	1.8	-3.7
		2000	6.3	-3.0	-0.4	1.0	-5.5
Coarse grains	Mln MT	1980	69.1	-26.1	-13.0	-1.7	-5.2
		2000	155.8	-73.5	-12.0	-1.8	-62.0
Bovine, ovine meat	Mln MT	1980	0.2	-0.9	–	0.1	-0.4
		2000	0.7	-1.2	–	–	-0.1
Dairy products	Mln MT	1980	4.6	8.8	0.6	-0.6	-12.1
		2000	16.2	9.0	0.8	0.4	-23.9
Other animal products	Mln MT of prot.equiv.	1980	0.4	0.2	–	0.1	-0.1
		2000	0.3	0.6	–	–	-0.2
Protein feed	Mln MT of prot.equiv.	1980	11.2	-9.2	-0.8	0.4	4.1
		2000	16.1	-13.8	–	-0.1	4.7
Other food	Billion '70 US$	1980	2.1	-5.5	-0.3	1.2	10.3
		2000	3.1	-7.6	-1.5	2.1	13.8
Non-food agric. products	Billion '70 US$	1980	1.1	-3.9	-1.2	–	1.8
		2000	1.4	-4.2	-2.1	–	2.8

Table 5.10: Agricultural trade balance and terms of trade, 1980-2000 in the reference scenario

		N. Amer. Oceania	W. Europe Japan	CMEA countries	China	Devel. countries
Agric. trade balance (mln 1970 US$):	1980	13,277	-8,564	-2,761	880	5,356
	2000	22,434	-12,105	-3,733	482	2,700
Terms of trade index (1970=100)	1980	100.9	94.2	97.6	108.9	-
	2000	102.7	92.0	88.3	123.2	-
Agric. trade balance (at current prices):	1980	13,162	-9,089	-2,829	997	6,373
	2000	21,835	-13,162	-4,237	836	5,051

market supplies; the other developed countries become more dependent on imports and the developing countries are gradually losing their export share in world trade.

Although we have seen that economic growth in the developing countries is maintained and agricultural growth does even accelerate, this has only limited impact on the number of people with inadequate food intake. Between 1980 and 1990 their absolute number increases by about 4 per cent, but declines thereafter by about 8 per cent until the end of the century. As a percentage of the total population of the developing countries, this is nevertheless an impressive improvement, declining from 25 per cent in 1980 to around 15 per cent in 2000.

4.   REMOVING BORDER PROTECTION IN THE EC

4.1   The notion of trade liberalization and the scheme of analysis

The analysis of trade liberalization in this study is restricted to removal of distortions between relative border prices and relative domestic prices at the level of raw materials. Not all distortion-creating measures from all markets and production activities are removed. Thus, the scenarios move towards free trade and not to total trade liberalization; one should characterize them as freer trade scenarios. The reason for restricting the analysis to removal of only border protection measures is the difficulty of obtaining accurate information on all trade distorting measures.

The results for the EC must be interpreted with some caution because the monetary compensatory amounts (MCA's) are still implicitly included in the producer prices. The kind of distortion resulting from this is very difficult to assess. Since, however, the MCA's are small in comparison to the EC's protection against third countries, one might argue that their impact is not very drastic. This is especially so if one works with the hypothesis that the MCA's only distort the (absolute) price levels between the EC member countries but not the relative prices of agriculture.

Tariff equivalents are removed only to the extent that they are made equal for all commodities. This is sufficient for the analysis because the model system is homogeneous of degree zero in prices so that only relative prices affect its outcome. Removal of tariff equivalents is not done in one step but successively over a period of five years beginning in 1982.

When interpreting the results of a trade liberalization scenario one has to be aware of some limitations of the analysis. The first is the uncertainty about the accuracy of the tariff equivalents. The tariff equivalents were calculated as differences between the domestic producer price and the corresponding border price. While the producer prices are taken directly from the FAO statistics, which is the main data base, the world market prices are derived statistics (Sichra (1984)). (4)

The world market price was determined as the export price of the product by the least cost major exporter, where a major exporter is defined as one exporting at least 3 per cent of the total world exports. The differences between prices of other exporters and this world market price are attributed to quality and composition differences. The details are given in Sichra (1984). In calculating the tariff equivalents, the quality and composition differences were accounted for. Some care should be exercised in interpreting the tariff equivalents calculated as above. In those cases where only tariffs, levies (fixed or variable), and quotas are applied at the border, no difficulty arises. If production of the commodity under study is assisted in ways which lower the costs of production, e.g. through input subsidy, storage subsidy, deficiency payment, etc., the calculated tariff equivalents measure in most cases both the border protection and the effect of the other measures. As the latter may have in the past led to a shift of the supply curve, it is important to be explicit about what exactly is meant when the tariff equivalent is set to zero. The logical position to take is that both border and other measures are removed, but it is important to note that this implies a shift of the supply curve again.

In the present analysis of trade liberalization the calculated tariff equivalents are removed. However, in our model this does not lead to a shifting of the supply curve; in turn this implies that in our approach assistance given for domestic production of commodities is maintained. We are aware of the basic inconsistency in our analysis but it would require a much more detailed treatment of the non-agricultural sectors (particularly those closely linked to agriculture) and of the government accounts to enable a more appropriate treatment of distortions and supply shifts due to measures reducing the costs of production. With available resources this was not possible.

Considerable effort has been made to account for transport, distribution and processing differentials in deriving export and import prices for each country so that they are not treated as part of the tariff equivalents. Also quality and commodity composition differentials have been taken into account in aggregating commodities. The results have been checked against estimates from other sources, wherever available. Nevertheless, the figures are subject to uncertainty, particularly for the country groupings, for which approximations had to be made. In treating all non-tariff barriers as tariff equivalents the incidence of the protection measure is distorted, e.g. an import quota increases the domestic price and the rent from this quota goes to the importer whereas the government gets the receipts from a tariff. However, for countries for which explicit trade quotas are used, such as the quota on import of bovine and ovine meat, removal of the quota does not lead to such a distortion.

A possibility that should be recognized in analysing the impact of a partial liberalization, as it is studied here, is that removing some trade distortions while leaving others in place might exacerbate the distorting effects of the latter.

Another limitation arises from the modelling of price responses for the country groupings of both demand and supply. Whereas the models and their implied price responses for individual countries, as well as the EC, are likely to be as realistic as models go, due to lack of data, the price response in the models of country groupings is ad-hoc. If the planned economies are excluded, which in practice are unlikely to participate in trade liberalization, the share of world agricultural output accounted for in models with not so reliable a price response is of the order of 20 to 30 per cent.

These limitations call for prudence in interpreting the results of a trade liberalization scenario. Figures should be considered as approximate rather than precise estimates and as indicating general directions of movement. The apparent precision in the tables is unavoidably higher than the results warrant, as is the case in any economic modelling exercise.

In the scenario the transition to trade liberalization is assumed to take place over a five-year period, from 1982 to 1986. Since a number of time lags are built into the various models of the BLS, several years of adjustment may be required to fully capture the impact of trade liberalization.

4.2 Consequences of removing EC border protection for world agriculture

Third countries criticize the EC especially for the impact the CAP has on the world market and because of lack of entrance into the EC market. The rather rigid price policy of the EC leads to a situation where the world market has to absorb to a large extent the annual changes in EC supply and demand balances. In other words, the EC exports the quantity variation it experiences on the domestic market. In order to sell growing surplus quantities on the world market, the EC is forced to finance high export subsidies because of its policy of high internal prices. This often makes it very difficult or even impossible for other exporting countries to compete in third country markets, or even in their own domestic markets.

In this section we describe the consequences of a liberalized CAP. Several attempts have been made to quantify the costs of the currently pursued CAP. One of the first to estimate the cost of the CAP were Koester and Tangermann (1976) who calculated the costs for the Federal Republic of Germany only. Their result indicates that the equivalent of around 0.3 per cent of the national income is the cost of the CAP for the FRG. More recent estimates are not confined to the FRG. Buckwell et al. (1982) estimate the welfare gains from a 'free market' policy at 11051 million European Units of Account for 1980 which are approximately equal to 0.5 per cent of GDP in the year. In a recent study, De Veer (1985) estimates the benefits from liberalized trade of the EC to be 0.38 per cent of the GDP. Engels et al. (1985) estimate the cost of the CAP to the consumer alone to be in the order of 36 billion ECU for 1982 by assuming an average protection for agriculture of 25 per cent and by using the value of production of this year which was 144.8 billion ECU. This figure, amounting to 1.3 per cent of GDP in 1982, is only a rough estimate since costs (or benefits) to the producer and tax-payer were not accounted for.

A recently published study goes one step further than those mentioned so far. It analyses the impact of EC trade liberalization in an international framework (Matthews (1985)). The advantage of this approach is that changes of world market prices are taken into account when calculating gains and losses from liberalized EC trade. In addition, the author also analyses the impact on other countries. Matthews arrives at the conclusion that both the developed

Table 5.11: Changes in prices* and volume traded at world market and in global production in 1990 and 2000 due to a unilateral trade liberalization by the EC, as compared to the reference scenario

	World market prices (% difference)		Global trade volume (net, % difference)		Production (global, % difference)	
	1990	2000	1990	2000	1990	2000
Wheat	6.8	8.7	-3.4	-2.2	0.9	0.6
Rice	5.9	1.5	1.2	-1.8	0.1	0.1
Coarse grains	7.4	3.7	-6.6	-5.0	0.5	0.6
Bovine and ovine meat	11.1	6.9	12.5	14.4	-0.1	0.7
Dairy	18.9	14.9	-9.7	1.9	-0.8	-0.5
Other animals	4.8	5.2	-1.1	5.2	-0.4	-0.6
Protein feed	2.9	0.3	0.4	-0.6	0.5	0.2
Other food	3.2	2.4	1.6	6.7	-0.1	-
Non-food agriculture	6.6	2.0	2.8	3.1	0.3	0.1
Non-agriculture	-	-	10.0	10.1	-	-
Total Agriculture	6.2	4.5	-	-	-	-

* Relative to the non-agricultural price

and the less developed countries would lose from the elimination of EC agricultural protection. As we will see in the next two sections, these conclusions are only partly supported by our analysis.

4.3 Trade liberalization by the EC increases world market prices

A removal of the EC's border protection leads to a price increase at the world market of about 5 per cent (Table 5.11). This effect is more pronounced in the initial years after the policy change than in later ones when other countries have time to adjust to the new situation. All relative agricultural prices increase but the strongest rise occurs for dairy products (about 15 per cent), the commodity for which the EC has a rather high level of protection. It is not surprising that bovine and ovine meat indicate the next strongest price increase because in many countries of the EC the dual purpose cow is prevalent. In other words, the production of milk and beef is interwoven so that assistance to dairy also means assistance to beef production. Among the prices which increase more than average are those of wheat and coarse grains. This does not come as a surprise either, knowing that the protection levels for these two products by the EC are relatively high (see Table 5.7) and the EC has a rather large share in the total world trade of these two products. The world market prices of all other commodities increase, but less than average.

Trade in grain contracts as a result of the EC's reduction of export of wheat and import of coarse grains. Dairy products are traded substantially less in the initial period and later the trade volume is slightly higher than in the reference run. This is a result of the rather sharp drop of EC's dairy exports which is not taken up by other countries. As can be seen from Table 5.11, production contracts as well but by a very small amount.

The strongest increase in trade volume is shown by bovine and ovine meat. Again, this is a direct impact of the EC which imports considerably more of this commodity because of lower production and higher demand.

Production at the global level changes only marginally. The non-EC countries do not take the price increase at the world market as an incentive to increase production beyond compensating for the reduction in the EC, although the price increase is (with various intensities) transmitted to the

Table 5.12: Changes in trade patterns by country- and commodity groups due to removal of EC border protection in comparison to the reference scenario in 2000 (volumes)*

	EC		Other develop. market econ.		CMEA-countries		Developing countries		World trade
	Exp.	Imp.	Exp.	Imp.	Exp.	Imp.	Exp.	Imp.	
Wheat	-16.5	–	10.8	-0.3	–	2.0	2.6	-4.8	-3.1
Rice	–	0.3	–	-0.3	–	–	-0.3	-0.3	-0.3
Coarse grains	–	-8.4	-6.7	-1.2	–	0.2	-1.9	0.8	-8.6
Bovine, ovine meat	–	1.6	1.1	-0.3	–	–	-0.2	-0.4	0.9
Dairy products	-8.7	3.0	7.8	-0.2	–	–	1.5	-2.2	0.6
Other animal prod.	-0.1	0.1	0.1	–	–	–	0.1	–	0.1
Protein feeds	–	-0.4	-0.3	0.1	–	0.1	0.2	0.1	-0.1
Other food	–	2.2	0.2	-0.2	–	0.5	1.4	-0.9	1.6
Non-food agr. prod.	–	0.3	–	–	–	–	0.2	-0.1	0.2

*for units, see Table 5.4.

domestic market.

The global response in the volumes traded and produced does not reflect the substantial changes which occur at the country level. Table 5.12 indicates how the trade pattern between countries changes by 2000 due to trade liberalization by the EC. The EC's share in wheat trade drops almost to zero together with a substantial reduction in wheat production and a simultaneous increase in demand.

Exports of wheat are reduced by 16.5 million tons as compared to the reference scenario. At the same time, Australia, Canada and the US increase their exports by 2.4, 4.9 and 3.5 million tons respectively, replacing together some 65 per cent of EC's reduced volume. An additional 15 per cent is taken up by a large number of other countries, small increases each. The remaining 20 per cent of the EC's export reduction is offset by diminished world imports. These are spread in small quantities over a large number of countries.

Trade adjustments for coarse grains show a substantially different pattern. The reduction of imports of coarse grains by the EC is matched almost completely by a global reduction of exports. This, however, does not mean that the other importing countries do not react to the changed structure of agricultural prices on the world market. There are many countries which alter their import of coarse grains. The strongest change occurs in Japan which reduces its import by more than a million tons. The countries which cut back their exports substantially are Argentina (2.2 million tons), Canada (1.3) and the USA (5.6). Together with Australia these are the nations which face the largest adjustments in the volume of grains (wheat and coarse grains) traded. The four together continue to increase their trade share both in wheat and coarse grains.

A different situation occurs for bovine and ovine meat. The EC increases its imports by 160 per cent of which more than half is additional supplies from Argentina whereas the remainder is compensated by reductions in imports elsewhere, notably by the USA. The case is similar for dairy products: the EC becomes an importer of 3 million tons instead of exporting 8.7 million tons. This additional import demand is met to the tune of 80 per cent by additional exports, mainly from the United States (75 per cent). The remaining 20 per cent is offset by import decreases, particularly in developing countries and most of all by India. New Zealand and Argentina contribute smaller additional export quantities. Canada continues to remain absent from the world market because it is assumed to maintain its dairy policy which restricts output to domestic demand.

Trade in other animal products is also strongly affected by the EC. Being a net exporter in the reference run with a share of 6 per cent of the world market the EC becomes an importer with a share of about 2 per cent under EC trade liberalization. Again, the USA replaces most of the EC's export (88 per cent) with Argentina, Canada and Japan also contributing to increased exports. Cuts in imports occur only in the developing countries.

With regard to protein feed the changes are small and amount to a slight loss for the USA. As expected, the EC's increased imports of other food opens up the market for the developing countries. They supply two thirds of the additional imports by the EC, whereas Japan and Canada reduce imports.

In summary, one can say that the EC influences the international trade structure quite substantially as evidenced by the changes in trade occurring due to its trade liberalization. The developed countries are more affected than developing ones. Since all countries, except China, the CMEA and the EC improve their agricultural trade balance - the surplus countries increase their positive balance and the net importers of agricultural goods decrease their deficit - non-agricultural products are increasingly imported with given trade deficits. The larger deficit in agricultural trade in the EC necessitates an increase of non-agricultural net exports by about 40 per cent. These additional exports (to which some more is added by the CMEA) is shared as increased imports by almost all countries.

4.4 Adjustments within the EC

The production, price and trade changes in the world and in the EC itself as a consequence of the removal of border protection by the EC have in turn effects on incomes, particularly in the European agricultural sector. On average, relative prices of agricultural products at the producer level are reduced by 12 per cent; the volume of agricultural production calculated with base-year weights is reduced by 10 per cent. Changes in the composition of output do, to some extent, mitigate these downward adjustments and at the same time there is a significant reduction of fertilizer inputs. Also in the animal husbandry sector substitution takes place between feeds, minimizing cost increases of dairy and meat products. As a result the downward adjustment of agricultural value added measured in constant prices remains limited to 9 per cent as compared to the reference scenario. Still, in current (producer) prices, agricultural value added drops by 21 per cent.

The effect of this decline on agricultural incomes is further reduced by accelerated out-migration from agriculture. The lesser income opportunities for farmers lead to an additional outflow of about 15 per cent of total agricultural labour, equal to some 800,000 workers. In the reference scenario this migration already takes place at a rate of 2.3 per cent per year; removal of border protection increases this rate to 3.1 per cent per year over the period 1980-2000. Or again expressed differently: in the reference scenario the agricultural labour force declines from 8.4 per cent of the total EC labour force to 4.7 per cent in 2000, whereas with the removal of border protection the share falls to 4.1 per cent in 2000.

Even with this decline of the number of people employed in agriculture, there remains an income decline in terms of current purchasing power of about 7 per cent. Expressed in terms of income parity with the non-agricultural sector there is a drop of 5.7 per cent. In other words, parity improves less for agricultural workers, rising from 0.61 in 1980 to 0.67 in 2000, slightly less than was the case in the preceding ten years from 1970 to 1980. Still, the loss is surprisingly small; if the remaining farmers were to be compensated for this loss as compared to the reference run, this would require an amount of the order of $4 billion in 1980-prices, or 0.14 per cent of total GDP. If, in addition, compensation were to be paid to those who left agriculture as a consequence of the removal of border protection, the amount would be some 0.5 per cent of GDP in the year 2000. In the first case this would be equivalent to a quarter of the gain which the EC obtains from the liberalization in terms of its non-agricultural GDP, whereas in the second case the cost of compensation just about equals the total gain.

These numbers seem rather small: non-agricultural GDP increases by 0.52 per cent when agricultural border protection is removed. Still, this is in line with a number of other estimates. The model used is stronger than those used for those other estimates because of its empirical general equilibrium approach, but still lacks in detailing the commodity composition of agricultural production (and even more for non-agricultural production) and in distinguishing categories of farmers. The latter is of particular significance in the context of the migration flows and the termination of farming when producer prices change.

Table 5.13 presents changes of internal EC prices, measured for EC removal of border protection compared to the reference scenario. Retail prices change less than producer prices as the latter receive the full impact of adjustment to world market prices and their margins to border prices are small, whereas retail prices include a substantial element of non-agricultural processing with only a small price decrease.

Table 5.13: Changes of internal EC prices due to removal of EC border protection in comparison to the reference scenario in 2000 (in %)

	Producer prices	Retail prices
Wheat	-33.7	-10.5
Rice	-37.2	-23.0
Coarse grains	-26.2	-25.6
Bovine, ovine meat	-6.7	-3.5
Dairy products	-6.9	-3.6
Other animal products	-9.7	-7.1
Protein feed	-26.1	-26.1
Other food	-10.6	-4.7
Non-food agriculture	-20.5	-20.5
Non-agriculture	-3.8	-3.8

These price changes reflect not only the level of protection at the outset, but also the changes in world market prices which to varying degrees compensate for the removal of border protection. This can for example be noted in the case of dairy products where internal prices decline only moderately as world market prices (see Table 5.11) increase substantially. However, in the case of rice, protein feed and non-food products there are no offsetting world market price increases and internal prices thus bear the full brunt of removing border protection.

On average (with Laspeyres weights) producer prices in agriculture decline by 15.4 per cent. (5)

The effects on production, demand and net export

volumes are presented in Table 5.14. The overall reduction of the volume of agricultural production is spread unevenly by commodity groups, with the largest reductions for rice and wheat, the smallest for pork and protein feed. There is a higher output registered for coarse grains notwithstanding substantially lower prices. As the producer price for wheat is reduced more than for coarse grains, substitution appears attractive to farmers and imports of coarse grains are reduced.

Changes in demand remain small, as could be expected as consumer demand for food in the EC is not very responsive to price changes. The combined changes of demand and production lead to substantial changes of external trade. Wheat exports virtually disappear, meat imports rise substantially and for dairy products the export surplus turns into a substantial deficit. Trade in coarse grains moves in the opposite direction as higher internal production and slightly less demand reduce the level of imports. The net trade balance in agriculture shows a larger deficit with border protection removed.

4.5 Consequences for developing countries

Generally speaking, the effects on the developing countries are small and diverse. To some extent this could already be read from Table 5.12 which shows the changes in the patterns of trade between countries for each of the commodity groups. Except for the 'other food' and 'non-food' groups, the share of the developing countries in export market opportunities resulting from trade liberalization by the EC remains small. As these countries are assumed not to participate in liberalization themselves, one cannot expect to find their domestic prices responsive to changes in world market prices and as a consequence their production responses are also rather small. The ratio of domestic agricultural to non-agricultural prices rises to some significant extent only in Argentina, Egypt, Kenya and Thailand (see Table 5.15), but even in those cases the changes amount to only 4-6 per cent. The effects of these price changes also differ a good deal: Argentina shows the most straightforward response in production (and exports) and the same applies to Egypt and Brazil where domestic production substitutes for previous imports. Production increases of 2-3 per cent are observed for Nigeria, Turkey, Pakistan and Mexico, notwithstanding very small increases

Table 5.14: Changes in the volumes of production, internal demand and net exports in the EC due to the removal of border protection by the EC in comparison to the reference scenario in 2000

	Production				Demand			
	1980	RO(e)	F6(f)	% diff.	1980	RO(e)	F6(f)	% diff.
Wheat (a)	51.42	64.56	48.33	-25.2	40.24	47.50	47.32	-0.4
Rice (a)	0.61	1.01	0.69	-31.1	0.91	1.20	1.21	+0.4
Coarse grain (a)	69.24	88.35	92.01	+4.1	71.51	108.06	103.20	-4.5
Meat (a)	9.27	10.31	9.06	-12.1	9.65	11.33	11.65	+2.8
Dairy (b)	106.13	117.39	104.22	-11.2	96.11	108.66	107.20	-1.3
Pork, etc. (c)	2.28	3.03	2.84	-6.2	2.23	2.95	2.97	+0.9
Prot. food (d)	0.98	1.28	1.20	-6.1	5.96	7.67	7.20	-6.1
Other food (d)	15.91	16.20	14.27	-11.9	20.08	23.35	23.61	+1.1
Non-food (d)	0.97	1.04	0.90	-13.1	3.05	3.08	3.23	+4.6
Non-agric. (d)	796.42	1481.76	1488.98	+0.5	792.37	1467.57	1469.04	+0.1
Agr. GDP (d)	39.78	45.01	41.01	-8.89	43.79	51.94	52.10	+0.3

Table 5.14: continued.

| | 1980 | Net Exports | | % diff. |
		RO(e)	F6(f)	
Wheat (a)	11.18	17.64	1.15	-93.5
Rice (a)	-0.30	-0.19	-0.51	+162.5
Coarse grain (a)	-2.27	-19.62	-11.24	-42.7
Meat (a)	-0.38	-1.03	-2.59	+152.9
Dairy (b)	10.03	8.70	-2.97	-134.1
Pork, etc. (c)	0.05	0.08	-0.13	-263.9
Prot. food (d)	-4.98	-6.39	-6.00	-6.1
Other food (d)	-4.17	-7.17	-9.34	+30.4
Non-food (d)	-2.08	-2.05	-2.33	+13.4
Non-agric. (d)	4.05	14.19	19.95	+40.6
Agr. GDP (d)	-4.01	-6.93	-11.09	+60.0

(a) In million metric tons
(b) In million metric tons of milk equivalent
(c) In million metric tons of protein content
(d) In constant (1970) US-dollars
(e) Reference scenario
(f) Removal of EC border protection scenario

189

Table 5.15: Changes in main economic indicators in selected developing countries due to removal of EC border protection, compared to the reference scenario for the year 2000 (in %)

Country	Volume of agricultural production	Agricultural employment	Terms of trade	GDP agric. (in constant prices)	GDP (in constant prices)	Ratio of agric. to non-agric. prices
Low-income countries:						
India	0.1	-	2.8	0.1	-	1.5
China	-	-	-1.3	-	-	-
Pakistan	2.2	1.1	3.2	1.6	-	-
Kenya	1.8	-	2.5	2.1	0.7	5.8
Middle-income countries:						
Thailand	0.6	-	2.3	1.0	0.1	4.4
Egypt	3.3	2.3	-1.2	1.9	-0.8	4.1
Indonesia	0.2	-	-3.2	0.2	-	1.1
Nigeria	2.8	2.2	-5.3	3.3	0.5	0.8
Turkey	2.6	1.5	3.2	3.6	-0.2	0.1
Brazil	1.7	0.3	-3.7	0.3	-0.1	3.8
Mexico	1.9	-	3.9	1.8	-0.8	0.6
Argentina	5.9	6.8	9.1	6.4	-	5.4

of relative agricultural prices.

The small increases observed in agricultural production volumes are reflected also in the agricultural GDP (in constant prices); differences between the two measures of agricultural growth are due to changes in (non-agricultural) input levels. Although the changes in production volumes and agricultural GDP are small, they are in the expected direction.

The crucial question to be answered concerns of course the evaluation of the overall effects of EC-liberalization on individual developing countries. But in deciding on appropriate indicators, one must recognise that there is more than one viewpoint that can be taken as there are different actors in the system. It is far from easy to combine those into a single social welfare function and for that reason a number of alternative measures are presented here. The simplest of those is the GDP, but at the same time it is affected by serious index number problems limiting the conclusions that can be drawn on its basis. Depending on the prices used, outcomes may differ. The direction of GDP change must be the same measured both at prices of the reference scenario and of the liberalization scenario before GDP can be accepted as an indicator.

In addition, consumer welfare is assessed through equivalent income measures. Equivalent income corresponding to a consumption bundle is defined as the income required under a reference set of prices to obtain the same utility as is provided by the given consumption bundle. Equivalent incomes corresponding to alternate consumption bundles may be compared; the one with higher equivalent income indicates an improvement in consumer welfare. Finally, as a measure of social welfare the number of persons in hunger is calculated on the basis of cross-country regressions.

GDP estimates are presented in Table 5.15; out of the twelve countries shown, five (including China) indicate no perceptible change of GDP, four show declines and only three indicate small increases. In the case of China, the rigidities of the model itself cause this result and therefore little significance should be attached to this outcome. Positive effects on GDP noted in the cases of Kenya, Nigeria and (marginally) Thailand are the result of opposing forces which affect non-agricultural production: higher food prices cause lower demand by consumers for non-agricultural products, but in these three countries this is more than compensated by a higher demand for non-agricultural goods and services by the agricultural sector (inputs, product processing, trade and transport).

Table 5.16: Gains and losses in some welfare indicators in the year 2000 due to removal of EC border protection, compared to the reference scenario*

	GDP	Equivalent income	People hungry
Low-income countries:			
India	NS	L	L
China	NS	-	-
Pakistan	NS	G	L
Kenya	G	-	G
Middle-income countries:			
Thailand	G	-	L
Egypt	L	L	-
Indonesia	NS	L	-
Nigeria	G	G	L
Turkey	L	NS	L
Brazil	L	L	L
Mexico	L	L	L
Argentina	NS	G	L

* G = country gains
  L = country losses
  NS = not significant
  - = not calculated

Negative outcomes in terms of overall GDP are noted for Egypt, Mexico and to a marginal extent Turkey and Brazil. Apparently in these cases the impact of higher agricultural prices on consumer demand for non-agricultural products is stronger than the additional demand for these products originating in the agricultural sector. In each of these countries the agricultural sector accounts for a relatively small part of total GDP, which may contribute to the unfavourable net effect. Judging on the basis of GDP alone, the conclusion must be that there is certainly no reason for bland optimism about effects of EC agricultural trade liberalization. The consequences are rather mixed from one country to another. In this connection one should also note the terms-of-trade estimates shown in Table 5.15, showing a deterioration in five cases. Particularly countries which are large grain importers face this problem, which calls for balance-of-payments adjustments and may delay the accrual of EC liberalization benefits to them.

Table 5.16 summarizes other welfare indicators mentioned earlier, and in comparison to GDP changes.

This broader set of measures does not in any way make the conclusions less mixed than the ones based on GDP alone. It strengthens the positive assessment for Kenya, weakens it somewhat for Nigeria and casts doubts on the welfare effects in Thailand.

5. CONCLUDING REMARKS

The findings presented here need to be somewhat qualified as a number of products which are of interest to developing countries and subject to market organization by the EC are not shown separately. This applies particularly to sugar, but to a lesser extent also to fruits and vegetables, fish and grains substitutes used for livestock feed. Also the number of countries for which reasonably detailed models are available is limited. Still, the analysis shows that broadly speaking the effects of removing EC border protection are not large and frequently negative. This is partly due to the fact that developing countries are large importers of agricultural products which are bound to show higher world prices. No doubt, their existing trade and production structures are distorted as a consequence of world prices which are strongly affected by protection of agriculture in the developed market economies. To adjust to a more liberal environment appears to take considerable time, and over the period covered by our projections the effects are to a significant extent negative.

In judging these results, one ought to be aware of the fact that the EC liberalization scenario does not include any provision to compensate losers, not within countries where particular groups suffer real income reductions, nor between countries where nations are affected by the removal of distortions to which they had adapted themselves in the base period. Compensation is an essential feature in any assessment of the implications of policy changes in terms of welfare.

For another part, the analysis points out how important the links are between the agricultural and non-agricultural sectors. Again in this respect, the adjustments needed to a different set of world prices take time and only few countries appear able to make those adjustments in ways providing early positive results for their overall economic growth. Removing their own border protection may accelerate this process of adjustment and speed up the time when gains are recorded. But that is another topic, and another analytical exercise.

Notes
This paper is based largely on findings obtained with the Basic Linked System (BLS) of national models constructed by a network of researchers who participated in the Food and Agriculture Programme (FAP) of the International Institute for Applied Systems Analysis (IIASA) in Laxenburg, Austria. To a substantial extent it derives from contributions written at IIASA by Klaus Frohberg, who also considerably improved the present paper through his comments.

In a collective effort like this one it is hard to attribute the final products to the large number of contributors. That applies to this one as to many others which are still forthcoming. While taking full responsibility for the content of this paper, the author wishes to mention particularly, and in alphabetical order, Günther Fischer, Klaus Frohberg, Michiel Keyzer, Kirit Parikh and Ferenç Rabar as major and continuous supporters of the project from which this paper derives.

1.   This is the term used in the Treaty of Rome, but in practice it would be more appropriate to speak about financial (co)-responsibility.
2.   Greece joined the EC only a few years ago, whereas in Spain and Portugal the CAP only begins to be introduced in 1986. Data refer to the remaining nine member countries.
3.   This logic is particularly apt in the case of the EC which pursues an agricultural income objective, with protection as a corollary.
4.   Sichra, U. (1984): World prices for the detailed and the small FAP commodity lists, WP-84-95, IIASA, Laxenburg, Austria.
5.   Input price declines lead to a smaller price

decrease applicable to agricultural GDP.

References

Bhagwati, J. and T.N. Srinivasan (1973), 'The general equilibrium theory of effective protection and resource allocation', Journal of International Economics, Vol. 3, No. 3, pp. 259-282.

Buckwell, Allan E., David R. Harvey, Kenneth J. Thomson and Kevin A. Parton (1982), 'The costs of the common agricultural policy', Croom Helm, London.

Commission of the European Communities (1985a), The situation of the agricultural sector in the community, Report 1984, Brussels/Luxemburg.

Commission of the European Communities (1985b), Perspectives for the common agricultural policy, (COM(85)333), Brussels.

Engels, W., A. Gutowsky, W. Hamm, W. Mäschel, W. Stützel, C.C. von Weiszäcker and H. Wilberoth (1985), Für eine neue Agrarordnung: Kurskorrektur für Europa's Agrarpolitik, Schriftenreihe, Band 8, Frankfurter Institut für Wirtschaftliche Forschung e.V., Frankfurt.

Jones, R.W. (1971), 'Effective protection and substitution', Journal of International Economics, no. 1, pp. 59-82.

Koester, U. and S. Tangermann (1976), 'Alternativen der Agrarpolitik', Landwirtschaft-Angewandte Wissenschaft, Heft 182, Landwirtschaftsverlag, Münster-Hiltrup.

Matthews, A. (1985), The common agricultural policy and the less developed countries, Gill and Macmillan, Dublin.

Meester, G. and A.J. Oskam (1983), Analyse van de wereldvraag naar zuivelprodukten uit de EG, Research report no. 2, Agricultural Economics Institute (LEI), The Hague.

Meester, G. and D. Strijker (1985), Het Europese landbouwbeleid voorbij de scheidslijn van de zelfvoorziening, Scientific Council for Government Policy (WRR), The Hague.

Ramaswani, V.K. and T.N. Srinivasan (1971), 'Tariff structure and resource allocation in the presence of factor substitution', in: J. Bhagwati et al. (eds), Trade, balance of payments and growth: papers of international economics in honour of Charles P. Kindleberger, North Holland Publishing Company.

Amsterdam.

Sichra, U. (1984), World prices for the detailed and the small FAP commodity lists, Working paper 84-95, IIASA, Laxenburg, Austria.

Thiede, G. (1984), '10 Jahre Versorgungsberechnungen für die EG'. Agrarwirtschaft, Jahrgang 33, Heft 6, pp. 136-142.

Veer, J. de (1985), National impact of different agricultural policy reform proposals developed within the socialist group of the European Parliament,' Paper presented at the Second Siena Workshop on Economic Integration, The Effects of the Common Agricultural Policy (CAP), Siena, May 1985.

World Bank (1982), World Development Report 1982, Oxford University Press, Washington.

Chapter Six

SOME POTENTIAL EFFECTS OF LIBERALIZING THE MULTI FIBRE ARRANGEMENT

K.A. Koekkoek and L.B.M. Mennes

1. THE MULTI FIBRE ARRANGEMENT

1.1 Short history and objectives

In 1961 a new textile and clothing régime - involving a formal departure from the basic articles of the General Agreement on Tariffs and Trade (GATT) - was created, governing an important part of world trade in textiles and clothing. This "Short Term Arrangement" (STA) referred to international trade in cotton textiles and pursued three goals: to increase significantly access to markets that were then restricted, to maintain orderly access to markets that were relatively open, and to secure a measure of restraint on the part of the exporting countries in order to avoid disruption.

The STA was followed by a "Long Term Arrangement" (LTA) in 1962, which was extended in 1967 for three years, and again in 1970 for a similar period. The LTA was followed by the first MFA (MFA I) in 1974. The MFA was renewed in 1977 (MFA II) and again in 1981 (MFA III) for a period of four years and seven months. [1] The MFA permits nine developed countries - the USA, EC, Canada, Austria, Sweden, Finland, Norway, Switzerland and Japan (though the last two do not apply the restrictions) - to restrict imports of textiles and clothing from 28 developing countries. Australia and New Zealand are not MFA members but have made their own arrangements with developing country exporters of textiles and clothing. Norway joined the MFA from July 1984, and prior to that had its own restrictions. The main characteristics of the various arrangements are summarized in Table 6.1.[2]

Table 6.1: Characteristics of arrangements affecting trade in textiles and clothing

	Period	Products	Regulations
STA	1961/1962	Cotton products	Short-term quantitative restrictions in case of market disruption.
LTA	1962/1974	Textile and clothing products with 50 per cent (or more) cotton in value or in volume	Where market disruptions occur or threaten to occur new restrictions permitted for products or sources hitherto unrestrained. Either with the agreement of the exporting country, or unilaterally. Quota levels not below imports preceding period; quota increase 5% annually.
MFA I	1974/1977	Textile and clothing products of wool, cotton or synthetic fibres	Article 3 involves in case of actual market disruption unilateral imposition of import restriction, in the event a mutually agreed solution is not possible. Article 4 makes bilateral agreements possible in case of a real risk of market disruption. Provisions dealing with base levels, annual growth rates (not less than 6%) and flexibility of quotas. If safeguard mechanism is employed, structural adjustment should be pursued.

Table 6.1: continued

	Period	Products	Regulations
MFA II	1978/1982	see MFA I	See MFA I. A provision for "jointly agreed departures" was introduced permitting derogation from MFA requirements (e.g. base levels and growth rates).
MFA III	1982/1986	see MFA I	See MFA I. Provision for "reasonable departures" was deleted. "Anti-surge procedure" to prevent sharp and substantial import increases was incorporated. If invoked, the resulting solution would include "equitable and quantifiable compensation" to the exporting country.

Although the MFA I extended coverage to textiles and clothing of wool and man-made fibres, as well as of cotton, it became more liberal and more favourable to the developing countries than the LTA with respect to the minimum growth rates for quotas, the flexibility provisions, and the rules, procedures and implementing arrangements.

MFA II became in many respects much more restrictive than MFA I. Most important, the introduction of the so-called "jointly agreed reasonable departure" clause led to reductions in quotas compared to their previous levels or actual trade, denials or reductions in the degree of flexibility and frequent use of growth rates below 6 per cent.

In MFA III the provision of "reasonable departures" was not included. On the other hand, the so-called "anti-surge procedure" was introduced, thus casting uncertainty on previously secured import opportunities. The EC reduced a number of quota levels of East Asian producers. In the US a large number of restraints on clothing were introduced.

On average, international trade in textiles and clothing has become considerably more restricted for developing countries, in particular for the dominant suppliers among them. Quotas have been reduced, flexibility conditions have been restricted, and the number of countries and products to which restrictive measures apply has increased. At present, it is not necessary for the industrialized countries' producers to prove that textile imports from developing countries are injurious to their industry for imposing restrictive measures.

The MFA had originally various objectives. In fact, it was supposed to prevent a general rush into protectionism which was expected because many developed countries had been taking unilateral, ad hoc actions against rising textile and clothing imports. Also, the MFA was considered as a device for increasing international trade in textiles and clothing. The premise was that if trade increased gradually and in an "orderly manner" the economic and social costs of the displacement of domestic production by imports from developing countries could be reduced so as to eliminate unilateral measures by restraints based on agreed criteria. In other words, the purpose was to increase world trade in textiles and clothing in such a way that the adjustment process in industrial countries was facilitated.

It has been already mentioned that instead of being reduced over time, protection in the textiles and clothing trade with the developing countries actually increased. It must be added that only the exports of developing or other "low-cost" countries are restricted by means of the MFA. Trade between developed countries in textiles and clothing, which forms 44 per cent of total world trade in those products, continued under normal GATT procedures and rules. Consequently, one of the effects of the MFA is to divert trade from poor to rich countries.

As for the MFA objective to develop world trade in textile products so as to lead to economic development of the developing countries and a substantial increase in their earnings from this trade, there is sufficient empirical evidence, e.g. Smallbone (1984) and Das (1985), that this aim has not been reached.

According to GATT (1984), Shepherd (1981) and de la Torre (1984) the adjustment process in the industrial countries - the third objective of the MFA - has occurred to a considerable extent. In Western Europe in 1980 the textile industry accounted for only 1.6 per cent of total employment and a further 1.3 per cent in the clothing industry, a decline of nearly one half since 1953. In the USA the corresponding figures were 1.1 and 1.2 per cent, a similar decline as in Europe. Profits for those companies still in textiles and clothing are currently reported to be healthy. This has been attributed, (The Economist 1984, p. 78), to investment in new technology, with the application of micro-processors to previously labour-intensive tasks, particularly in clothing.

1.2 The MFA and the EC

Broadly speaking, three general régimes apply to imports of textile products into the EC depending on the products and the countries in which they originate. The MFA régime, the preferential régimes for a number of Mediterranean countries and the partners in the association of Lomé, and finally the autonomous EC régime on imports which applies to textile products not covered by the MFA régime or a preferential régime.(3)

How the actual division of power between the Community and member states is with respect to the various import régimes on textile products is somewhat unclear, with one exception. As far as the MFA régime applies, no problems seem to arise because this régime is entirely operated by the EC institutions, either the Council or the Commission. (4)

The EC import policy regarding textile products is based on the concept of "cumulated market disruption". Within the framework of the MFA the Commission has negotiated under Article 4 bilateral agreements with 21 developing countries - exclusive of China and Taiwan - and 6 East European countries. The main characteristics are as follows. The agreements are applicable to the total range of the MFA products, which are divided into 114 categories and are grouped together into three groups. Group I contains the "very sensitive" products.

The quotas at Community level are further subdivided into 8 country quotas: one for each member state where the Benelux is considered to be one member state. There is a provision for transfer of unutilized regional quotas from one member state to another on request. Apart from the quotas at the Community level, the unrestrained categories may be restricted for one or more member states separately.

The remaining categories are subject to the so-called "basket exit procedure". If exports from a given country reach a specified percentage of the total imports of the product into the EC in the previous year, the EC can call for consultations so as to arrive at an agreed quota level; in the absence of agreement a quota may be imposed unilaterally. The procedure can also be applied for a single member state, if imports reach a prescribed share of total imports.

In addition to the quotas at Community level and the country quotas, the member states may, if approved by the Commission, apply Article 115 of the Treaty of Rome to restrict imports of the products under quota from third countries through other member states.

Finally, the "anti-surge procedure" can be applied so as to regulate the level of imports in previously under-utilized quotas for highly sensitive products in such a manner that sharp and substantial increases in imports are prevented.

Summarizing, nearly all textile and clothing products imported into the EC from the MFA countries are subject to some restriction: either by means of quotas or via the basket exit and anti-surge procedures. According to UNCTAD (1984) the 27 bilateral agreements between the EC and 21 developing countries as well as 6 centrally planned economies contain 377 community-wide quotas and 28 specific country quotas; 127 community-wide quotas refer to the group of very sensitive products. Because there exist 8 country quotas for each of the quotas at Community level the total number of quotas for the 27 exporting countries amounts to more than 3000.

According to the Commission the basket exit procedure was used in 145 cases by one or more of the member states between 1978 and 1985. This resulted in 38 cases in quotas at Community level; in a large majority of the cases the procedure was used for fixing specific country quotas.

The anti-surge mechanism has not been invoked to date. The importance of this procedure is, however, that it implies the principle that in specific circumstances the exporting countries have no unconditional access to the EC within the jointly agreed quotas.

1.3 **Protective effect**

1.3.1 **Tariff equivalents.** There is no doubt that the MFA is devised and meant to protect the domestic textile and clothing industry in the industrial countries. On the other hand it is very difficult to measure to what extent the MFA actually provides protection. Obviously this is due to the intricacy and lack of transparency of the system, which does not allow for an all-embracing approach.

In this section the extent of the MFA's protective effect will be considered in two ways. First, some empirical evidence on the tariff equivalent of the MFA's quota protection will be summarized. Secondly, trade coverage and quota utilization rates indicating the degree to which the MFA actually performs as a protective barrier, are analysed.

There are some studies in which the price or tariff equivalent of quantitative restrictions under the MFA, for selected clothing products, are estimated by the premiums paid on transfer of quota rights among firms in the exporting countries. Such quota premiums appear to be significant only for exports from Hong Kong, South Korea and Taiwan, which might indicate that the restrictions are not binding on the other exporters.

First, there is a study by Jenkins (1980)(5) in which he estimated for 16 garment categories the total nominal protective rates - consisting of tariff protection and the effect of quotas - on Canada's imports from Hong Kong, South Korea and Taiwan in 1979. For these product groups tariff protection ranged from 12 to 26 per cent, but in most cases it was more than 20 per cent. The range of tariff equivalents of quotas was between 2 and 54 per cent; for 3 product groups only they were lower than 10 per cent, whereas 8 categories showed rates of 15 per cent and higher.

Taking both rates together, total nominal protection amounted to between 24 and 74 per cent; comparing tariff and quota protection for each product group, the quota effect varied between 10 and 250 per cent of the corresponding tariff protection.

A second study is by Cable (1983) who used Hong Kong quota premiums information for a limited number of products so as to arrive at estimates of the total protective effect of tariffs and quotas in 1981 on garments exported to the EC. Cable calculated total nominal protective rates for four product groups, which amounted to between 29 and 68 per cent; the range of tariff equivalents of quotas was between 12 and 51 per cent. The quota effect varied between 70 and 300 per cent of the corresponding tariff protection.

Another study is by Hamilton (1984) who similarly used 1980-1983 Hong Kong quota premiums on exports of 4 to 11 clothing product groups to 8 European countries. During this period the average import tariff equivalent of the various quotas was equal to 18 per cent, about the magnitude of the average tariff rate (17 per cent). Hamilton found that the tariff equivalents varied between importing countries with Sweden highest with 31 per cent and Austria at the lower end with 4 per cent. Further analysis showed that for the countries concerned total nominal protection amounted to some 40 per cent and that, with the possible exception of Italy, variations of the tariff of 17 per cent were inversely related to the tariff equivalents of the corresponding country quotas.

Finally, some recent estimates by the IMF, Kirmani, Molajoni and Mayer (1984), are mentioned. In this study the 1980 tariff equivalents of tariff (post-Kennedy Round) and non-tariff barriers in the United States and the EC were estimated to amount to 68 and 59 per cent for textiles and 79 and 59 per cent for clothing, respectively. According to Yeats (1979) post-Kennedy tariffs for the United States and the EC were equal to 18.7 and 14.9 per cent for textiles and 30.0 and 15.2 for clothing. In this way one can estimate the tariff equivalent of the MFA for textiles to be about 42 (USA) and 38 (EC) per cent, and for clothing about 38 per cent for both the USA and the EC.

It is clear that, despite the extraordinary complexity of the system, tariff and quota escalation still prevails. All these studies show that the protective effect of MFA quotas is considerable and on average at least as important as tariff protection. As an order of magnitude one could, on the basis of GATT (1984, p. 69), put post-Kennedy, trade weighted, tariff protection in the EC at around 16 per cent for clothing and at between a half (fibres) and 14 (fabrics) per cent, say around 10 per cent, for textile products. Taking the tariff equivalent of the MFA in the same order of magnitude, this leads to total nominal protection in the seventies for the EC of 35 per cent for clothing and 21 per cent for textile products.

1.3.2 Trade coverage and quota utilization rates. Another approach towards considering the effectiveness or protectiveness of the textile arrangements consists of looking at the trade coverage of the system and the rate of quota utilization. This has been done, among other things, in a recent study of the Netherlands Economic Institute (1985). In that study the following figures regarding trade coverage and quota utilization can be found.

The first figures refer to the potential influence of the textile policy. (6) They represent the share of those products, which are potentially regulated by the MFA, in EC textile and clothing imports, irrespective of their origin. In volume terms this share was around 73 per cent, both in 1977 and 1983. In value terms this share increased from 83 to 87 per cent, between 1977 and 1983. Out of this trade, around 75 per cent, in volume terms, came from MFA suppliers in 1983, with the textile share slightly below 70 per cent and the clothing share slightly above 90 per cent, i.e. this share originated from MFA countries. Limiting the analysis to the most sensitive products for the EC, groups I and II, their share in MFA-products imports, from all sources, increased between 1977 and 1983, from 43 to 48 per cent for textiles and from 85 to 92 per cent for clothing in value terms.

Now the analysis regarding the quotas is further limited to the developing countries among the MFA-suppliers. The number of quotas, for the most sensitive products, groups I and II, directed against these suppliers, increased from 177 in 1978 to 194 in 1983. (7) During this period the share of trade under quotas in the imports of these products, coming from these suppliers, decreased from 91 to 87 per cent for textiles and from 94 to 92 per cent for clothing. Regarding the utilization rates of the quotas the figures in Table 6.2 apply.

Table 6.2: Frequency distribution of the utilization rates for the quotas in groups I and II, directed against MFA developing countries; 1978, 1983

Rate of utilization	Number of quotas	1978		1983	
		177	100%	194	100%
0 - 30%		45	25	42	22
30 - 50%		23	13	42	22
50 - 70%		35	20	36	18
70 - 90%		27	15	39	20
90 - 100%		47	27	35	18

From this table it is clear that the share of highly utilized quotas in the total number of quotas has decreased between 1978 and 1983. With regard to the trade coverage of the quotas with a utilization rate above 50 per cent the figures in Table 6.3 apply. From this table it is clear that less trade is covered by higher utilized quotas in 1983 than in 1978. After looking at the trade coverage and frequency distribution of the quotas now some figures regarding average quota utilization will be given, in particular again for the MFA developing countries, in the sensitive product groups.

Table 6.3: Share of imports under quotas in groups I and II, with a utilization rate of 50 per cent or more, from MFA developing countries, in total imports under quotas of these product groups from these suppliers

Utilization rate	1978			1983		
	90%	70%	50%	90%	70%	50%
Share in quota imports	.55	.77	.93	.42	.74	.85

Table 6.4 gives average quota utilization rates for these countries, where the value of trade under quotas is used for weighting the volume rate of utilization. In this table it can be seen that the average quota utilization rate, for all developing MFA suppliers together, has decreased from 100 per cent in 1978 to 82.2 per cent in 1983.(8)

Table 6.4: Average quota utilization rates for MFA developing countries, in product groups I and II

	1978	1983
Brazil	72.4	94.3
Colombia	69.4	42.3
Egypt	66.1	73.5
Hong Kong	101.0	89.8
India	71.2	50.1
Indonesia	-	76.9
Macao	90.3	87.1
Malaysia	84.5	53.5
Mexico	22.5	24.8
Pakistan	89.2	102.9
Peru	31.6	102.9
Philippines	82.5	64.1
Singapore	81.1	57.6
South Korea	137.1	82.9
Sri Lanka	42.2	80.8
Thailand	83.2	68.4
Total	100.0	82.2

Another way of looking at average quota utilization is by calculating average utilization rates per product instead of per country. Application of this type of calculation shows that in 1983, for 6 out of the 38 categories of products, in groups I and II, the average quota utilization is above 90 per cent, covering 42 per cent of total imports in product groups I and II, from MFA developing countries. Additionally, 10 out of the 38 product categories have an average utilization rate between 70 and 90 per cent, representing 38 per cent of corresponding imports. Taking these categories together, some four-fifths of imports in product groups I and II from MFA-developing countries takes place under quotas with a utilization rate above 70 per cent.

Summarizing the above figures it can be said that a very substantial amount of textile and clothing trade of the EC is under the potential or actual impact of the MFA. The data on quota utilization can be interpreted as at least being consistent with some of the known by-product distortions of the MFA, viz. trading up - increase in value with static volume - trade diversion - fall in recorded utilization of some quotas - diversification in LDCs and monopolistic pricing in LDCs (Murray et al., 1978). On the other hand, although a considerable amount of trade is covered by the higher utilized quotas, the figures also show a surprising amount of underutilization of the quotas. Conclusions along these same lines can be found in GATT (1984). There one can also find a number of reasons for this underutilization, which will be shortly summed up here, GATT (1984, p. 154/155). First, quotas may be redundant, e.g. because of recession in the importing countries, supply bottlenecks or other reasons. Secondly, there may be a mismatch between demand and supply, e.g. if quotas are negotiated in order to secure future access to a market, or because of fashion changes. Thirdly, the quotas may lead to reduced competitiveness of the foreign suppliers, e.g. by offering disincentives for investment, or because of administrative inexperience in allocating the quota. With regard to the EC, it must be kept in mind also that EC-wide quota are distributed over the EC countries, thus in effect leading to eight sub-quotas for each quota. This may also lead to underutilization of quotas at the EC-level. Finally, the possibility of evasion of the system cannot be discarded. There are many possibilities in this respect. It follows that in calculating the utilization rates of the quotas, there is a bias towards underutilization. Figures below 100 per cent may thus indicate genuine non-restrictiveness, but this need not be the case at all. It may also indicate that a quota is binding below a 100 per cent utilization rate.

2. ABOLISHING THE MFA; EFFECTS FOR LDCS, THE EC, AND THE NETHERLANDS

Abolishing or liberalizing the MFA will have effects on the economies of both the developing and the developed countries. Such effects will be discussed in the present section where the analysis is confined to the effects of a possible liberalization of the MFA by the EC only.

2.1 Effects for the EC and the Netherlands

In the present sub-section the effects of abolishing the MFA for the EC and the Netherlands will be discussed. The analysis will be as comprehensive as possible in the sense that welfare effects of abolishing the MFA will be presented. For the Netherlands a complete welfare effects analysis will be made which is for all components but one derived from a similar analysis for the EC. The welfare effects estimated for the EC are not complete in the sense that estimates of one component - adjustment costs - are lacking.

2.1.1 Methodology. To estimate the welfare effects of abolishing the MFA must be considered a rather difficult task, not in the least because one has to make a considerable number of assumptions regarding price effects, elasticities, tariff equivalents and market behaviour. The approach used in this section is based on Pearson (1983), with some adjustments. (9) In this approach imperfect substitution is assumed between foreign and domestic supply. (10) There are two types of foreign supply distinguished, viz. imperfectly elastic supply, under the restriction of tariffs only, and perfectly elastic supply, which, in addition to the tariff, is subject to a Voluntary Export Restraint (VER). Abolition of the VER leads to lower foreign supply prices and changes in efficiency, welfare and transfers between foreign suppliers, domestic consumers and the government. Figure 6.1, taken from Pearson, shows such a situation.

Figure 6.1

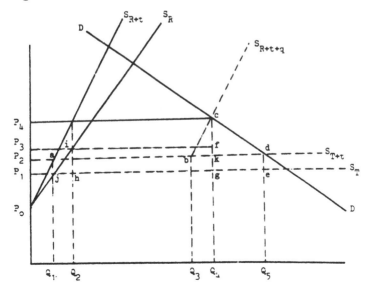

In Figure 6.1 DD represents the import demand curve. S_R represents the imperfectly elastic foreign supply curve. S_T represents the total foreign supply curve, including the perfectly elastic supply at price P_1. Application of a tariff would alter these foreign supply curves into S_{R+t} and S_{T+t} respectively, where $P_2 = P_1$ (l+t).

If, in addition to the tariff, a VER would be imposed on the perfectly elastic supplier, the foreign supply curve would change into the double-kinked curve P_2 a b S_{R+t+q}, leading to equilibrium at a price P_4. P_3 would be the price received by the exporters, where $P_4 = P_3$ (l+t). This implies that the tariff-equivalent of the VER is equal to P_3/P_1, which is also equal to P_4/P_2.

In order to apply this methodology one has to assume that the MFA acts like a single VER, restricting supply from certain countries and pushing up import prices. (11) In other words, in terms of this methodology, the restricted supplier represents all MFA restricted countries, the unrestricted supplier represents the rest of the world. (12) Still, this methodology cannot be applied straightaway so as to estimate the effects of abolishing the MFA upon the Netherlands, because in effect, the MFA is an EC-wide protective system and there is a third source of foreign supply on the Dutch market, viz. completely unrestrained supply from other EC producers. Estimating the effects of abolishing the MFA for the Netherlands will therefore be done in two stages. The first stage is a calculation of the effects for the EC as a whole. The second stage consists of regionalizing these resulting effects.

What happens in the first stage will be explained in terms of Figure 6.1. Elimination of the VER leads to a decrease in the foreign supply price from P_4 to P_2 (tariff included). The quantity imported will increase from Q_4 to Q_5, with a redistribution between the two types of foreign supply. Perfectly elastic supply will increase from $Q_2 Q_4$ to $Q_1 Q_5$. The other foreign supply will decrease from Q_2 to Q_1. With regard to the various parties involved the following effects can now be distinguished. The consumer surplus increases with the area $P_2 P_4$ c d. Tariff revenues for the importing country increase with $P_1 P_2$ d e minus $P_3 P_4$ c f. This leads to a total welfare gain for the importing country of $P_1 P_3$ f g plus g c d e. The supplying countries under the VER lose a transfer of f g h i. The other foreign suppliers lose a transfer of $P_1 P_3$ ih, partly compensated by lower resource costs, j h i. Together these effects lead to a global welfare gain of g c d e + j h i.

Finally, these effects still have to be augmented with the costs of an increase in unemployment, for some period, in the importing country. (13) In calculating the domestic employment loss it is assumed that total consumer expenditure remains constant. The increase in imports then leads to an equal decrease in domestic production, which can then be translated into a corresponding employment loss via the appropriate labour intensity coefficient.

The various effects, indicated in terms of the areas above, are now calculated in the following way. We assume a tariff rate t and a tariff equivalent of the VER of τ. The increase in consumer surplus is equal to

$$V_m^{cif} \left(\frac{\tau}{1+\tau} \right) \cdot (1+t)(1+\tfrac{1}{2}\eta_m \cdot \frac{\tau}{1+\tau}) \tag{1}$$

in which V_m^{cif} is total imports, Q_4, valued at price P_3, in other words the cif-value of total imports before liberalization, and η_m is the absolute value of the price elasticity of import demand. The effect on government revenue can be calculated as

$$V_m^{cif} \frac{t \cdot \tau}{1+\tau} \left(\frac{m-1-\tau}{1+\tau} \right) \tag{2}$$

leading to a national welfare gain of

$$V_m^{cif} \cdot \frac{\tau}{1+\tau} (1+\tfrac{1}{2}\eta_m \cdot \frac{1+t\tau+2t}{1+\tau}) \tag{3}$$

The countries under MFA lose a rent of

$$V_{MFA}^{cif} \cdot \frac{\tau}{1+\tau} \tag{4}$$

in which V_{MFA}^{cif} is the cif-value of the imports from the

MFA-countries before liberalisation.

The other foreign suppliers lose

$$\frac{\tau}{1+\tau} \cdot V^{cif}_{other} \cdot (1 - \tfrac{1}{2}\varepsilon_m \cdot \frac{\tau}{1+\tau}) \tag{5}$$

in which V^{cif}_{other} is the cif-value of the imports from the other foreign suppliers before liberalization and ε_m is their price elasticity of supply. From formulas (1) - (5) it follows that for the first stage of the calculations one needs the values of cif-imports for the EC, of both MFA-suppliers and others, the EC tariff rate and the EC tariff-equivalent of the VER, the EC import price elasticity and the price elasticity of the unrestricted foreign supply.

In the second stage the Dutch share in these welfare effects has to be calculated. From the formulas it seems logical to assume that the Dutch share in the EC-wide consumer surplus increase, and national welfare increase, should be taken to be proportional to its share in EC imports as represented in the various formulas.

Finally, the welfare loss connected with the increased unemployment has to be calculated. The calculations are confined to the factor labour. For this purpose it is assumed that the increase in EC-wide imports replaces national production according to the existing distribution of production over the member countries. This may reflect a too static, and thus optimistic, assumption regarding Dutch comparative advantage in these industries compared with other EC suppliers, in particular Italy. It is not inconceivable that the brunt of adjustment within the EC would be borne by the relatively high-wage countries among the EC suppliers. This would apply more to clothing than to textiles, in view of the net trade position of the two product groups. Anyway, the adjustment costs calculated on the basis of this assumption probably reflect a lower limit. Next, on the basis of national labour-intensity coefficients the loss of employment can be calculated. Together with an assumption about the length of the unemployment period this leads to the estimation of the concomitant welfare loss. Assuming the productivity of labour can be equated with the labour costs, the calculation can be simplified in the following way. Displaced production times labour intensity times labour cost per man is equal to displaced production times labour cost as a percentage of production. The welfare loss is then equal to this amount for the duration of the unemployment period.

2.1.2 Data and parameters: values and sources. The MFA group of countries includes both developing and state trading MFA-countries plus Taiwan. Textiles consists of SITC groups 26 and 65. Clothing is represented by SITC 82. Trade data are from the UN, for the year 1983.

The tariff figures used are 8 per cent for textiles and 14 per cent for clothing. These are reasonably representative values for 1983, for the EC. Regarding the tariff equivalent of the quota system, the figures reviewed in section 1.3.1 hardly allow for a unique choice. They represent a wide range, sometimes including rather high values. It must be kept in mind that the analysis is applied to the whole of textiles and clothing, reasonably ruling out the use of high values. (14) We chose to apply therefore three alternative values of the tariff equivalent, viz. 15, 10 and 5 per cent.

With regard to the import demand elasticities there is a range of values to be found in the literature. Stern et al. (1976) show for textiles values ranging from -.71 to -2.98 and for clothing -3.77 to -4.06. Kirmani et al. (1984) use -2.61 for both textiles and clothing for the EC. Stone (1979) presents estimates for the EC of around -.8 for textiles and an insignificant (positive) value for clothing. In view of these figures we chose -1.5 for textiles and -2.5 for clothing. For the export supply elasticity of unrestrained suppliers, for want of a better assumption, Hamilton (1980, p.17) was followed in assuming supply to be as flexible as demand, i.e. the absolute values of their price elasticities were assumed to be equal.

The Dutch share in the EC production of textiles and clothing was calculated to be 2.5 per cent in 1981. (15) The length of the unemployment period for textile labourers was estimated to be 14.5 months. (16) The labour cost coefficient (labour costs as per cent of production value) was 25.2 per cent for both sectors in 1980. (17)

2.1.3 Results. The results of the liberalization exercise will now be presented in two parts. First, the EC-wide effects

Table 6.5: Welfare effects for the EC of abolishing the MFA, in million US dollars, 1983*

Alternative tariff equivalent	Textiles			Clothing		
	0.15	0.10	0.05	0.15	0.10	0.05
Consumer surplus	1,594	1,081	549	1,473	983	490
Government revenue	33	27	17	183	138	78
National welfare gain	1,627	1,108	566	1,656	1,121	568
MFA rent loss	-401	-279	-146	-665	-464	-243
Other suppliers' loss	-852	-613	-332	-373	-275	-153
Global welfare gain	374	216	88	618	382	172

* Recurrent annual values

will be given in Table 6.5. No estimates of adjustment costs are included, as the necessary information for the ten countries is not available to us. Then the effects for the Netherlands are given, derived from the effects for the EC under the assumptions mentioned above.

Regarding the EC, Table 6.5 shows that the consumer surplus gain and the national welfare gain are both of the same order of magnitude in textiles and clothing. Depending on the assumption regarding the tariff equivalent the gains are around 0.5, 1 or 1.5 billion dollars. The difference between the sectors can be found in the extent to which the national welfare gain is at the expense of foreign producers. In textiles, depending on the value of the tariff equivalent, between 75 and 85 per cent of the national welfare gain is a transfer from foreign producers, leaving a global welfare gain of between 374 and 88 million dollars. In clothing the national welfare gain consists for in between 63 and 70 per cent of a transfer from abroad, leading to a global welfare gain ranging from 618 to 172 million dollars. For the world as a whole, liberalizing imports of clothing is thus more advantageous than liberalizing imports of textiles.

Table 6.6 give the results of the liberalisation exercise for the Netherlands. In textiles the consumer surplus gain ranges between 23 and 65 million dollars. The same applies, approximately, to the national welfare gain. This national welfare gain consists of more than 75 per cent of a transfer from foreign producers. The remainder represents a global welfare gain. The adjustment costs, although not negligible, are rather low, especially when one keeps in mind that these are non-recurrent, whereas the welfare gains are annual values.

The same picture can be seen in clothing, albeit that the figures involved are somewhat higher. The consumer surplus gain ranges between 42 and 126 million dollars. The national welfare gain ranges between 48 and 141 million dollars. This national welfare gain consists again of a substantial, although in this case lower, part of a transfer from producers abroad, viz. more than 60 per cent. Again the adjustment costs are comparatively low.

Comparing the results for the Netherlands with those for the EC, it can be seen that approximately 4 per cent of the welfare increase in textiles and 8.5 per cent of the welfare increase in clothing takes place in the Netherlands. Similarly, as in the case of the EC above, the global welfare gains are larger when imports of clothing are liberalized

Table 6.6: Welfare effects for the Netherlands of abolishing the MFA for the EC as a whole, in million US dollars, 1983*

Alternative tariff equivalent	Textiles			Clothing	
	0.15	0.10	0.05	0.10	0.05
Consumer surplus	65	44	23	84	42
Government revenue	1	1	1	12	7
National welfare gain	67	45	23	96	48
MFA rent loss	-20	-14	-7	-44	-23
Other suppliers' loss	-31	-23	-12	-20	-11
Global welfare gain	16	8	4	32	14
Adjustment costs	3	3	2	9	5

* Annual values, except for adjustment costs which are non-recurrent.

Table 6.7: Additional trade flows in case of abolishing the MFA by the EC; in million US dollars, 1983

	Textiles			Clothing		
Alternative tariff equivalent	0.15	0.10	0.05	0.15	0.10	0.05
Additional imports EC	409	341	210	1,304	985	560
Additional exports						
MFA countries	2,584	1,896	1,047	2,717	2,000	1,100
demand effect	1,754	1,287	701	2,414	1,759	966
substitution effect	1,231	897	492	968	705	387
rent loss	-401	-279	-146	-665	-464	-243
Additional export						
other suppliers	-2,175	-1,555	-837	-1,413	-1,015	-550
substitution effect	-1,231	-897	-492	-968	-705	-387
rent loss	-944	-658	-345	-445	-310	-163

Imports EC 1983	Textiles	Clothing
from MFA countries	3,073	5,100
from other suppliers	7,237	3,415

than when doing so for textiles.

2.3 **Effects for LDCs**

In order to estimate the welfare effects for the EC of abolishing the MFA, which were presented in Table 6.5, one needs to calculate estimates of the additional exports of textiles and clothing from the MFA countries as well as from other suppliers. These values together with some other relevant estimates are presented in Table 6.7 on the basis of which some effects for LDCs can be calculated.

The export gains for the MFA countries consist of additional exports to the EC due to an increase in import demand (demand effect), plus additional exports to the EC because of substitution for EC imports from other suppliers, minus the rent losses. These gains amount to 1-2.5 billion US dollars for textiles and 1-2.7 billion US dollars for clothing, depending on the assumption regarding the tariff equivalent.

It is also interesting to have an estimate of the effects of abolishing the MFA by the EC on the MFA countries' volume of employment. Before doing so first something will be said on the role of textile and clothing activities of LDCs.

It is well known and well documented, e.g. GATT (1984), that textiles and clothing are important in LDCs' production, employment and trade. For this reason only a few figures indicating this importance will be presented here.

The share of LDCs in textiles and clothing production and employment in all market economies has been increasing continuously since the Second World War. LDCs have now (1980) a share of 35 per cent in the world production of textiles; for clothing this percentage is 25. The LDCs share in world textile employment is 73 per cent (1980), and for clothing 61 per cent.

The importance of textiles and clothing in manufacturing production in LDCs has been decreasing, but is still considerable. The shares of textiles and clothing production in total manufacturing are 11.5 and 4.5 per cent, respectively (1980). The share of textiles in LDCs' manufacturing employment has been decreasing also, but is still very high: 24.0 per cent. On the other hand, the share of clothing has been increasing somewhat to 10.9 per cent.

The share of textiles in LDCs' manufactured exports

has been decreasing regularly, but is still 10.6 per cent (1982). The share of clothing has increased till 1973 and then remained stable: 13.6 per cent.

The importance of the developed countries' markets for LDCs' exports of textiles and clothing is quite substantial. In 1980 51 per cent of LDCs exports of textiles and 70 per cent of their exports of clothing went to these markets.

It has been already mentioned in section 1.2 that in the framework of the MFA the EC has bilateral agreements with 21 developing countries and 6 state trading countries. With the aid of available information on and own estimates of the direct and total labour requirements per unit of textile and clothing output in each of these countries (plus Taiwan) the following estimates of the employment involved in exporting textiles and clothing to the EC were made in the study by the Netherlands Economic Institute mentioned before. Such employment in the EC MFA régime countries plus Taiwan amounted to 285,000 persons directly employed in the textile industry and 485,000 persons directly employed in the clothing industry, in 1980. Including indirect employment effects the total number of persons employed in these countries associated with exports of textiles and clothing to the EC amounted to about 1.25 million in 1980.

From Table 6.7 one can easily derive that abolishing the MFA may involve additional exports by the MFA countries amounting to 1.2-3.0 billion US dollars for textiles and 1.4-3.4 billion US dollars for clothing, depending on what is assumed regarding the tariff equivalent. This implies an export increase of 39-97 per cent for textiles and 27-67 per cent for clothing.

With the aid of the information on the direct and total labour requirements per unit of textile and clothing output in each of the MFA countries, provided in the study by the Netherlands Economic Institute, one can calculate the effects on employment corresponding with the export increases mentioned above. For textiles the direct employment effect amounts to 43,000-106,000 persons; total employment effect amounts to 103,000-254,000 persons. For clothing the direct employment effect is 75,000-185,000 persons; the total employment effect is 122,000-303,000 persons. In other words, in case the EC would abolish the MFA completely, the present employment in the MFA countries associated with exports of textiles and clothing to the EC, which equals about 1.25 million persons, would increase by some 20-45 per cent due to increased exports to the EC.

Notes

This chapter is a modified and extended version of an article published in the 'Journal of World Trade Law', Volume 20, Number 2, March/April 1986. Permission given by the editor of that journal to include the chapter in this volume is gratefully acknowledged.

The authors want to thank David Greenaway and Carl Hamilton for their comments on an earlier version of this article.

1.   The last renewal, MFA IV, which took place in July 1986, is beyond the scope of this article.

2.   Complete information on the Multi-Fibre Arrangement can be found in: GATT (1984) and Keesing and Wolf (1980).

3.   For a detailed survey see van Dartel (1983).

4.   See Timmermans (1983).

5.   As reported in Wolf (1983).

6.   All figures in this section refer to extra-EC trade.

7.   Only community-wide quotas are considered here.

8.   A word of caution is in order here. One must be careful in interpreting these changes in average rates, as these do not only reflect changes in volume utilization rates, but also the accompanying changes in value weights. It is not difficult to construct examples, where increasing utilization rates of individual quotas are accompanied by a decrease in their value-weighted average.

9.   Pearson applies this methodology to a particular type of footwear, imported in the USA under a VER from Taiwan, in 1980.

10.   This is not uncommon. Silberston (1984, p. 30) though criticizes many studies of this kind that assume imported and domestically produced textile products to be perfect substitutes.

11.   In view of the share of EC imports of textile products consisting of MFA-type products and the actual share of trade covered by the MFA, as presented in section 1.3.2, this is not an unreasonable assumption. It also reflects the position taken in Wolf (1983, pp. 481/482).

12.   The assumption of perfectly elastic supply from the MFA countries reflects the belief that, in these rather capital-extensive industries, producers in the MFA countries

would be quite capable of expanding output with marginal cost equal to average cost. Insofar as pressures on the cost side would not allow this, especially in the more advanced MFA countries, producers might very well relocate production facilities towards other lower-wage LDCs.

13. In this analysis no price effect on domestic output is assumed, which may well be unrealistic. Insofar as the domestic price level decreases upon liberalization, consumer surplus gains will be underestimated. These additional consumer surplus gains will be mainly at the expense of domestic producers and will not so much influence the national welfare gain, depending of course on the values of the parameters involved.

14. For a discussion about the likely price effects see also Silberston (1984), p. 29 ff.

15. This figure represents the share in EC value added in both sectors combined. The source was National Accounts ESA (1984).

16. This was estimated on the basis of figures on the duration of registration at the unemployment office. The source was Sociale Maandstatistiek (1983) p. 22.

17. Source: Nationale Rekeningen (1982), Supplement on the input-output table.

References

Cable, V., (1983), Protectionism and Industrial Decline, Hodder and Stoughton/ODI, London.

Cline, W.R., ed., (1983), Trade Policy in the 1980s, Institute for International Economics, Washington.

van Dartel, R.J.P.M., (1983), 'The Conduct of the EC's Textile Trade Policy and the Application of Article 115 EC', in Völker (1983), pp. 99-123.

Das, D.K., (1985), 'Dismantling the Multifibre Arrangement', Journal of World Trade Law, vol. 19, no. 1, pp. 67-80.

The Economist, (1984), 15 September, London.

GATT, (1984), Textiles and Clothing in the World Economy, Geneva.

Hamilton, C., (1980), Effects of Non-tariff Barriers to Trade on Prices, Employment and Imports: the Case of the Swedish Textile and Clothing Industry, World Bank Staff Working Paper no. 429, Washington.

Hamilton, C., (1984), Voluntary Export Restraints on Asia: Tariff Equivalents, Rents and Trade Barrier Formation, Seminar Paper no. 276, Institute for International

Economic Studies, Stockholm.

Jenkins, G.P., (1980), Costs and Consequences of the New Protectionism: the Case of Canada's Clothing Sector, North-South Institute, Ottawa.

Keesing, D.B. and M. Wolf, (1980), Textile Quotas against Developing Countries, Thames Essay no. 23, Trade Policy Research Centre, London.

Kirmani, N., L. Molajoni and Th. Mayer (1984), 'Effects of Increased Market Access on Exports of Developing Countries', Staff Papers, International Monetary Fund, Volume 31, No. 4, pp. 661-684.

Murray, T., W. Schmidt and I. Walter, (1978), 'Alternative Forms of Protection against Market Disruption', Kyklos, vol. 31, no. 4, 1978, pp. 624-637.

National Accounts ESA, (1984), Eurostat, Luxemburg.

Nationale Rekeningen, (1982), Centraal Bureau voor de Statistiek, Voorburg.

Netherlands Economic Institute, (1985), Het Multivezelakkoord en de Ontwikkelingslanden, Rotterdam.

Pearson, C., (1983), Emerging Protection in the Footwear Industry, Thames Essay no. 36, Trade Policy Research Centre, London.

Shepherd, G., (1981), Textile-industry Adjustment in Developed Countries, Thames Essay no. 30, Trade Policy Research Centre, London.

Silberston, Z.A., (1984), The Multi-Fibre Arrangement and the UK Economy, Her Majesty's Stationery Office, London.

Smallbone, T., (1984), Consumers' Interests in Textile and Clothing Policy, paper for the OECD Symposium on Consumer Policy and International Trade, Paris.

Sociale Maandstatistiek, (1983), vol. 31, no. 10, Centraal Bureau voor de Statistiek, Voorburg.

Stern, R.M., J. Francis and B. Schumacher (1976), Price Elasticities in International Trade, MacMillan Press, London.

Stone, J.A., (1979), 'Price Elasticities of Demand for Imports and Exports: Industry Estimates for the US, the EC and Japan', Review of Economics and Statistics, vol. LXI, no. 2, pp. 306-312.

Timmermans, C.W.A., (1983), 'Community Commercial Policy on Textiles: A Legal Imbroglio', in Völker (1983), pp. 125-145.

de la Torre, J., (1984), Clothing-industry Adjustment in Developed Countries, Thames Essay no. 38, Trade

Policy Research Centre, London.

UNCTAD, (1984), <u>International Trade in Textiles with Special Reference to the Problems Faced by Developing Countries</u>, document TD/B/C.2/215/rev. 1.

Völker, E.L.M., ed., (1983), <u>Protectionism and the European Community</u>, Kluwer Law and Taxation Publishers, Deventer.

Wolf, M., (1983), 'Managed Trade in Practice: Implication of the Textile Arrangements', in <u>Cline</u> (1983), p. 455-482.

Yeats, A.J., (1979), <u>Trade Barriers facing Developing Countries</u>, Macmillan, London.

Chapter Seven

FOLLIES OF POLICIES FOR TEXTILE IMPORTS IN WESTERN EUROPE

Carl Hamilton

1. INTRODUCTION

World trade in textiles, clothing, fibres and textile machinery currently constitutes more than 10 per cent of the value of world trade in manufactures.(1) Trade in these commodities is of about the same magnitude as world trade in raw materials, ores and other minerals (excluding fuel and both ferrous and non-ferrous metals). Most of this trade, 55-60 per cent, takes place among developed countries. As is well known, since the mid-1960s there has also been a rapid increase in textile and clothing exports from developing countries.(2)

Imports by developed countries of textiles and, in particular, clothing have become increasingly regulated through a complex set of multilateral and bilateral agreements. (3) Since 1974 the Arrangement Regarding International Trade in Textiles, better known as the Multi-fibre Arrangement (MFA), has provided the multilateral framework for the restraints on exports from so-called 'low cost' suppliers to developed countries. At present, the third MFA is in force, it having come into effect in 1981. Articles of the MFA stipulate the conditions that must be satisfied by any restrictions unilaterally imposed by an importing country on exports from a 'low cost' supplier or by any bilaterally-agreed restraints on exports. The articles of the MFA and the protocols of renewal specify conditions for substitution between commodity categories and between periods which are supposed to be met by the bilateral agreements. The bilateral agreements also cover technical matters like rules of origin which are of great importance in determining the actual working of the textile agreements. Today the overall MFA system has become extremely complex and non-transparent. This in itself acts as an obstacle to trade since exporters incur costs in trying, first, to discover the obstacles they face and, then, to arrive at commercial arrangements which would allow them to fill the quotas they are allotted. (4) Such costs lower the profitability of exports.

In brief, the MFA has become the living embodiment of the notion of 'managed trade'. Its principal characteristic is the superimposition of bureaucratic allocation and intervention on the forces of the market. The European Community, in particular, distinguishes among products, sources and destinations in its bilateral agreements and, as a result of this attempt at bureaucratic 'fine tuning', has at least three thousand distinct restraint levels to police. In addition, the Community is committed to the surveillance of a still greater number of distinct flows of particular products from particular suppliers to particular destinations.

Bureaucracy has its own logic and this logic rarely has much to do with economics. One familiar process is the need to create new regulations (and, usually, new distortions) to deal with the unintended by-products of previous regulations. The history of the MFA has provided an object-lesson in such an 'interventionist's progress'. Discriminatory restrictions on exports from particular suppliers have led, through trade diversion, to the spread of such restrictions to an ever-increasing number of new suppliers.

The regulators must always give the appearance of control, but in ways that are also seen to be 'fair'. After all, having agreed to protect the production of some product or other, the government can hardly turn round and say it is impossible. Yet the constraints under which governments operate often mean that much of their frenetic activity and consequent appearance of control over economic forces is no more than a facade. Their actions either have no consequences at all or even have unintended consequences that undermine the stated goal.

In few cases are the unintended or misunderstood consequences of regulatory trade policy more noteworthy than that of protection of the textile and clothing industries by the countries of Western Europe. Accordingly, examination of this case is of great interest not only in itself - textiles and clothing being of great importance in the world economy - but also for the lessons that may be learned about 'managed trade'. In the face of market forces the bureaucratic regulation of trade merely gives the appearance of rationality. In reality, though, its costs are unknown and its consequences often quite distinct from its pretensions.

The purpose of this article is to demonstrate these points by focusing on the free trade area in manufactures that consists of the member countries of the European Community and the European Free Trade Association (EFTA) together, hereafter referred to as 'the West European free trade area'. The analysis focuses mainly, but not exclusively, on one particularly futile intervention, namely the attempt to control imports of textiles and clothing from outside the West European free trade area into particular national markets. Both theoretical considerations and the evidence suggest that this is an almost entirely futile activity. A number of intriguing points follow:

(a) The practice of allocating the total quota for imports of a particular product category among the member countries of the Community is almost always pointless.

(b) Imposition of controls on imports of a particular product into just one member or even several members of the Community under the so-called 'exit from the basket' provisions of the Community's textile agreements is also likely to prove futile if a substantial portion of the total Community market remains open to imports of the products in question.

(c) The attention paid by the EFTA countries to their own national restrictions on imports of textiles and clothing is misplaced. What really matters to them is the restrictiveness of the Community's policies.

The point about the futility of national measures in the context of a free trade area is one aspect of the general problem of trade diversion. But trade diversion would occur even without attempts at national controls and, in general, is an important aspect of the lack of point of much policy making in Western Europe. This important issue, too, is discussed below, although space prohibits more than a cursory consideration.

Finally, policy that is futile in certain respects can, nevertheless, be costly in others. Indeed, it is the problem of much trade policy for textiles and clothing that it is either inexpensive but futile or effective but expensive. The existence of controls on imports into Western Europe of textiles and clothing imposes costs which are both high and essentially invisible. It is one of the purposes of the present discussion to illustrate those costs from the limited evidence which is available.

In order to clarify these points, the article is organized as follows. First, a theoretical framework is developed for consideration of some of the effects of export-restraint agreements on importing countries, especially when they are members of customs unions and free trade areas. Secondly, the implications of restrictions on imports that are specific to individual member countries of the European Community and EFTA are analysed. Thirdly, quantitative estimates of the economic impact of export restraints on clothing are presented for the West European free trade area. Fourthly, the trade-diverting effects in Western Europe of export-restraint agreements are discussed. Finally, the effects of export restraints on consumer prices and employment in the case of Sweden are considered.

2. EXPORT RESTRAINTS AND TARIFF EQUIVALENTS

The economic effects of export restraints in a free trade area are complex. For the benefit of those who are relatively unfamiliar with the relevant analysis, it may be useful first to recall the economic effects of restraints on exports from one supplier to a given market. Most important will be an explanation of the concept of the tariff equivalent of an export restraint. (5)

A tariff increases the price of an imported commodity and its domestically-produced substitute. This is a familiar phenomenon. A quantitative restriction has the same effect. By restricting the supply of imports, total supply in the importing country is reduced and the domestic price rises to a higher level than it would otherwise have attained.

An increase in price affects consumers in two ways. First, consumers who are unwilling to pay the higher price start purchasing less of the commodity, perhaps switching to substitutes. Secondly, all the consumers who still buy the commodity have to pay the higher price. The mechanism is reversed for domestic producers. Some who would otherwise have to close down are willing to produce at the higher price and all producers can increase their profits because of the higher price of their output.

Since both a tariff and a quantitative restriction raise the domestic price in the importing country, the effect of a restraint may be expressed as a tariff equivalent. Because there is such a tariff equivalent (unless the restraint is redundant or, in other words, the permitted level is greater than actual imports), there is also an implicit tariff revenue, usually known as the quota rent. The total quota rent equals the difference between the price paid for licensed output and the marginal cost of supplying it (before taking account of the cost of acquiring licences themselves) multiplied by the quantity licensed. The quota rent accruing to licensees equals the total rent less their cost of acquiring the licences. If a government puts quotas up to open auction, the rent will normally accrue to it. Thus the quota rent is equivalent to a tariff, although one which is likely to vary over time, with the difference that some (or even all) of the revenue may accrue to private licensees.

The above analysis applies whether the restraint is an import restraint - that is, is administered in the importing country - or an export restraint - that is, is administered in the exporting country, as is normal in the case of restrictions under the MFA. There are important differences, however, between the two. First, import restraints can be discriminatory, whereas export restraints normally are discriminatory (unless the distribution among suppliers happens to duplicate the pattern that would occur under non-discriminatory instruments like tariffs or global quotas). Secondly, under import restraints the tariff revenue implicit in the quantitative restriction accrues to the importing country, while under export restraints it accrues to the exporting country.

To give an example of the tariff equivalent of a restraint: if the foreign producer's marginal costs of supply for the licensed exports were 90, the costs of freight and insurance were 10 and the landed import price were 120, then the tariff equivalent of the export restraint would be 20 per cent. In other words, the same import price as that generated by the quota could have been achieved by a tariff of 20 per cent imposed on the price of imports.

Incidentally, it must not be assumed that a quota with a tariff equivalent of 20 per cent actually raises prices in the importing country by 20 per cent over what they would be in the absence of the quota. That is only true if the importing country is a small one - or, more precisely, a price-taker in world markets. If the country were a large one (for example, the United States or the European Community as a whole), lifting the quota would so expand the demand for exports from the restrained suppliers that their marginal costs of production could be expected to rise, at least in the short run. In that case, the reduction in prices in the liberalizing markets would be smaller than might be expected from the observed tariff equivalent of the quota.

3. RESTRAINTS IN CUSTOMS UNIONS AND FREE TRADE AREAS

With these points in mind it is possible to turn to a few of the interesting issues that arise when restraints are imposed on outside suppliers to customs unions and free trade areas. (A customs union differs from a free trade area by having a common external tariff, while the free trade area permits national sovereignty over tariffs.)

First, consider a customs union with free circulation both of goods produced in the customs union and of imports, but with a (non-redundant) quota on the total level of imports into the customs union. Assume, also, that imports and goods produced in the customs union are perfect substitutes for one another. It is then evident that, ignoring the effect of transport costs, the prices of the good subject to restriction - both the imports themselves and the internally-produced substitutes - will be equalized (under competition) throughout the customs union and will also be above the price that would have existed without the restriction.

Then assume that the partners in the customs union also divide up the total level of external imports into the customs union by setting a maximum share for each member country and prohibiting the re-export of imported supplies from one member to another. In other words, the assumption of free circulation of imports within the customs union no longer holds, although there continues to be free circulation of internally-produced goods. What would happen to prices of the restricted product in the customs union?

In order to answer this question, suppose that, after the allotment of import quotas, some of the consumption in each member country is supplied by domestic producers or by producers from other member countries or by both. The sub-division of the total quota into sub-quotas for member countries will then make no difference to prices in any member country. These will continue to be exactly the same as if there were only a global restraint equal to the sum of the restraints on imports into the markets of individual member countries and no such restraints for individual countries as well. Why is this so? Just remember that, under competition, a profit-maximizing producer will charge the same price in all the markets he supplies (except for differences arising from transport costs), for otherwise he could increase his profits by shifting sales from markets with lower prices to markets with higher prices.

Consider then the interesting possibility of one of the member countries of the customs union allowing imports to supply the whole of its market. (Maybe restraints on imports into this particular market are abolished altogether.) This will occur if restrictions on imports into this country are such that the price of imports in the market (the marginal cost of production plus the tariff equivalent of any quotas plus transport costs plus the tariff - hereafter 'the tariff-inclusive world market price') is less than the price at which any producer in the customs union would supply the market. In that case, the customs union will have two prices: one for consumers in the liberalized market - the tariff-inclusive world market price - and another for consumers elsewhere and all internal producers - the common price in the other member countries. The existence of such a situation depends on effective control over the internal circulation of imported supplies.

The existence of one price for consumers in the liberalized market and another for producers and consumers selling and buying elsewhere in the customs union suggests a disequilibrium, but this would not be the case. The goods that supply the liberalized market could not be exported elsewhere in the common market (because of restraints on the free circulation of external supplies), while such imports would still be restrained effectively in other member countries. The tariff equivalents of quotas in the liberalized market, if any, would be below the tariff equivalents in the markets of other members. Profit-maximizing producers located in the rest of the customs union would supply nothing at all to the liberalized market and, at any given moment, would therefore still be selling at the same prices in all the markets they do supply. They would find, however, that prices in the customs union are generally lower than before the liberalization as sales are displaced from the liberalized market onto other markets of the customs union. This latter point has important implications to which I return below.

If two prices do emerge in the customs union, suppliers located in the liberalized market may continue to produce, but they would not sell any of their output in their own domestic market. That output will go to other markets in the common market. It is a strange paradox that, if the most liberal country were also to have an industry which is competitive with producers elsewhere in the customs union, its output might not be affected to any significant extent by the loss of its domestic market. All that would happen would be a shift in the destination of sales of its national producers.

The conclusions this far are two:

(a) If a non-redundant restraint on external suppliers to a customs union were to be divided up (along with restrictions on the internal circulation of imports) in such a way that internal suppliers were still present in each of the now-segmented markets, a common price would remain. There would also be no reason to expect a change in the price from that created by the overall restraint alone, unless the aggregate quota were also altered.

(b) If one of the markets were to be so liberalized that external suppliers would take it all, consumers in that market would normally pay the tariff-inclusive world market price, while producers throughout the customs union and consumers elsewhere would transact at a higher price in the markets of other members. There would no longer be a common price throughout the customs union.

The emergence of two prices following liberalization by one member of a customs union would be the expected effect, but there are two important exceptions.

The first would occur if the restraint on total imports into the customs union had been redundant in the first place. Liberalization would then make no difference at all. (While improbable in the context of a customs union, this becomes an important point in the context of free trade areas, as will be seen.)

The second exception could occur as a result of the effect of liberalization by one member of a customs union on the common price itself. If one of the members were to liberalize quantitative restrictions at its border against external suppliers, some of the supplies previously sold on the now-liberalized market would be displaced onto the markets of other members. As has been mentioned, the effect of this displacement would be to lower prices in the customs union as a whole, the scale of the reduction depending inter alia on the scale of the displacement in relation to the market of the customs union as a whole. It is possible (and, if the liberalizing member country is large enough, even likely) that the effect of the liberalization would be to make a previously effective restraint on external suppliers redundant, unless offsetting reductions in quotas were made elsewhere. In other words, the common price would fall to the tariff-inclusive world market price, even though before liberalization it had been above it. In this case, even complete liberalization in one member would not lead to the existence of two prices, for it would be equivalent to liberalization by the customs union as a whole.

The last is not a remote possibility. If, for example, there were to be a complete liberalization of quantitative restrictions on clothing imported into Ireland from outside Western Europe, there would be little effect on the price level for clothing in the European Community, even if quotas in the remaining members were unchanged. Liberalization of the markets of the Federal Republic of Germany, the United Kingdom, France or Italy, however, could have a significant effect. Liberalization by one or two of these large countries might make the restrictions on most products redundant, unless quotas were tightened elsewhere.

For present purposes, a free trade area is not fundamentally different from a customs union, what differences there are, result from the fact 'that tariffs on external suppliers are not identical. Again, within a free trade area in which suppliers from within the free trade area supply all markets, prices will be equalized. This implies, in turn, that the effect of the restraint and the tariff taken together (the combined trade barrier) would be the same in all the markets of the free trade area. In consequence, if a given member country has a relatively high tariff then the import-tariff equivalent of any restriction on exports to its market would be relatively low. (This is another way of saying that an export restraint is a way of exporting the revenue which would accrue under a tariff to the government of the importing country.)

In the event that a member of a free trade area did liberalize a restraint at the border, the result would tend to be exactly as analysed in the case of a customs union. (In fact, this situation is more likely to occur than within a customs union, since members of free trade areas normally have greater discretion over trade policy than members of customs unions). But there is one important difference. If the tariff level in the member concerned were actually equal to or higher than the combined trade barrier in the rest of the free trade area, the restraint on exports to its market would have been redundant in the first place. The tariff equivalent of the restraint would have been zero and, correspondingly, lifting it would make no difference. In fact, if the tariff were actually higher than the combined trade barrier in the rest of the free trade area, a part of the tariff itself would have been redundant; that is, it would have provided no protection to domestic producers. If, however, a restraint were to be redundant in a particular member of a free trade area, because its tariff was above the combined trade barrier of other members, then liberalization would not create two prices. Indeed, liberalization would not make any difference.

The key conclusion from the analysis is that, under most circumstances, the sub-division of quota levels among member countries of customs unions or free trade areas would be irrelevant. This conclusion must be qualified, however, in the following respects.

(a) If individual member countries introduce administrative obstacles to the full utilization of the quota specific to their markets, then the effect is similar to a reduction in the aggregate quota for the customs union or free trade area as a whole. Prices would then tend to rise throughout the customs union or free trade area.

(b) If the market of one of the members were to be sufficiently liberalized to allow external suppliers to take it all, there would normally be two prices in that country: one for consumers and another, higher one, for producers able to sell in the rest of the customs union or free trade area. The consumer price in the market of that member would be the tariff-inclusive world market price. The producer price, however, would be the common price in the customs union or free trade area. This dual-price outcome would occur unless it became redundant throughout the customs union as a result of the price-lowering effects of liberalization by the country concerned.

4. EVIDENCE ON TARIFF EQUIVALENTS IN WESTERN EUROPE

Average tariff equivalents of export restraints on clothing exported from Hong Kong to Western Europe and the United States are presented in Table 7.1. The method used exploits the fact that there is a market for export quotas in Hong Kong. The procedure adopted is to relate the quota rent, which is known from the prices for quotas in the export-quota market in Hong Kong, to the unit value of the corresponding imports. In addition, Table 7.1 shows average tariffs on clothing imported from Hong Kong, tariff preferences also being taken into account. The external tariff is the same for all member countries of the European Community, while external tariff rates differ between Austria, Finland and Sweden, which are member countries of EFTA. (There is free trade in internally-produced manufactures, including clothing, between Community and EFTA countries.) Since export restraints are, by definition, administered in the exporting country (in this case, Hong Kong), the quota rent is collected in the exporting country. In Hong Kong, this rent is usually captured by producers or exporters (frequently one and the same) who are established 'quota holders', a position which they have typically been able to acquire by virtue of their 'past performance' as exporters. The following observations can be made on the basis of Table 7.1.

First the countries of the European Community not only have a common tariff level but also had approximately the same combined trade barrier of 32-35 per cent between 1980 and 1983. This means that France, for example, was in effect no more protected against exports from Hong Kong than the Federal Republic of Germany, in spite of the tighter restrictions on imports to France under the Community's bilateral agreement with Hong Kong.(6) Sources of clothing supply in France, however, can be (and are) different from the sources of supply to the market of the Federal Republic. Nevertheless, just as should be the case within a customs union, the aggregate quota for the Community gives rise to a common price, which reflects a common level of protection to producers in the Community

Table 7.1: Trade Barriers against Clothing Exported from Hong Kong, 1981-84 (per cent)

	Average import-tariff equiv-alent of export restraints	Average import tariff	Average combined trade barrier
Denmark	14	17	33
France	13	17	32
West Germany	13	17	32
United Kingdom	15	17	35
Austria(a)	4	33	38
Finland	6	35	43
Sweden	26	13	42
Switzerland	0	13	13
United States(b)	25	23	54

(a) 1982 only.
(b) 1982 and 1983.

Source: Carl Hamilton, 'An Assessment of Voluntary Restraints on Hong Kong Exports to Europe and the USA', Economica, August 1986.

countries. In short, the present procedure of dividing up the overall quota for the Community into national quotas would seem to be pointless.

Secondly, the average tariff equivalent of the export restraints for the European Community was 14 per cent. Tariffs are calculated on the rent-inclusive import price and the combined rate was very high in 1981-83 as compared with the Community's external tariff on other types of manufactures.

Thirdly, the free trade agreement between the European Community and EFTA (excluding Portugal) implies that the common price level in the Community could also be expected to have been shared by Austria, Finland and Sweden. Table 7.1 seems to indicate that the domestic price levels and combined trade barriers of the EFTA countries were slightly higher than those of the Community countries. The seemingly higher combined trade barriers of EFTA members, however, may be explained by the existence of hidden barriers in the Community, which lower the rent to exporters. (7)

Fourthly, within the West European free trade area, tariff equivalents of export restraints are inversely related to the tariff levels of importing countries - as, indeed, would be expected given the almost equal price level within this free trade area for manufactures. Thus the high tariffs of Finland and Austria - 35 and 33 per cent, respectively - do not protect producers in these two countries any more than the 13 per cent Swedish tariff protects Swedish producers. The effect of the high tariffs is merely to ensure that the Finnish and Austrian governments obtain more of the benefit of protection than does the Swedish Government. But if the common price level in the West European free trade area should fall below the tariff-inclusive Finnish price, as it did in 1981, Finland could be expected to be the first market in the West European free trade area from which Hong Kong would withdraw. Then the Finnish market would be served by domestic producers, by producers in lower-cost developing countries and by producers in countries of the European Community or EFTA able to exploit their free access to Finland. Nevertheless, even then the price in Finland would remain at the common level of Western Europe, with a part of the high Finnish tariff simply being redundant.

Fifthly, the national agreements to restrict imports of the EFTA countries can only have a marginal effect on the common price in the West European free trade area, because of the small size of the EFTA countries as compared with the countries of the European Community. This means that the decisions on quota volumes taken in Brussels are much more important to producers in the EFTA countries than decisions taken in Vienna, Helsinki or Stockholm. Furthermore, in the event that an EFTA country should decide to 'go it alone' by liberalizing imports from developing countries, an interesting situation would arise. Rules on trade between EFTA and Community countries would prevent the re-export to the Community of products originating in developing countries. Domestic producers, however, would still have free access to the markets of the Community and of other EFTA countries. With relatively small domestic markets and positive quota premiums prior to liberalisation, producers and consumers in a liberalizing EFTA country would trade at different prices. (On the basis of Table 7.1 the tariff-inclusive world market price would appear to have been lower than the common price in

Western Europe, even for high-tariff countries like Austria and Finland.) Consumers would pay the tariff-inclusive world market price and producers would receive the common price in Western Europe. (Under competition they can never get more within the West European free trade area). As has been explained, a wedge would then be driven between the price paid by consumers and the (higher) price received in export markets in Western Europe by the EFTA country's own producers.

Sixthly, the combined trade barrier for the United States seems to have been slightly higher than that for the West European free trade area. It has increased even further since 1982-83. Both the average tariff level and the average tariff-equivalent level for the United States were higher than the corresponding levels in Western Europe, resulting in an average combined trade barrier of approximately 50 per cent in 1982-83.(8)

5. EFFECTS ON TRADE AMONG WEST EUROPEAN COUNTRIES

When the supply of clothing from developing countries to the European Community and EFTA countries is reduced, for example, through restrictions, the common price level within the West European free trade area goes up. This, in turn, stimulates increased imports from the United States, Canada and Japan. Above all, it stimulates trade within the West European free trade area so that there is trade diversion away from the globally lowest-cost producers, for example those in South-east Asia towards the lowest-cost unrestricted producers, those located in Italy being the main beneficiaries in the context of Western Europe.

The important implication is that the protectionist actions taken by the higher-cost countries in Western Europe, such as the Federal Republic of Germany, Benelux, France and the Nordic countries (excluding Finland), cannot after an adjustment period be expected to protect primarily the textile industries in these countries. Instead, the restrictions of higher-cost countries will tend to protect jobs and profits in the lower-cost countries in Western Europe against competition from developing countries. It seems strange that in this way consumers in, for example, France and Sweden should pay higher prices for their clothing to boost textile production in, for example, Italy

Table 7.2: Normalized Changes in Trade Patterns for Textiles, Clothing and Footwear (a) between 1970 and 1979

	(1) Change in share of imports in domestic demand between 1970 and 1979 (percentage points)	(2) European Community and EFTA members excluding Portugal (b)	(3) Other developed countries (c)	(4) All developed countries (2)+(3)	(5) Established developing-country exporters of textiles, clothing and footwear excl. Taiwan (d)
		Distribution of increased share of imports among groups of exporters (per cent)			
European Community or EFTA members					
France	10	47	8	55	20
West Germany	11	5	6	11	54
Italy	13	9	20	29	27
Sweden	17	40	-2	38	46
United Kingdom	8	-18	16	-2	63
Other countries					
Australia	10	5	-15	-10	45
Japan	5	18	6	24	47(f)
United States	2	-30	-80	-110	117

Table 7.2 continued

	(6) Rest of the world (e)	(7) Total increase in import share of home demand
	Distribution of increased share of imports among groups of exporters (per cent)	
European Community or EFTA members		
France	25	100
West Germany	36	100
Italy	44	100
Sweden	16	100
United Kingdom	39	100
Other countries		
Australia	65	100
Japan	29	100
United States	93	100

(a) Defined as ISIC 32.
(b) Portugal is excluded since quantitative restrictions have been used against Portugal by member countries of the European Community and EFTA.
(c) Australia, Canada, Japan, the United States and the centrally-planned economies of Eastern Europe.
(d) Portugal, Greece, Yugoslavia, Spain, Malaysia, Philippines, Singapore, Thailand, Hong Kong, Republic of Korea, India, Pakistan, Sri Lanka and Indonesia.
(e) Includes Taiwan.
(f) Excluding Malaysia.

Source: Carl Hamilton, 'Voluntary Export Restraints and Trade Diversion', Journal of Common Market Studies, June 1985

and Finland.

Another important aspect of the situation is that the lower-cost countries in Western Europe have a strong interest in maintaining the present system of protection in Western Europe and, once the group of lower-cost producers has been enlarged with Spain and Portugal, the lobbying group in the European Community against imports from developing countries will be considerably strengthened. Consequently, if the Community's citizens wish to get rid of the limitation of their freedom to buy goods they like best, they seem to stand a much better chance today than in the 1990s, say, when Spain and Portugal will have become fully integrated members of the Community.

The effects on the trade pattern in Western Europe are analysed in Table 7.2. The emergence of the European Community and EFTA during the 1960s was followed by a strong trend towards economic integration as free trade in manufactures was established during the 1970s. Measuring trade creation in the usual way as changes in the shares of partner countries in domestic demand (apparent consumption), such a trend causes the shares to increase - with or without bilateral trade restrictions. To isolate a trade-creating effect due to the restrictions on textiles an underlying trend towards integration was 'weeded out' (normalized) by using manufactures other than textiles, clothing and footwear as a control group. (The percentage point increase in the share of imports in domestic demand for 'other manufactures' was deducted from that of textiles, clothing and footwear.) Columns 2-6 show how the increase in import share of home demand was distributed among sources of supply.

It is found that, during the 1970s, for France and Sweden the bilateral trade restrictions had a comparatively strong trade-diverting effect: 47 and 40 per cent, respectively, of the increase in the share of imports in domestic demand came from partner countries in the Community or EFTA (column 2). In the case of France no less than 55 per cent of the increase came from non-restrained developed countries (column 4). For Sweden the figure is somewhat lower, 38 per cent. Of the increase in the share of Community and EFTA producers in Swedish consumption, no less than two thirds came from Finland.(9) In short, the more the Swedish Government restricted imports from the Far East, the greater became the stimulus to imports from the very near East on the other side of the

Baltic! The increases in the shares of imports in domestic consumption in the Federal Republic of Germany and the United Kingdom were captured primarily by developing countries during the 1970s, the bilateral trade restrictions at the time not appearing to have had much, if any, trade-diverting effect.

6. EFFECTS OF LIBERALIZATION IN SWEDEN

Suppose all quantitative restrictions on imports of clothing from developing countries were abolished. What would happen to producers and consumers? This question may be illustrated by some calculations regarding Sweden in the early 1980s. (10)

Let us begin by considering the producers. Several Swedish producers would not be affected, for they produce products which are not substitutes for products from, for example, Hong Kong. This segment is perhaps 20 per cent of the market. In the remaining 80 per cent of the Swedish market, prices facing producers would fall to the world market level plus the Swedish tariff, currently 13 per cent. Since Sweden is a small market, however, the increase in supply would be so low on the integrated and much larger combined market of the West European free trade area that the common price in Western Europe would fall by only two percentage points (trade deflection being prevented by the rules of origin). Owing to the free trade agreement between the Community and EFTA, Swedish producers could turn to other markets in Western Europe, where they would receive the higher common West European price for their exports.

The gains to Swedish consumers are perhaps of greater general interest. The maximum reduction in prices at the retail stage would have been 11 per cent in 1981-82 (17 per cent if the tariff was also abolished). For the household of an average wage-earner with children, this would mean a saving on clothing expenses of approximately £100 per year (at the January 1985 exchange rate). The household's gain would, of course, increase according to the number of children.

What is the maximum transfer which consumers and importers would be willing to give to each employee if import restrictions were abolished? In other words, what are they currently losing per employee in clothing as a result of the restrictions on imports? It turns out that the losses per employee were between £12,500 and £24,000 per year in 1981 and 1982.

When considering effects on employment, it should be kept in mind that an increase in the real incomes of households due to reduced prices of clothing would stimulate employment and, in particular, that employment in the clothing retail trade would expand if the volume of trade were to increase. In the case of Sweden, the expansion of employment in the retail trade could be almost as large, in terms of man-years, as the number of potential jobs lost in the competing domestic industry (in any case, not the same as the number of people who actually lose their jobs) as a result of the liberalization of imports from developing countries. It is even possible that the number of jobs in the economy would increase as a result of this purely micro-economic effect without relying on the general stimulus to the demand for labour that would be caused by an increase in the real income of households.

7. IMPLICATIONS FOR COUNTRIES OF WESTERN EUROPE

The principal implication of the points developed in this article is that policy makers in Western Europe probably do not know what they are doing. Much of their activity seems futile and, where it is not futile, it is costly. While not the subject of this article, one implication is that a comprehensive reconsideration of policy towards imports of textiles and clothing is required, starting with the MFA itself and on down to the small print of the bilateral agreements.

So far as policy in Western Europe is concerned, one obvious implication of the arguments developed above is that the internal sub-division of the overall quota for the European Commmunity is unnecessary and, accordingly, should be done away with. Equally, action by just one member to restrict imports into its own market, as happens under the so-called 'exit from the basket' provisions of the Community's bilateral agreements or invocation of Article 115 of the Treaty of Rome, is pointless so long as the same imported products have free access to other Community markets. No benefit can be gained for the supposedly protected industry and this may explain the general frustration of producers who believe - wrongly - that they are relatively well protected by measures at the national border.(11)

Most intriguing possibility of all, one of the smaller countries of Western Europe might show up the absurdity of the current structure of restrictions on imports of textiles and clothing into Western Europe by proposing the complete liberalization of restrictions at its border, in order to benefit its own consumers, combined with tighter restrictions on external imports into all other West European markets, in order to allow its producers to exploit the protectionism of other West European countries. A detached observer, unacquainted with the current jargon of trade policy, might protest against such overt exploitation, but hardly the remaining countries of Western Europe. They have talked too long about the 'burden' of cheap imports to make such a protest credible. After all, what does the whole policy of export restraints amount to? It consists of compelling competitive suppliers to do the importers a supposed favour by forming an exploitative cartel against the importers' citizens. The policy recommended here would, indeed, represent exploitation by one astute West European country of the remaining West European countries. Far from being outrageous, however, this policy would be the logical reductio ad absurdum of the prejudices and misconceptions whose apotheosis is the MFA itself.

Notes and References
This chapter has been published as an article in 'The World Economy', Volume 8, Number 3, September 1985. Thanks are due to Basil Blackwell, the publisher of 'The World Economy' for permission to include the article in this volume.

1.   I am indebted to Martin Wolf for his valuable comments and suggestions on the presentation of the ideas in this article.
2.   See Textiles and Clothing in the World Economy (Geneva: GATT Secretariat, 1984); and International Trade 1983-84 (Geneva: GATT Secretariat, 1984).
3.   See Martin Wolf, 'Managed Trade in Practice: Implications of the Textile Arrangements', in William R. Cline (ed.), Trade Policy in the 1980s (Washington: Institute for International Economics, 1983).

4. See ibid.

5. See Carl Hamilton, 'An Assessment of Voluntary Restraints on Hong Kong Exports to Europe and the USA', Economica, August, 1986.

6. Under the current textile policy of the European Community, France's share of extra-Community imports is set at 18.5 per cent, compared with 28.5 per cent for the Federal Republic of Germany and 23.5 per cent for the United Kingdom.

7. See Hamilton, 'An Assessment of Voluntary Restraints on Hong Kong Exports to Europe and the USA', loc. cit. For a discussion of additional non-tariff barriers in the European Community, see Rolf Langhammer, 'ASEAN Manufactured Exports in the EEC Markets: an Empirical Assessment of Common and National Tariff and Non-tariff Barriers', in Narongchai Akrasanee and Hans Christoph Rieger (eds), ASEAN-EEC Economic Relations (Singapore: Institute for Southeast Asian Studies, 1982). It is difficult to compare the combined trade barriers of the European Community and EFTA countries because the special clothing commodity classification used by the Community, which is common to all member countries of the Community, differs from the classification systems employed by the EFTA countries.

8. One important finding is the considerable fluctuation over time in the rates of the tariff equivalents of restraints on exports from Hong Kong. See Hamilton, 'An Assessment of Voluntary Restraints on Hong Kong Exports to Europe and the USA', loc. cit. The reasons for the observed variations are not yet fully understood, but fluctuations can be expected to depend on the level of aggregate demand in the importing countries, on expectations of available quota volumes and on changes in rates of exchange. Having estimated the tariff equivalents, it is possible to calculate the rent income accruing to Hong Kong, for the protection is partly implemented through export restrictions rather than only through import tariffs.

9. See Hamilton, 'Voluntary Export Restraints and Trade Diversion', Journal of Common Market Studies, June 1985.

10. See Hamilton, 'Swedish Trade Restrictions on Textiles and Clothing', Skandinaviska Enskilda Banken Quarterly Review, No. 4, 1984.

11. On the general inefficacy of much trade policy, see Robert E. Baldwin, The Inefficacy of Trade Policy,

Essays in International Finance No. 150 (Princeton: International Finance Section, Department of Economics, Princeton University, 1982).

Chapter Eight

SOME ESTIMATES OF THE COSTS OF PROTECTION IN
TWO IMPORT SENSITIVE SECTORS IN THE UK

David Greenaway

1. INTRODUCTION

The UK, like other developed market economies has relied
upon voluntary export restraints (VERs) and source specific
quotas (SSQs) to an increasing extent over the past decade
or so. The forces which have increased the popularity of
VERs are well known, and well understood, (by economists
anyway). From the standpoint of the policy-maker VERs are
attractive because they serve to transfer income from one
group of voters to another in a well disguised manner. The
invisibility of the instrument to consumers ensures that
potential votes forgone are minimized, the higher profile to
domestic producers however ensures that potential gains in
votes may be maximized. Moreover, since rents generated
by the instrument tend to be transferred overseas, the
instrument is often more acceptable to trading partners
than a tariff, or global quota. These statements obscure
many of the subtleties of the political economy of VERs.
Nevertheless the central argument that VERs have
increased in importance as a result of their political
attractiveness is a cogent one. (For a detailed analysis of
political economy aspects see Jones (1984), and Hamilton
(1985a).)

The exact economic effects of VERs are difficult to
identify and quantify. In this paper an attempt is made to
estimate the costs and benefits of VERs/SSQs in two sectors
where the instruments are used alongside tariffs to regulate
the flow of imports from NICs/LDCs into the UK. The
sectors in question are non-leather footwear and woven
clothing, and the approach is partial equilibrium. Section 2

of the paper gives details of the estimation procedure used and reports the results. Section 3 summarizes the implications for 'the South' and finally section 4 offers some concluding comments. The model employed to gain estimates of the dead-weight losses and transfers associated with tariffs and VERs is the standard partial equilibrium model. This analysis has been widely deployed by inter alia Morkre and Tarr (1980), Jenkins (1981), Morkre (1984) and Greenaway (1986). Its main features are well known as are the principal problems associated with its application. Accordingly a detailed outline of the methodology will be eschewed. (1)

2. DATA AND ESTIMATION

2.1 Made-up clothing
The UK, like most other developed market economies, restricts the volume of made-up clothing imported under the terms of the Multi-Fibre Arrangement (MFA). European Community (and therefore UK) restrictions apply to some 114 product categories. Under the NIMEXE system these are classified into groups according to the degree of sensitivity of the items.

Data constraints (in particular the availablity of quota premium data) precluded calculation of estimates of the cost of protection for the entire set of restricted commodities. For purposes of calculation a subset from the most heavily restricted group forms the sample. This comprises woven trousers (Nimexe Category 6), woven and knitted blouses (Nimexe Category 7) and woven shirts (Nimexe Category 8). These items however account for some 30% of all clothing imports into the UK, and details of the quotas applied to these commodities between 1978 and 1982 are reported in Table 8.1. (A more comprehensive study of the clothing sector in the UK is provided by Silberston (1984).)

As in all studies of this type a problem arises with respect to estimating the price raising effect of the quotas. A common response is to rely upon information provided indirectly by transactions in quotas i.e. quota premiums. Relying upon quota premiums to ascertain an estimate of the price raising effect of source specific restrictions is not without difficulty. For example, it has been observed that the value of quota premiums varies from one time of the

Table 8.1: Total Quotas on Imports into the United Kingdom of Certain Clothing Items (number of items)

Category number	Category description	1978	1979	1980	1981	1982
6	Woven trousers	27,214	27,732	28,220	28,460	28,832
7	Woven and knitted blouses	26,781	26,986	27,191	27,427	27,582
8	Woven shirts	36,281	36,823	37,259	37,694	38,133

Source: Official Journal of the European Communities, L149/36, Brussels, June 1979.

year to another, and moreover there is a tendency for quota premiums to vary cyclically. (See Hamilton (1984).) Another objection to their use, raised by Silberston (1984) is that because only a proportion of the total quota is traded at any one time, quota premiums are biased in an upward direction. The last point is not a serious objection, in part because the proportion of quota traded is not insubstantial,(2) but, more importantly because in most markets arbitrage occurs at the margin and the prices generated by such activity can, and are reasonably interpreted as providing signals regarding relative scarcities.

The variability of quota premiums over the year and over the cycle is a more serious issue. In response to the former the figure used in the calculations below is an average of the premiums reported over the year; in the case of the latter, 1982 is used as the reference period since premiums appeared to be at a cyclical low then. (See Hamilton (1984).) Any bias from cyclical variation should therefore be in a downward rather than an upward direction.

To obtain the quota free price a trade weighted average of the quota premiums was simply subtracted from a weighted average of UK cif unit values of the commodities in question. The ad valorem tariff equivalent of the quota premiums was almost 15% of the unrestrained price.(3) In addition to the quota an average tariff of 17% was levied on imports. Thus the combined effect of the tariff and quota was to raise prices in the United Kingdom by up to 34%. Price elasticity of demand was taken as -1.086 as estimated by Deaton (1976). No comparable information on domestic supply elasticity is available and assumed values of 1 and 2 were used, although the former is likely to be more plausible. (4) Details of these and other data are provided in Greenaway and Hindley (1985).

2.1.1 **Costs of protection.** The estimated economic costs and transfers of income in the United Kingdom associated with the tariff and the source-specific quotas are summarized in Tables 8.2 and 8.3. Table 8.2 reports the results for one year on the basis of a supply elasticity of 1. Table 8.3 reports values for a variety of periods, using supply elasticities of 1 and 2. It can be seen from Table 8.2 that the estimated total loss to UK consumers from protecting producers of woven trousers, woven shirts and blouses amounted in 1982 to over £170 million. (5) Over £21 million of this was transferred to

Table 8.2: Estimated Costs of Clothing Protection in the United Kingdom from Tariffs and Quotas Combined, 1982 (£ million)

a.	Dead-weight loss to consumers	7.1
b.	Production efficiency loss	2.0
c.	(i) Transfer to Hong Kong suppliers	21.6
	(ii) Transfer to European Community and EFTA suppliers	19.2
	(iii) Transfer to others	18.4
d.	Tariff revenue	53.0
e.	Increase in profits to domestic producers	49.1
f.	Total loss to United Kingdom consumers	170.4
g.	Total loss to United Kingdom economy	68.4

Notes

a. Calculated as: loss = $\frac{1}{2} (^{ta}/1 + ta)^2 (n_d)(D_o)$.
b. Calculated as: loss = $\frac{1}{2}(^{ta}/1+ta)^2 (n_s)(P_o)$.
c. (i) Calculated as the quota premium per unit multiplied by the number of units imported from Hong Kong.
   (ii) Calculated as the quota premium per unit plus tariff per unit multiplied by the number of units imported from the European Community and EFTA suppliers.
   (iii) Calculated as the number of units imported from all other sources, times the quota premium per unit.
d. Calculated as the tariff per unit, times the number of units imported from sources outside the European Community and EFTA.
e. Calculated as the quota premium plus tariff per unit, times the number of domestically supplied units.
f. Calculated as the sum of the values derived in notes a to e.
g. Calculated as the sum of items a, b, c(i), c(ii) and c(iii).

suppliers in Hong Kong, whilst a further £37.5 million was transferred to other overseas suppliers (£19 million to suppliers in the European Community and EFTA and £18 million to suppliers elsewhere). In total these transfers abroad accounted for 35 per cent of total losses to consumers. In addition to transfers overseas there are transfers to recipients of tariff revenue and to domestic

Table 8.3: Present Value of Consumer Losses and Losses to the United Kingdom from Clothing Protection for Alternative Discount Rates and Periods

Time period	Discount rate (%)	Consumer losses (£ million)	Net losses (£ million) Elasticity of supply=1	Elasticity of supply=2
1 year	-	170.4	68.4	70.3
5 years	5	737.7	296.1	304.3
	7	698.6	280.4	288.2
10 years	5	1,254.1	528.2	542.9
	7	1,143.4	480.4	493.8
25 years	5	2,178.2	964.0	990.8
	7	1,819.0	797.1	819.3
Permanent	5	3,410.0	1,370.0	1,410.0
	7	2,430.0	977.1	1,000.0

producers. The tariff revenue is estimated to have been almost £53 million whilst the gain to domestic producers is estimated to have been £49 million. From the standpoint of calculating the net losses to the United Kingdom these internal transfers are assumed to cancel each other out.(6) The net losses after eliminating internal transfers are presented as the total loss to the United Kingdom economy in Table 8.2. These losses are estimated at £68 million and are for one year only. They will be sustained for as long as the import restrictions remain in force. Table 8.3 provides estimates of consumer costs and net losses to the United Kingdom for a variety of time periods. If the restrictions are maintained indefinitely, total consumer costs are £3.41 billion or £2.43 billion depending on whether one discounts at 5 per cent or 7 per cent. (7) Net losses to the United Kingdom are somewhere between £977 million and £1.41 billion depending on the elasticity of supply assumed and the discount rate used. At the other extreme, if all controls were to be unilaterally dismantled after five years, total costs to consumers of woven garments of a further five years of protection at current levels would be around £700 million, while the net costs to the economy would be between £280 million and £304 million. Thus, even in the 'short term' losses from protecting this part of the clothing industry are substantial.

2.1.2 **Benefits of protection.** It is often argued that as a result of import protection, employment in the protected activity (though not in the economy) would therefore be higher than otherwise. Even in a partial equilibrium setting the employment implications of import protection are far from obvious, not least because of the conceptual and practical difficulties of identifying the impact of induced technical change. To gain some impression of orders of magnitude it will be assumed that import protection is completely effective in preserving employment. Thus, if protection is removed we can infer that domestic output and employment would contract. The precise magnitude of any contraction being dependent upon domestic elasticity of supply. If this is unity then the fall in output would be estimated at some 15.8 million units of woven garments, with a combined value (at 1982 prices) of £84 million. (8) Clearly, if the domestic supply elasticity is 2, then the fall in output would be twice this amount. The average value of made-up clothing per worker in 1982 was £10,500. Hence, with a supply elasticity of unity about 8,000 jobs would be lost if protection were withdrawn on the three product categories under examination. If the supply elasticity were 2, then some 17,000 jobs would be lost. (It might be noted parenthetically that Silberston (1984) estimates total job losses from the removal of quotas on all textiles and clothing to be between 24,000 and 48,000 for supply elasticities of 1 and 2.)

The cost to the United Kingdom of protecting the industry for one year are £68.4 million (if the domestic supply elasticity is 1), or £70.3 million (if the domestic supply elasticity is equal to 2). Thus if the domestic supply elasticity is equal to 1 and protection is completely effective in preserving a job the cost per job saved is £8,500, while if it is 2, the cost per job saved is almost £4,500. Even the lower of these figures exceeds the average annual wage (weighted by male/female participation rates) in the industry (of £4,205) while the latter figure is twice the annual wage. Moreover, it must be remembered that these figures are for one year only. For as long as the protection remains, these costs are incurred.(9) The cost to buyers of made-up clothing is even greater. For example, in a single year the cost to consumers assuming a supply elasticity of unity is £21,300 per job. If supply elasticity were 2 then the annual costs would be £10,600. (10)

2.2 Non-leather footwear

The footwear industry has enjoyed a degree of tariff protection in the United Kingdom throughout the period since World War II. Currently, average tariffs range from 8 per cent on leather shoes to 20 per cent on non-leather shoes. In addition, imports from some planned economies namely Poland, Czechoslovakia, Bulgaria, China, the Soviet Union and Romania are restricted by non-tariff means. More importantly, so are imports from Taiwan and the Republic of Korea. Details of the restraints on Taiwan and Korea are provided in Table 8.4.

The costs of protection are estimated for non-leather footwear only. This serves to narrow the range of products covered by the study (although it is obvious that there remain considerable differences between products within the category). Over 60 per cent of non-leather footwear imports into the United Kingdom are subject to tariffs and over 30 per cent are subject to tariffs and VERs. It could be argued that a high substitutability between leather and non-leather footwear may result in the price effects of the VER being minimal. It can be seen from Table 8.4 however, that leather footwear is also restrained, and moreover the quotas are far smaller than those for non-leather footwear.

The tariff rate on non-leather footwear imported into the United Kingdom is 20 per cent. In order to gain some indication of the magnitude of the price raising effect of the VERs unit values of footwear imported from Taiwan into the United Kingdom were compared with unit values of footwear imported from Taiwan into Hong Kong. Exports of footwear into the latter country are completely unrestrained and furthermore the commodity composition of Hong Kong imports is broadly similar to that found in Britain. (11)

As one would anticipate the U.K. import unit value is in excess of the Hong Kong import unit value. The difference between the two can be partly accounted for by higher transport costs to the United Kingdom and partly by the VER premium. To adjust for transport costs just over 12 per cent of the c.i.f. value of imports into Hong Kong was added to the price in Hong Kong. (12) The difference between the resulting price and the unit value in the United Kingdom was taken to be the VER premium or rent per unit. For 1982 this amounted to 31p per pair, (13 per cent of the cif price to the United Kingdom).

Price elasticity of demand, as estimated for footwear

Table 8.4: Breakdown of United Kingdom VERs with South Korea and Taiwan

South Korea (pairs)				
	1979	1980	1981	1982
Leather footwear	1,150,000	1,150,000	775,000	810,000
Textile footwear	9,000,000	9,500,000	11,000,000	11,500,000
Rubber footwear	400,000	420,000	450,000	450,000
Plastic footwear	1,800,000	1,850,000	2,200,000	2,300,000
Slippers	2,400,000	2,400,000	2,400,000	2,800,000
Total	14,750,000	15,320,000	16,825,000	17,860,000

Taiwan (pairs)					
	1978	1979	1980	1981	1982
Leather footwear	na	na	na	750,000	770,000
Textile footwear	na	na	na	3,100,000	3,850,000
Plastic footwear	na	na	na	3,550,000	4,050,000
Rubber footwear	na	na	na	50,000	60,000
Slippers	na	na	na	500,000	530,000
Total	5,500,000(a)	5,500,000(a)	5,500,000(a)	7,950,000	9,260,000

Note: In the table 'na' signifies not available.
(a) This is the quota level for 1978, 1979 and 1980.

Source: Compiled from information obtained from the Department of Industry and from trade associations.

by Deaton (1976) was assumed to be -0.25. An elasticity which applies to both leather and non-leather footwear will almost certainly be an underestimate of the price elasticity for non-leather footwear alone. Clearly, if the price of non-leather footwear were to alter, while prices for leather footwear remain unchanged, the change in demand for non-leather footwear would be greater than if the price of all footwear were changed. Thus the estimate of price elasticity of demand used here is probably an underestimate although as noted above, imports of leather footwear are restrained and one would expect some price raising effects as a consequence. As in clothing, supply elasticities of 1 and 2 were assumed. (13)

2.2.1 Costs of protection. The results of estimating the costs and transfers associated with the tariff and VERs for one year are summarized in Table 8.5. The total loss to British consumers from protecting non-leather footwear in 1982 is estimated in £117 million. Of this some £3.9 million is the value of the dead-weight losses. A further £7.5 million represents a transfer to Taiwanese and Korean exporters which is a direct consequence of the VER. The price raising effect of the quotas and tariff combined results in a transfer of some £22.3 million to suppliers in the European Community, EFTA and the Mediterranean who face neither quota nor tariff, while the VER alone transfers up to £9.7 million to other suppliers. Since a tariff is levied on suppliers outside the European Community, EFTA and the Mediterranean, tariff collections from these countries amount to £24 million. By far the largest single transfer, £49.9 million, occurs between domestic consumers and domestic producers. As in the clothing estimates these internal transfers are taken as cancelling each other out. The net losses to the British economy are then estimated at £43.5 million, which is about 14 per cent of final expenditure on non-leather footwear.

As in the case of woven garments estimates of present values can be arrived at by assuming that the protective instruments remain in force for various periods. Table 8.6 presents a range of estimates of both consumer losses and net losses for several time periods. In each case the losses are discounted at 5 per cent and 7 per cent. For instance, if all forms of protection are assumed to remain in force for five years, and it is further assumed that 7 per cent is the

Table 8.5: Estimated Costs of Footwear Protection in the United Kingdom from the Tariff and VER Combined, 1982 (£ million)

a.	Dead-weight loss to consumers	1.4
b.	Production efficiency loss	2.5
c.	(i) Transfer to Taiwanese and South Korean suppliers	7.5
	(ii) Transfer to European Community, EFTA and Mediterranean suppliers	22.4
	(iii) Transfer to other suppliers	9.8
d.	Tariff revenue	24.1
e.	Increase in profits to domestic producers	49.9
f.	Total loss to United Kingdom consumers	117.5
g.	Total loss to United Kingdom economy	43.5

Notes:
a. Calculated as loss = $\frac{1}{2}$ $(ta/1 + ta)^2 (n_d)(D_q)$ where
ta = ad valorem tariff equivalent of the tariff and quota
n_d = price elasticity of demand
D_q = apparent consumption in 1982.
b. Calculated as loss = $\frac{1}{2}$ $(ta/1 + ta)^2 (n_s)(S_q)$ where
ta = ad valorem tariff equivalent of the tariff and quota
n_s = price elasticity of supply
S^s = domestic supply of non-leather footwear
c. (i)   Calculated as the VER premium per unit, times the number of units imported from Taiwan and the Republic of Korea.
   (ii)   Calculated as the VER premium plus the tariff per unit, times the number of units imported from the European Community, EFTA and Mediterranean suppliers.
   (iii)   Calculated as the VER premium per unit, times the number of units imported from all other suppliers.
d. Calculated as the tariff per unit, times the number of units imported from suppliers outside the European Community, EFTA and the Mediterranean.
e. Calculated as the VER plus tariff per unit, times the number of units produced domestically.
f. Calculated as the sum of the values derived in notes a to e above.
g. Calculated as the sum of items, a, b, c(i), c(ii) and c(iii).

appropriate discount rate, then the present value of consumer losses would be estimated at £481.6 million whilst the present value of net losses would be £179.2 million. Thus as in clothing losses remain substantial even under the assumption that protective instruments remain in force for a comparatively short period and are discounted at a relatively high rate.

Table 8.6: Present Value of Consumer Losses and Losses to the United Kingdom from Footwear Protection for Alternative Discount Rates and Periods

Time period	Discount rate (%)	Consumer losses (£ million)	Net losses (£ million) Elasticity of supply=1	Elasticity of supply=2
1 year	-	117.5	43.5	45.9
5 years	5	508.5	188.1	198.6
	7	481.6	179.2	189.1
10 years	5	907.1	335.6	354.1
	7	825.1	305.3	322.1
25 years	5	1,660.0	612.5	646.3
	7	1,370.0	506.5	534.4
Permanent	5	2,350.0	869.2	918.0
	7	1,680.0	620.8	655.7

2.2.2 Benefits of protection. As in the clothing case it will be assumed that the benefit of protection is employment preservation. If domestic elasticity of supply were unity and all tariffs and quotas were abolished imports would increase by 28.2 million pairs. Part of this increase would be caused by expansion of demand. The remainder would be due to the contraction of the production of domestic import substitutes, which is estimated at 17.8 million pairs. Average output per head in the production of footwear in the United Kingdom was 2,374 pairs in 1982. (14) Given the ratio of output to employment in the United Kingdom, complete import liberalization would result in the loss of some 7,500 jobs. If an elasticity of 2 were assumed then the loss in employment would be 15,000 jobs.

The net costs to the United Kingdom of protecting the industry for one year are £43.5 million (if the domestic supply elasticity is 1), or £45.9 million (if the domestic supply elasticity is equal to 2). Thus, if the domestic supply elasticity is equal to one, the cost per job saved is almost £6,000, while if it is 2, the cost per job saved is just over £3,000. (15) The cost to buyers of non-leather footwear is about three times as great. For example in a single year the cost to consumers assuming a supply elasticity of unity is £15,600 per job. If supply elasticity were 2 then the annual cost would be almost £8,000. (16)

2.2.3 **Evaluation.** These estimates suggest that the costs of import protection in the clothing and footwear sectors in the UK could be relatively high, both to consumers and to the UK economy. For example, the cost of protection to footwear consumers would appear to amount to some 14% of footwear expenditure in 1982. It could be argued that protection preserves employment. If it does so the cost per job saved in both activities would appear to be relatively high. Even on the most conservative of estimates the costs to the economy exceed annual average wages in the industries concerned.

The results reported in this paper, along with further analysis of the data, (see Greenaway and Hindley (1985)), are not intended to provide definitive estimates of the costs of protection in the UK, but rather to provide approximate orders of magnitude. Data imperfections mean that some margin of error is inevitable. On the one hand it is possible that the welfare effects are overestimated. In clothing this could result from conducting the experiment on the small open economy assumption. The UK is certainly a small open economy. It is however, unlikely that unilateral liberalization in clothing is a realistic prospect. European liberalization is more likely, in which case there would be possible terms of trade losses (see Koekkoek and Mennes (1986)). With regard to footwear Hamilton (1985b) argues that unilateral restraints may have a minimal impact on prices in a situation where the restraining country is a member of a customs union. Although import tariffs on footwear are Community-wide, the British VERs are unilateral raising the possibility that the UK may be unable to sustain higher price levels than prevail elsewhere in the EEC for any length of time. If this is so then our estimates of VER price effects may be overstated.

On the other hand, however, there are various reasons why the estimated effects may be understated. The elasticity estimates in each case are intentionally conservative. So too are the estimated price effects. Thus in the clothing case observations of quota premia were taken for a year when these premia were at a cyclical low. In the case of footwear secondary evidence on import unit values suggests that a price effect of 14% may be on the low side, (notwithstanding the Hamilton point made above). With regard to total consumer costs, and total costs to the economy, it is important to remember that the sample in each case comprises a sub-group of the relevant industry's product range. Finally, regarding employment effects, in using a partial equilibrium methodology we abstract from secondary employment effects. If prices fell in the event of liberalization, there would be responding effects associated with the growth in real disposable income which would presumably have employment creating effects.

It is impossible to say a priori exactly how these biases will net out. The key data input is the estimated price effects and one would hope that this still errs on the side of caution. If Hamilton (1985b) is correct in his argument that the VERs have a minimal effect on prices then this merely leads one to question further the rationale for their existence. Moreover it is probable that EEC enlargement will make the arrangements even more redundant.

3. SOME IMPLICATIONS OF SOURCE SPECIFIC RESTRAINTS FOR THE SOUTH

The implications of source specific interventions for restraint facing countries have not been widely explored. A certain amount of documentary work directed at identifying the trade barriers faced by LDCs has been completed, (see for instance Nogues, Olechowski and Winters (1986) and the references cited therein); some cross-section econometric analysis has also been completed (for example Hughes and Newbery (1986)), but there are to date few country specific analyses. Since the VERs/SSQs on footwear and clothing which have been discussed in this paper affect a number of LDCs and NICs some comment on the implications of the restraints for these countries is in order.

3.1 Restraint facing LDCs/NICs
For those countries directly faced by source specific

interventions there are several direct and indirect effects associated with the instruments. The most obvious direct effect is the provision of rents to restricted producers. Estimates of the rents accruing to Hong Kong as a result of the MFA have been reported above, as well as estimates of rents to Taiwan and Korea as a result of footwear VERs. In the case of the latter the rents amounted to 15% of the total value of footwear imports into the U.K.; in the Hong Kong clothing case rents amounted to 13% of the value of exports of the restrained commodities. Hamilton (1985a) estimates that total rent income to Hong Kong amounted to 1% of the state's GDP in 1981-82, or 16% of the clothing industry's value added.

It can be argued that the existence of such rent transfers is a desirable by-product distortion of source specific restraints on the grounds that it constitutes a source of untied aid. Even if this were so it is difficult to make out a case for reliance on source specific restraints as there are other more efficient instruments available. Moreover, as a means of transferring income it is singularly inequitable. For the commodities examined in this study source specific restraints constitute a regressive tax, and it is difficult to contend that the proceeds of the tax are distributed according to 'need' (however defined). It must also be remembered that the presence of substantial rents creates an incentive for those countries who benefit from quota rights to maintain the status quo and thereby use the instruments as a means of pre-empting competition from newly emerging producers. When arguments regarding 'certainty' of access are advanced this consideration should be borne in mind.

'Upgrading' is a further by-product of VERs/SSQs which is well documented and quite well understood. Faced with quantitative restraints which apply to a complete category of products exporters have an incentive to specialize in higher value added products with higher margins. Insofar as this expedites the process of moving up-market for a given exporter it may be regarded as a beneficial by-product of this form of restraint. On the other hand, however, since the restraints by raising profitability may serve to maintain producers in particular activities longer than would otherwise be the case there is an associated efficiency loss.

It is also known that source specific interventions influence market structure and firms' behaviour in the restrained country. This follows as a result of the fact that restrained suppliers administer the system and, in order to do so effectively they must cartelize (whether formally or informally). The usual price/output effects, the implications of which have been discussed above, can be expected to follow. In addition, however, a barrier to the entry of new firms is created in that a prerequisite to exporting to restrained markets is access to quota. If quota rights are not tradeable/transferable, new entrants can effectively be excluded. If quota rights are transferable entry is possible. However, competition for quota rights then means that at least some part of the rents is being absorbed in efficiency losses.

One further effect which should be mentioned is the impetus given to trade deflection. Restricted access to some markets often serves merely to deflect exports to other markets. This phenomenon has been noted as being an especially prevalent feature of trade in clothing, (see Keesing and Wolf (1980)). From the standpoint of the exporting country this may raise the probability of the introduction of additional restraints in other importing countries.

3.2 **Non-restraint facing LDCs/NICs**

The introduction of VERs has indirect effects on unrestrained exporters. By restraining market access for the most successful exporters (invariably the NICs) and raising the profitability of exporting, VERs can serve to facilitate entry for new exporters. Again, this is a phenomenon which has been observed with respect to the MFA. Thus in the UK case MFA restrictions may have facilitated entry into the UK market by new exporters such as Mauritius and Bangladesh. It is of course impossible to be certain on this issue, given almost total ignorance regarding the 'anti monde'. It is nevertheless a possibility and one which has led some commentators to conclude that the MFA has had beneficial side effects in this regard. Even if the regime of restraints does encourage the entry of new exporters, its institutionalization invariably means that new exporters find themselves restrained at relatively low levels of market penetration.

4. CONCLUDING COMMENTS

This paper has attempted to examine some of the economic effects of tariffs and source specific import restraints in two sectors where UK producers face competition from NIC and LDC exporters. The approach is what may be described as 'unsophisticated partial equilibrium' and is designed to provide estimates of various orders of magnitude. In particular the domestic transfers, the deadweight losses, and the rents associated with the use of source specific restraints are identified. These estimates are then used to provide some indication of the possible costs per job preserved in woven clothing and non-leather footwear both to UK consumers and to the UK economy. If these figures are within a reasonable margin of error they suggest that import protection is a relatively costly form of job preservation.

From the standpoint of NICs and LDCs it can be argued that some of the by-product distortions of the source specific restraints may be beneficial. As the discussion in Section 3 showed this may pertain to upgrading, the provision of rents, and the incentive effects on new exporters of artificially inflated prices. No attempt at a cost-benefit appraisal of the restraints from the standpoint of NICs/LDCs has been undertaken. While recent research has shown that source specific restraints may not have arrested the growth of NIC/LDC exports in the aggregate by as much as is sometimes asserted, due to trade deflection and the emergence of new exporters, (see Hughes and Newbery (1986)) it is difficult to believe that net benefits can be positive for LDCs/NICs. Even if they were positive they would probably have to be very high indeed to outweigh the costs of a two-tier regime of trading 'regulations'.

Notes
An earlier draft of this paper has benefited from discussion at the 'European Trade Policies and the South' Conference, The Hague, September 13th and 14th 1985. The remarks of Carl Hamilton, Patrick Messerlin and Alexander Sarris were especially helpful. The author alone is responsible for the contents of the paper.

1.   An   evaluation   of the basic principles can be

found in Jones (1984), Hamilton (1985a) or Greenaway (1983). The latter also details the technical problems implicit in the application of the methodology. Surveys of evidence are available in Milner (1985) and Pelzman (1983).

2.   According to Silberston (1984) some 18.5% of quotas for the EEC were traded in 1982, and 22% in 1983. Morkre (1984) estimates that 22.14% of US quotas were temporarily transferred in 1979.

3.   Silberston (1984) contends that removal of MFA restrictions would result in price increases of less than 10 per cent in the UK. This conjecture is partly based on Hong Kong production data and partly on information about quota premiums. In comparing Professor Silberston's estimate with the one presented here, it must be remembered that the sample used here comprises only items drawn from the most restrained categories. One would therefore expect it to be higher.

4.   Faced with a lack of information on elasticity of supply other researchers have also invoked the assumption of unit elasticity (see, for instance, Jenkins (1981)). In the present context such an assumption is quite consistent with a plausible implied import elasticity of demand. The relationship between import elasticity of demand, own (compensated) price elasticity of demand and price elasticity of supply is as follows:

$$e_i^m = e_i^d (Q_i^d/Q_i^m) - n_i (Q_i^s/Q_i^m)$$

where e_i^m and e_i^d refer to import and own price elasticity of demand respectively and n_i refers to domestic elasticity of supply. Q^d, Q^m and Q^s refer, respectively to quantities demanded, imported, and domestically supplied. In the United Kingdom (Q^d/Q^m) in clothing is around 3, while (Q^s/Q^m) is about 2. With an elasticity of demand of -1.086 and an assumed elasticity of supply of unity, this implies an import elasticity of demand of -5.2. If domestic elasticity of supply is assumed to be 2, the implied import elasticity is -7.2. Vincent Cable believes a 'conservative estimate' of import elasticity of demand for imported clothing in the United Kingdom to be about -3.5 (Cable 1983).

5.   Cable (1983) estimated total consumer losses from protection of all MFA restricted products to be £500 million in 1980 prices. In 1982 prices this would be around £600 million. The estimate provided here for the three quota restricted categories we are dealing with is just under 30

per cent of Vincent Cable's estimate. Coincidentally the commodities being examined account for just under 30 per cent of import of British clothing. Since, however, the present sample is drawn from the most restricted categories this suggests that the results reported here are likely to under-estimate consumer losses.

6.   Under the 'Own resources' system for financing the European Community, customs collections from member countries go directly to Brussels. If the United Kingdom has less than its full contribution returned (which is likely since Britain is a net contributor), then treating the entire tariff revenue as an internal transfer understates the net losses to the United Kingdom.

7.   The discount rate of 5 per cent is used because this is the real rate of return recommended by the Treasury in the evaluation of Nationalized Industry investments (see Cmnd 7131). A higher rate of 7 per cent is used by government departments for the appraisal of public service investments. This higher rate is used where the output of public services is not sold and where benefits may be exaggerated. A discount rate of 7 per cent includes a 'premium' to offset 'appraisal optimism'. See <u>Investment Appraisal and Discounting Techniques and the Use of the Test Rate of Discount in the Public Sector</u> (London: Her Majesty's Stationery Office, for the Department of the Treasury, 1980). Calculations based on the rate of 7 per cent will be reported for comparability. Given the magnitudes involved, discounting at the higher rate does not significantly affect the results.

8.   This is calculated on the basis of a British weighted average unit value of items from Nimexe 6/6p, 7 and 8 of £5.37.

9.   For instance, if protection remains for five years the cost per job (discounting at 5 per cent) would be between £19,000 and £37,000. Over 10 years the cost per job would be between £34,000 and £66,000. If protection is maintained permanently, and if this serves to preserve these jobs permanently, the cost per job amounts to between £88,000 and £171,000.

10.   The respective costs for five years would be £92,000 and £46,000, for ten years £157,000 and £78,000, and for permanent protection £426,000 and £213,000. Clearly the cost of job preservation to buyers could be very great indeed.

11.   In 1982 non-leather footwear accounted for 92 per

cent of total footwear imports from Taiwan in both countries. Furthermore, the largest categories for both countries were textile footwear and plastic footwear. South Korea is a relatively unimportant supplier of footwear to Hong Kong. In 1982 imports from South Korea (by volume) were a mere 4 per cent of the quantity imported from Taiwan. Moreover, whereas leather footwear accounted for less than 8 per cent of imports from Taiwan, it accounted for over 25 per cent of imports from Korea. Hong Kong imports from Taiwan were therefore more directly comparable to British imports than are Hong Kong imports from Korea. See Hong Kong Trade Statistics 1982 (Hong Kong: Census and Statistics Department, Government of Hong Kong, 1982).

12.   Industry sources indicate that freight charges for importing footwear from the Far East range from 15 pence a pair for textile footwear to 30 pence a pair for leather footwear. For the purpose of these calculations a simple average of the two was used (of 22 pence a pair). It should be noted that this probably over-estimates freight costs since 92 per cent of British footwear imports from Taiwan are of the non-leather variety. Potential prices at British ports are probably overstated therefore.

13.   An assumption of unit elasticity, together with an assumed demand elasticity of -0.25 is consistent with a plausible short-run import elasticity of demand. As in footnote (4) (e^m) can be defined as follows:

$$e^m_i = e^d_i(Q^d_i/Q^m_i) - n_i(Q^s_i/Q^m_i)$$

where e^d_i refers to price elasticity of demand and n_i price elasticity of supply (for commodity i). Q^d_i, Q^m_i and Q^s_i refer to quantities of i demanded, imported and supplied domestically. In the United Kingdom (Q^d/Q^m) in footwear is around 1.8 whilst (Q^s/Q^m) is around 0.80. With a demand elasticity of -0.25 and an assumed supply elasticity of unity, the implied import elasticity of demand is -1.25. With an elasticity of supply of 2 the implied import elasticity is -2.05. Barker (1983) has estimated import elasticity of demand for footwear in the United Kingdom at -1.48. For the United States, Szenberg (1977) has estimated import elasticity of demand at -1.5, although Buckler and Almon (1972) estimated it to be somewhat higher at -4.0.

14.   It is assumed that the average value of output produced per unit of labour is equal to the marginal value of

output. This is a common assumption in cost of protection studies, in spite of the likelihood that marginal product will be less than average product. Data limitations generally preclude calculation of the marginal product. One notable exception is J. Pelzman and C. Bradberry (1980).

15. If protection remains for five years the cost per job (discounting at 5 per cent) would be between £13,000 and £25,000. Over 10 years the cost per job would be between £22,000 and £45,000. If protection is maintained permanently, and if this serves to preserve these jobs permanently, the cost per job amounts to between £61,000 and £116,000.

26. The respective costs for five years would be £68,000 and £34,000; for ten years £121,000 and £60,000 and for permanent protection £313,000 and £156,000.

References

Barker, T. (1983), UK Import Functions Revised: Estimates 1956-75, Working Paper GPP 483, Department of Applied Economics, University of Cambridge.

Buckler, M. and C. Almon (1972), Imports and Exports in an Input-Output Model, American Statistical Association Proceedings, pp. 167-184.

Cable, V. (1983), Protectionism and Industrial Decline, Hodder and Stoughton, London.

Deaton, A. (1976), Models and Projections of Demand in Post War Britain, Chapman and Hall, London.

Greenaway, D. (1983), International Trade Policy, Macmillan, London.

Greenaway, D. (ed.) (1985), Current Issues in International Trade, Macmillan, London.

Greenaway, D. (1986), 'Estimating the Welfare Effects of Voluntary Export Restraints and Tariffs: An Application to Non-Leather Footwear in the U.K.', Applied Economics, Vol. 18, pp.1065-1083.

Greenaway, D. and B.V. Hindley, (1985), What Britain Pays for Voluntary Export Restraints, Thames Essay 43, Trade Policy Research Centre, London.

Hamilton, C. (1984), Voluntary Export Restraints on Clothing from Asia; Price Effects, Rent Incomes, Trade Barrier Formation and Quota Allocation Systems, mimeo.

Hamilton, C. (1985a) 'Economic Aspects of Voluntary Export Restraints', in: Greenaway (ed.) (1985).

Hamilton, C. (1985b), 'Follies of Policies for Textile Imports in Western Europe', The World Economy, Vol. 8, No. 3, pp.219-234.

Hughes, G. and D. Newbery (1986), 'Protection and Developing Countries Exports of Manufactures', Economic Policy: A European Forum, Vol. 7, pp.409-454.

Jenkins, G. (1981), 'Costs and Consequences of the New Protectionism', in: Canada in a Developing World Economy, Oxford University Press, Oxford, 1981.

Jones, K. (1984), 'The Political Economy of Voluntary Export Restraint Agreements', Kylos, Vol. 37, pp.82-101.

Keesing, D. and M. Wolf (1980), Textile Quotas Against Developing Countries, Thames Essay 23, Trade Policy Research Centre, London.

Koekkoek, K.A. and L.B.M. Mennes (1986), 'Liberalizing the Multi Fibre Arrangement', Journal of World Trade Law, Vol. 20, pp.142-167.

Milner, C.R. (1985), 'Empirical Analysis of the Costs of Protection', in: Greenaway (ed.) (1985).

Morkre, M.E. (1984), Import Quotas on Textiles: The Welfare Effects of United States Restrictions on Hong Kong, Bureau of Economics Staff Report, Washington.

Morkre, M.E. and D.G. Tarr (1980), Effects of Restrictions on United States Imports, Bureau of Economics Staff Report, Washington.

Nogues, J.J., A. Olechowski, and L.A. Winters (1986), 'The Extent of Non Tariff Barriers to Imports of Industrial Countries', World Bank Staff Working Papers, No. 789, World Bank, Washington.

Pelzman, J. (1983), 'Economic Costs of Tariffs and Quotas on Textile and Apparel Products Imported into the United States: A Survey of the Literature and Implications for Policies', Weltwirtschaftliches Archiv, Vol. 119, pp.523-542.

Pelzman, J. and C. Bradberry (1980), 'The Welfare Effects of Reduced Tariff Restrictions on Imported Textile Products', Applied Economics, Vol. 12, pp.445-465.

Silberston, Z.A. (1984), The Multi-Fibre Arrangement and the U.K. Economy, H.M.S.O., London.

Szenberg, M. et al. (1977), Welfare Effects of Trade Restrictions: A Case Study of the U.S. Footwear Industry, Academic Press, New York.

Chapter Nine

A EUROPEAN COMMUNITY PRECEDENT: EXPORTS OF VCRs FROM JAPAN

Brian Hindley

1. THE FIRST VER BETWEEN THE EC AND JAPAN: A TRADE POLICY BACKGROUND

In February 1983, as part of the so-called Tokyo Agreement, video cassette recorders (VCRs) became the subject of the first VER between the European Community, as such, and Japan. (1) The VER formally lapsed on 1 January 1986 but reports of its demise may have been exaggerated.

In the latter part of 1985, as the end of the VER agreed in Tokyo approached, the Community announced its intention of increasing its tariff on VCRs from 8 to 14 per cent. One interpretation of this move is that it provides a substitute for the lapsed VER. The <u>Financial Times</u> (16/12/85), however, has reported that the Ministry of International Trade and Industry (MITI) in Japan will restrain sales of VCRs to the EEC even after the end of the formal VER. The article notes that "EEC officials (in Tokyo) emphasized that the Japanese announcement was 'unilateral' and had not been 'negotiated' with the EEC". Nevertheless, there is no record of protests by EEC officials at this apparent monopolistic exploitation of the EEC market.

The origins and effects of this curious situation are of interest in their own right. Yet the VCR restriction has a significance that extends far beyond the market for VCRs in the European Community. Since the VER was a precedent, it is rightly regarded as holding lessons for the future conduct of European Community trade policy. Some members of the European Commission evidently regard the restraint as a 'success'. That view would imply that the VCR restrictions are a precedent to be built upon: that the EEC should 'solve its trade problems' with Japan by a more extensive use of such instruments. Yet if the EEC adopts this course in its trade relations with Japan, it is very difficult to imagine that it will not pursue VERs even more enthusiastically in its trade with other and weaker trading partners. The claim of 'success' for the VCR restriction calls for careful assessment.

This paper, naturally, focuses on the economic consequences of the VER, and initially will judge 'success' in those terms. In fairness to the European authors of the VCR restraint, it therefore must be said that there is little ground for any belief that thought about economic consequences played any substantial role in its creation.

As noted above, this was the first VER negotiated between the European Commission and the Government of Japan. There are, however, a large number of VERs between Japan and the governments of member states of the European Community, and this creates a major policy problem for the European Commission. Under the Treaty of Rome, it is the Commission, under the Council of Ministers, that is responsible for the external trade relations of the Community. But since so much of the actual commercial policy affecting the Community has taken the form of bilateral agreements between individual member states and non-members, especially Japan, the Commission's role has been seriously undermined.

The Commission had been concerned for some time prior to 1983 with the problem of re-establishing its authority in matters of trade policy. Yet what kind of trade policy? If the Community followed a liberal path, the protectionist member states would continue to undermine it by negotiating restrictions bilaterally.

In these circumstances, the conclusion that the Commission could restore its authority in matters of trade policy only by negotiation of Community-wide VERs must have been tempting, even for Commissioners or officials of relatively liberal views. Of course, member governments opposed to protection of manufactured goods, in particular the Federal Republic, would have to be persuaded into that course of action. To view that as an easier task than that of persuading the protectionist members to adhere to a liberal policy, however, is not a sign of defective judgement.

The events leading to the VER can be interpreted in the light of this conflict between liberal and protectionist states within the Community. A convenient starting point for a précis of these events is the requirement of the French government that all VCRs imported into France should be cleared through a single small customs post at Poitiers. This occurred in October 1982.

This action led to a Japanese complaint in GATT under Article XXIII, which concerns the right of a party to the GATT when a benefit accruing to it under the GATT is nullified or impaired by the actions of another party. (2) The complaint was not addressed to the French government, however, but to the European Commission, which acts as the representative of the governments of the member states in GATT, and is therefore in GATT terms the responsible party.

It is difficult to see any plausible ground upon which the French action could have been defended in GATT. The de facto position is that the Commission has no means of controlling the actions of the French government. (3) Nevertheless, a lack of power to affect relevant events within the Community is hardly a satisfactory plea for the Commission to make in GATT or in any other international forum in which it negotiates for the European Community.

The Commission therefore appears to have been caught in a trap of French manufacture, even though the ostensible collector of the prey was Japanese. So long as the French government persisted in its action (which it showed every sign of doing), the Commission was trapped in a position of potential high embarrassment. Much of the subsequent political activity in the VCR industry is plausibly interpreted in terms of the struggles of the Commission to escape from that trap. (4) Allegations by the European manufacturers of VCRs that the Japanese producers were dumping VCRs in Europe provided the basic escape route, and the Commission has consistently represented the VER as a solution for 'the dumping problem'.

Yet why did the French government create the trap in the first place? What policy objective was served by insisting and continuing to insist that VCRs coming into France should be routed through Poitiers? (5) In the light of the analysis above, an obvious conjecture is that it was a step in the process of persuading the government of the Federal Republic of the need for a Community restraint agreement with Japan. And if one such VER could be agreed, the principle of an active Community policy with regard to restrictions on exports from Japan would be established.

Seen from that standpoint VCRs were a clever choice. All European Community manufacture of Video 2000 sets (the European format that would be protected by a VER) was located in the Federal Republic. (6) Moreover, Japanese companies had established plants for video assembly in West Berlin. If exports of finished sets from Japan were restricted, West Germany could look forward to more such investment.

But the circumstances surrounding the VER allowed the issue to be represented in less parochial terms. The government of the Federal Republic is highly communautaire - it is concerned with the maintenance of the powers and dignity of the Community and the Commission. The proposition that a VER was necessary to avoid humiliation for the Commission (via the Japanese Article XXIII complaint) therefore possessed a persuasive power that mundane parochial considerations alone could not have had. In any event, the upshot was the appearance of the first Community VER with Japan.

These political conjectures become relevant again later on. If they are correct, account must be taken of them in any final assessment of the VER, for the restraint then represents more than appears at first sight. For the moment, however, this is enough of political analysis. Whatever the depth of the Commission's concern with the economic consequences of the VER at the time of its negotiation, it inevitably did have such consequences. I now turn to them.

2. ECONOMIC ASPECTS OF THE VER: MARKET SIZE AND SHARES

2.1 Permitted Japanese sales

Table 9.1 provides information on the announced limits on Japanese exports of VCRs to the European Community, divided between kits for assembly in Europe and complete sets, for 1983, 1984, and 1985. The table also gives outturns for the first two years. A comparison of the limit for 1984 with the actual number of sets exported from Japan during that year shows that actual exports failed by a large margin to reach the announced number of permitted sets. This might be taken to suggest that the VER was redundant. Before that conclusion is drawn, however, two other aspects of the agreement require consideration.

The first of these aspects is that the permitted quantity of Japanese sales during a year was not independent of events during that year. Specifically, whether that maximum remained in force throughout the year appears to have depended upon the number of VCRs sold by Philips and Grundig. The second is that the restraint agreement incorporated a system of minimum selling prices for the Japanese producers.

Table 9.1: Quantity Restrictions on Japanese Exports of VCRs to the European Community

Year	Complete Sets	Kits	Total	Outcome
1982	No Restriction			4.95m
1983	3.95m	0.6m	4.55m	4.65m
1984	3.95m	1.1m	5.05m	3.76m
1985	2.25m	1.7m	3.95m	?

Sources: Text and Japan Exports and Imports (Tokyo: Japan Tariff Association)

The upper limit on Japanese sales agreed at the beginning of a year, as presented in Table 9.1, was widely reported and easily verified from official sources either in Japan or the European Community. Details of the minimum price system and the relationship between Philips-Grundig sales and adjustment of the announced limit were not widely reported; when reported they were often represented in contradictory ways by different sources; and were very difficult to confirm from official sources, either in Japan or the European Community.

In Europe, the VER is for legal reasons represented as a unilateral action of the Japanese government. Officials in Europe therefore tend to deny any knowledge of the administration of the VER. This may strain belief: its effect, nevertheless, is that the details of the agreement and its administration (which on the basis of the 1984 figures in Table 9.1 may be the crucial aspect of it) are in some degree a matter of informed conjecture. (7)

2.2 European output and permitted Japanese exports

At the time of the Tokyo Agreement, reporting of it made

clear that the video cassette recorder VER was designed to 'guarantee' Philips-Grundig sales of 1.2 million units in 1983 (the word 'guarantee' was used by both the Times (14/2/83) and the Financial Times (editorial 15/2/85). Japanese reports were couched in similar terms. Nihon Kezai (13/2/83), for example, reported that the restraint agreement called "... for both parties to work together to enable European VCR manufacturers to produce and sell at least 1.2 million units this year". However, none of these reports mentioned any means by which these plans were to be made effective.

One possibility, suggested by the form of many reports (and most explicitly in the Economist of 13/10/84) is that a forecast was made for total European Community sales for the next 12 months and 1.2 million deducted from it to obtain the Japanese quota. This would in itself be a very weak guarantee, however.

In the first place, sales of VCRs were in most parts of the world in 1983 growing at extraordinarily high rates. Table 9.2 gives figures for Japanese exports to selected regions. These suggest - in addition to the abberant behaviour of exports to the European Community following 1982 - a market whose future size would be very difficult to predict with confidence.

Table 9.2: VCR Exports from Japan to Selected Markets (thousands)

	1981	1982	1983	1984
European Community	2855	4946	4646	3755
United States	2374	2504	5437	11906
Canada	160	367	766	1277
Rest of World (exc. EC and US)	2126	3202	5155	6410

Source: Japan Exports and Imports (Tokyo: Japan Tariff Association)

In the second place, units offered by Philips and Grundig in the Video 2000 format clearly are not perfect substitutes for VHS and Betamax sets made in Japan. Even if an accurate forecast was available for the size of the market without quota restriction on the Japanese producers (who held some 85 per cent of the market in 1983), it does not in any way follow that cutting X million units from projected Japanese sales would increase European sales by X million units.

According to informed industry sources in Japan in late 1983, however, the arrangement (or perhaps this was merely MITI's plan; that is not clear) was that if the combined sales of Philips and Grundig fell short of 1.2 million by x million units, then the Japanese quota would be cut by x million units. These were still the early days of the VER: what would happen in the event that Philips-Grundig sales rose by less than x million units following the cut in the Japanese quota was obscure.

According to British government sources in late 1984 and 1985, the arrangement was less formal than this. It was said merely to consist of a six monthly review of the working of the VER by representatives of MITI and the European Commission. Philips-Grundig sales would be 'one of several considerations' to be discussed at those meetings.

In the event, Philips-Grundig sales appear to have failed to reach the target of 1.2 million. No official figures on actual Philips-Grundig sales are available. They are, however, widely reported to have been 0.8 million in 1982; 0.6 million in 1983; and 0.7 million in 1984. (8) Nevertheless, the target was increased to 1.3 million for 1984 (Economist Intelligence Unit: Multinational Business No. 4 1983) and to 1.4 million for 1985 (Financial Times 11/12/84). It is a plausible conjecture that the discrepancy between targets and performance has some bearing on the failure of the Japanese producers to achieve the maximum agreed at the beginning of 1984 and also on the sharp drop in the quota for 1985.

In any event, it does seem clear that official action was taken in 1984 to reduce the flow of VCRs from Japan to the EEC below the level agreed at the beginning of the year. On 1/10/84, the Financial Times reported that:

> Japan's Ministry of International Trade and Industry said at the weekend that it has asked Japanese manufacturers of VCRs to curtail their exports of finished sets to the European Community by at least 10 per cent this year to maintain "proper prices" ... The new cut has been decided upon to avoid price competition among Japanese makers because of slackening demand for VCRs in Europe, said the MITI official. Each maker is to be required to cut back more

than 10 per cent of its current allotment.

This action might have been unilateral, or an outcome of the EEC-Japan meetings to review the progress of the VER, or have been required to meet the terms of the minimum price agreement negotiated in 1983. Information to discriminate between these alternatives is lacking.

The account above, of course, refers only to institutional arrangements. It takes no account of the incentives created for Philips and Grundig by those arrangements. It will be necessary to return to that issue.

3. ECONOMIC ASPECTS OF THE VER: PRICE BEHAVIOUR

3.1 The minimum selling price for Japanese producers

Details of the minimum price aspects of the VER are if anything vaguer than those of the relation between the size of the Japanese quota and the sales of Philips and Grundig. According to the BEUC (p.9), "The Japanese producers undertook not to sell at stock prices lower than the factory prices of the European producers". The Financial Times (15/2/83) spoke of the price of European and Japanese machines being 'aligned' (its quotation marks). It continued "While details have yet to be worked out, this could mean that Philips and Grundig will in effect set the price which the Japanese ... will charge for their VCRs."

The Economist Intelligence Unit (Multinational Business No. 3 1983) stated that "The Japanese agreed to raise their wholesale prices by £50 per unit ..." This seems a plausible version of the initial form of the VER. Certainly it would be possible to give it administrative effect.

Nevertheless, it appears that the system that emerged defined three classes of VCR: top quality, medium quality and standard recorders. It appears to be the case that each of the characteristics or quality of the characteristics of a particular model (whether it has stereo sound or the timing options offered for example) carried points. The total points earned by a particular model determined the category it entered, and therefore its minimum price.

This raises the possibility that the VER affects the characteristics of models exported from Japan to the European Community (since, for example, a manufacturer may be able to avoid a higher minimum price by removing or worsening characteristics). Were details of the points system available, a potentially interesting study would be possible. They are not available, of course. Nor are reliable details of the minimum prices. (9)

Either the system of minimum prices or a mid-year renegotiation of permitted exports in the light of lagging Philips-Grundig sales (or some combination of these two) is capable of explaining the failure of Japanese sales in 1984 to approach the maximum announced at the beginning of that year. It is not possible to discriminate between these alternatives with available data, though the sharp fall in the permitted quantity of exports for 1985 suggests that the Commission was not content to rely upon the minimum price system. A third possible explanation is that the VER was redundant in 1984.

The comparison of exports of VCRs to the European Community compared with the rest of the world, as contained in Table 9.2, rather strongly suggests that the VER was not redundant. Nevertheless, it would be useful to have evidence on the behaviour of prices of VCRs in the European Community as compared with their behaviour in other, unrestricted, markets. Two relevant pieces of information are in fact available.

3.2 **The behaviour of VCR prices in the European Community**

The first piece of evidence is the behaviour of the unit values of Japanese exports. Table 9.3 gives information on these.

Table 9.3: Unit Values of VCR Exports from Japan (thousands of yen)

	1981	1982	1983	1984
European Community	110.1	94.9	80.8	77.8
United States	112.7	105.7	80.6	70.8
Canada	113.4	95.4	74.8	67.0
Rest of World (exc. EC and US)	127.8	107.8	86.8	75.8

Source: Japan Exports and Imports (Tokyo: Japan Tariff Association)

Although all of the unit values displayed in the table fall over time, a comparison of the rate of change of the unit value of exports to the European Community makes apparent the rise in that figure <u>relative</u> to the unit value of Japanese exports to other areas. Comparing 1984 with 1982, for example, the figure for the European Community falls by 18 per cent. For the United States, however, it falls by 33 per cent and for the rest of the world by 30 per cent. These figures imply that the unit value of Japanese exports to the European Community rose by some 12-15 per cent relative to the unit value of exports to other areas.

Unit values, of course, are difficult to interpret in the absence of information on the quality mix of exports. <u>Ceteris paribus</u>, it should be expected that a VER will shift the composition of exports to the restricted market towards units with a higher selling price, or, alternatively stated, that the price of high priced units will rise by a smaller percentage than the price of low priced units (Falvey (1979), Feenstra (1984)).

However, the minimum prices for exports from Japan to Europe (and in particular those on high priced units) may impede the Japanese producers in shifting their sales mix in Europe to the extent that they would wish. Moreover, in a market as dynamic as that for VCRs, it is risky to assume that quality up-grading is the major factor affecting the European Community quality mix, or that the quality mix to areas other than the European Community is constant. Finally, kits to be assembled in the Community presumably carry a lower price than fully assembled sets, and since these form an increasing proportion of Japanese exports to the Community, this factor is likely to give a <u>downward</u> bias to the average value of exports to the Community as compared with those to other areas.

Without further support, therefore, it would be unwise to make any stronger claim for these figures than that are consistent with the hypothesis that the VER raised the price of VCRs in the European Community. It clearly would be useful to have more evidence of the price effects of the VER.

Hindley (1985a) compares the rate of change of retail prices of VCRs on the Japanese market with the rate of change of the retail prices of similar sets in the United Kingdom between March 1983 and March 1984. Using data collected by the Electronics Industries Association of Japan and by specialist Video magazines in the United Kingdom, he examines both the change in price and the change in quality of the most basic set offered by each Japanese manufacturer for whom data was available. In local currency terms, the retail price of such sets on the British market rises by 24.28 per cent relative to those offered in Japan and the quality of the Japanese sets rises relative to the quality of those offered on the British market. Over this period, the yen appreciated by 5.5 per cent against the pound. Hence, these data suggest that the retail price of basic sets was increased by the VER by a minimum of 18.76 per cent in the first twelve months of its actual operation; and taking account of quality changes, by rather more than that.

There is, of course, ground to expect that the price of basic sets will rise by a larger percentage than the price of higher quality models, although, as already noted, application of that proposition in this particular case is complicated by the minimum prices imposed under the restraint agreement. Ignoring that difficulty, however, the theory of the effect of a VER on the price structure of restricted imports suggests that a VER on a particular category of goods will act as would a specific tariff. On the British market, an expensive VCR carries a retail price that is roughly twice that of a basic set, and this suggests, for example, that the retail price of expensive VCRs might have risen by 10 per cent relative to Japanese prices. In the absence of information about the product mix or changes in it, therefore, a plausible guess is that retail prices rose by an average of 15 per cent as a result of the VER in its first year of operation. This is broadly consistent with the comment of the Economist Intelligence Unit, noted above, that the restraint agreement required the Japanese to raise their prices by £50 per unit. At first sight, however, it may appear inconsistent with the behaviour of unit values of Japanese exports.

Average unit values of Japanese exports to the European Community fell by 15 per cent in calendar year 1983 as compared with calendar year 1982. Unit values of exports to the United States fell by 24 per cent over the same period, and those to the rest of the world by 19.5 per cent. However, while unit values of exports to the European Community fell by only 2.7 per cent in calendar year 1984, those to the United States fell by 12.2 per cent and those to the rest of the world by 12.7 per cent.

That the comparative unit value figures show a smaller

rise in calendar year 1983 than the Hindley comparison is not unduly disturbing. Quite apart from the difficulties in interpreting the unit value figures noted above, the VER was agreed in mid-February 1983, and several months elapsed before it was given administrative effect. Hence, a considerable proportion of sales in 1983 would have been on pre-VER terms, an effect exaggerated by the fact that since the VER applied to calendar year 1983, exports fell sharply in the latter part of that year. Average unit values for calendar year 1983 are therefore on that account alone likely to underestimate the effect of the VER on prices to the European Community. Moreover, Hindley compares prices in March 1984 with those of March 1983, thus covering at least part of the calendar year 1984 in which relative unit value figures do rise sharply for the European Community.

There is therefore no major discrepancy between the pictures conveyed by the unit values of exports and by the Hindley comparison. The unit value figures do suggest, however, the possibility that European Community prices continued to rise (in relative terms) after March 1984.

Casual observation of the market for VCRs in the United States, where imports are free of quantity constraints and subject to a 4 per cent tariff, supports this conjecture. In Britain in October 1985, Which Video? reviewed a new Sanyo model under the sub-title 'A video recorder for less than £300? There has to be a catch - or has there?' At that date, VCRs were commonly advertised in the U.S. for less than $300 (which was 40 per cent less than £300 at the current exchange rate). The Economist (12/10/85) reported that "in Texas and the Midwest, a Sanyo machine is already on sale for $157" (that is, for well under half the price that causes surprise in the British magazine).

4.   WELFARE EFFECTS

4.1 Welfare costs

Hindley (1985a) estimates a 15 per cent increase in retail prices between March 1983 and March 1984. To avoid the risk of over-estimation, however, he estimates welfare costs on the basis of a 15 per cent increase in Japanese fob prices. In fact, there is no reason to suppose that Japanese producers would share the quota rents with European retailers, so that a 15 per cent increase in retail prices is consistent with a considerably larger percentage increase in fob prices. Nevertheless, if fob prices rose on average by 15 per cent, this would on 1983 figures imply a payment of rents to Japanese producers by European Community buyers of £175,000,000 per annum.

A market as new and growing as rapidly as that for VCRs poses major problems for the estimation of demand functions, or even for guesses of what the level of Japanese exports to the European Community would have been in the absence of the VER (although Table 9.1 makes clear the plausibility of the proposition that they would have been very much greater). For this reason, no estimate of foregone consumer surplus is presented by Hindley. £175,000,000 therefore is a lower bound on the welfare loss for the first year of the VER.

Although detailed figures on the price movements of specific sets are not available for 1984 and 1985, it seems most unlikely that welfare losses in those years can have been less than that calculated for 1983. That suggests that the VER costs residents of the European Community at least half a billion pounds by the end of 1985. What did Europeans get in return?

4.2 Welfare gains

In Hindley (1985a) four possible benefits of the restraint agreement are discussed in some detail. Two of these can be quickly disposed of in the present context.

The first easily disposed of 'benefit' is the contention of the European Commission that the VER was entirely about the settlement of the dumping complaint by Philips and Grundig against the Japanese producers. No evidence has been published to support the contention that there was dumping; the complex form of the VER and its pre-set duration are incompatible with the notion that dumping was the central problem in this action; and had there been proof of dumping, it surely would have occurred to the Commission that it would be better from a European point of view to collect revenue from antidumping duties than to pay rents to Japanese producers.

The second putative benefit not requiring extended discussion is that implied by the notion that the VER was a means of providing infant industry protection for the fledgling European V2000 format. It is neither necessary to re-state here the strict conditions that must be met if a satisfactory case for infant industry protection is to be constructed, (10) nor to argue that these conditions are unlikely to be met by the makers of V2000.

The dominant fact in this case is that Philips and Grundig are abandoning the V2000 format and are turning instead to the manufacture of VHS sets under licence from Matsushita. If protection of the V2000 format per se was an objective of the VER, it has failed.

The remaining two potential benefits are worth more detailed discussion. They are, first, the effects of the VER in inducing Japanese investment in video assembly plants in the European Community and second, protection of the output of Philips and Grundig (of whatever format that output consists) and/or its associated employment.

4.2.1 Employment in assembly of Japanese kits. In considering this topic, numbers are useful but not easy to obtain. In the United Kingdom at the end of 1984, the Department of Trade and Industry reported that some 580 persons were directly employed in the assembly of Japanese video kits, and it was estimated that a similar number were employed in supplying components of one kind or another. Of the 580 persons directly employed, however, 280 were in the J2T (a consortium of JVC, Thorn EMI and Telefunken) plant at Newhaven, which was established before the VER. Employment in that plant, therefore, cannot be attributed to the VER.(11)

Officials in the European Commission deny that any similar figures are calculated for the European Community as a whole. British officials, however, suggest that elsewhere in the European Community, there were probably around twice as many persons employed in assembly of Japanese kits as in the United Kingdom: on the order of magnitude of 1100 directly employed in Video assembly and a roughly similar number supplying components. The J2T plant in Berlin, however - which - like Newhaven, predates the VER, employed 800 of these.

Excluding the J2T plants, therefore, the expansion in employment in assembly by the end of 1984 appears to amount to some 300 jobs in Britain and probably a similar number elsewhere in the Community. The figures on employment in component-supplying industries suggest that jobs there match jobs in direct employment. Hence, for the European Community as a whole, a plausible estimate of the number of jobs that appeared in video manufacture and related industries between the institution of the VER and the end of 1984 is on the order of magnitude of 1200.

This figure, even if its statistical validity is accepted, is open to query from a number of directions. In the first place, the VER may have caused an expansion of employment in J2T plants. On the other hand, Japanese companies might have opened assembly plants in the Community even in the absence of the VER (Japanese producers have often denied that their plants in the Community are a consequence of the VER. The prior establishment of the J2T plants adds credibility to at least some of these denials).

Finally, insofar as the VER reduced the stock of VCRs in the EEC below the level it would otherwise have had, it slowed the appearance of jobs in ancillary sectors - for example, in the distribution of tapes for home use. To obtain a true figure of the net job creation in the EEC of the VER, these lost jobs should be deducted from those created in assembly.

The VER clearly should not be credited with the creation of all of the jobs that existed in video assembly by the end of 1984. In view of the uncertainty of the figures, however, it is a useful precaution to calculate 'costs per job created' as though the VER were responsible for all 3300 of them. On the basis of the welfare estimates noted earlier, the VER had by the end of 1984 imposed costs upon European residents amounting to a minimum of £350 million. At that stage, therefore, each job that the VER is assumed to have created had cost residents of the European Community around £106,000 - even calculating on the basis of an absurdly high estimate of employment created and a much lower estimate of welfare loss than could plausibly be sustained. The true figure of the costs so far incurred per job actually created in video assembly therefore is likely to be much greater than £106,000: probably in excess of £300,000.

Moreover, the jobs created are for the most part likely to be unskilled. A Financial Times report (13 March 1984) notes that:

> Most of the Japanese operations are so-called 'screwdriver' assembly plants. The first materials to be purchased locally are usually packaging and cases - the VCR items unlikely to cause quality problems.

Certain electronic components may also be produced locally. The precision built tape mechanism, the single most costly item in a VCR, is built only in Japan. Thomson in France is the only company with plans to make the mechanism in Europe other than Philips.

The creation of video assembly employment in Europe via protection-induced inward investment by Japanese producers cannot by itself possibly justify the economic costs of the VER. This comment stands, moreover, even under the assumption that whatever employment was created in video assembly was a net gain for overall employment. There is little warrant for that assumption, (12) but pursuit of the issue seems unnecessary here.

4.2.2 Output and employment in Philips and Grundig. As noted above, the reported figures suggest that Philips-Grundig output not only has failed to reach the level targeted for it in the restraint agreement: it has even fallen below its pre-agreement level. In Europe, where it is frequently said that V2000 is technically superior to VHS and Betamax, widely cited reasons for this failure are a comparative lack of software in the V2000 format, and the lack of appeal in the design of V2000 sets. No doubt there is much to be said for these hypotheses and for a variety of others that have been put forward. In a discussion of trade policy, however, it would be foolish to ignore the fact that the VER probably did not provide Philips and Grundig with any economic incentive to expand output.

The basic point was made by Bhagwati (1969) in his discussion of the equivalence of tariffs and quotas. Even when there is only one domestic producer, he is, when protected by tariffs, constrained in his pricing policy on the domestic market by the threat of an increase in imports. A quota or VER, however, removes that constraint. The single domestic producer is then able to raise his price without any threat to his sales from imports: he becomes a monopolist on the domestic market and therefore may have an incentive to reduce his output.

In 1983, Philips owned a 25 per cent share in Grundig, and later acquired a majority interest. From this point of view, therefore, they should be regarded as a single producer. In 1983, Philips and Grundig were the only indigenous producers of VCRs in the Community.

Hindley (1985b) calculates the restriction on imports necessary to provide a single domestic producer with an incentive to produce the same output after the VER as before it when imports and home-product are perfect substitutes in consumption. For a producer with the same market share as Philips and Grundig prior to the VER (15 per cent), it turns out that if the overall elasticity of demand for the product in the domestic market is 1.5, imports must be cut by 74 per cent to hold domestic output constant; with an elasticity of demand of 2 by 53 per cent; of 3 by 42 per cent; of 4 by 38 per cent; and of 5 by 36 per cent. VERs giving imports a larger market share than implied by these figures give the domestic producer an incentive to reduce output.

These figures, combined with the market position of Philips and Grundig, strongly suggest the possibility that the VER, at least initially, did not cut imports by enough to provide Philips-Grundig with an incentive to increase output. Instead, it seems likely that it provided the linked firms with an incentive to reduce output. Moreover, this effect is reinforced by the apparent dependence under the VER of the Japanese quota on Philips-Grundig sales.

Judged as a means of encouraging European manufacture of European VCRs, therefore, the VER was a disastrously poor piece of policy. Not only has it failed in this respect but, worse, there was never reason to suppose that it would succeed.

With respect to Philips and Grundig, one certain effect of the VER has been to increase their profits (or reduce their losses) from VCR manufacture. That objective in itself is unlikely to command widespread assent for a very expensive policy. It does open the route to another argument, however, which is that the two firms would have exited from the VCR business in the absence of the VER, thus eliminating European production of VCRs.

Clearly, whether this would in fact have happened, and whether it was anyway an outcome worth avoiding, are both issues open for debate. (13) The dominant fact, however, is that to regard increased profits (or reduced losses) of the European producers as the major achievement of the VER is to take an indefensible position. To force or allow all producers to raise their prices must be an enormously expensive means of increasing the revenue of producers holding 15 per cent of the market. Only lack of imagination could lead to the view that the VER was an appropriate means of achieving that end.

5.   THE VER AS AN INSTRUMENT OF ECONOMIC POLICY

5.1   **The dynamics of the VER**
It is tempting to speculate on the development of the VER over its three year history.

From its start, its operation was affected by two major interests of national governments within the Community. One of these was an interest in the manufacture of complete VCRs. The other was in Japanese inward investment in the assembly of basically Japanese sets.

These two interests, however, are to some extent competitive with one another. Both are served by a restriction on Japanese exports; but the assembly of Japanese kits in Europe conflicts with the objective of increasing European production of complete VCRs.

A tempting conjecture, however, is that the VER has been driven in an increasingly restrictive direction by the failure of Philips and Grundig to expand output by the 50 per cent or so envisaged in 1983. One explanation of this failure is that the European Community market for VCRs is close to saturation. This explanation appears to be favoured in the Commission. In any event, it has responded with sharp reductions in permitted exports of complete sets from Japan.

An alternative explanation for the Philips-Grundig failure lies in the increasing unpopularity of the V2000 format. Another alternative, not inconsistent with this, is that the VER did not provide Philips and Grundig with any incentive to expand output, and certainly not to expand output by 50 per cent. As noted above, it appears from Hindley (1985b) that the restriction required to supply such an incentive may be very severe.

If the VER did not permit exports of kits, the cut in the quantity of complete sets exported from Japan might now be sufficient to give the European producers an incentive to expand output. But the VER did not exclude kits; and these increasing indirect imports undercut the possible effect of the tightness of the VER in expanding the output of Philips and Grundig. The Commission therefore saw fresh evidence of saturation and felt increased pressure to tighten the VER further.

Yet it is not evident that even a total ban on the import of complete sets from Japan would have provided a pecuniary incentive for the European producers to expand output so long as the Commission acceded to the pressures for the import of kits. Under these circumstances, Philips-Grundig output may be an extremely perverse indicator of the state of the European market.

5.2 The VER as a precedent for policy

As economic policy, the video cassette recorder VER has little to recommend it. But, as argued in the introduction to this paper, it is probable that economic considerations played only a very small role in the activity and thinking that led to the VER. In view of that, a question might arise as to whether it is appropriate - or even quite fair - to assess the VER solely from an economic point of view.

It is possible, perhaps, to be succinct. Politicians and civil servants everywhere claim higher duties and causes than can be encompassed by mere pecuniary assessments of the costs and benefits of their actions. It is unlikely, however, that this methodology is anywhere pursued with more solemnity than in the European Commission.

For politicians to be obliged to bow to the power of special interest groups is one thing. It is another thing to represent such obeisance as part of a crusade for European unity, and yet another to believe it. The effects on clear thinking of such beliefs are much more likely to be the death of European unity than its foundation.

Notes

An earlier version of this chapter has been published in the 'Journal of World Trade Law', Volume 20, Number 2, March/April 1986. Permission given by the editor of that journal to include the chapter in this volume, is gratefully acknowledged.

I am grateful to Carl Hamilton for his extensive comments when an earlier draft of this paper was presented at a conference on "European Trade Policies and the South" in The Hague, September 1985. If errors and omissions remain, he certainly is not to blame!

1.   The Tokyo Agreement was announced on 14

February 1983, after bilateral talks between the European Community and Japan. In addition to the restraint on VCRs, the Agreement set a ceiling on exports to the Community of large colour TV tubes and established bilateral monitoring of Japanese exports to the EEC of cars, quartz watches, fork lift trucks, hi-fi equipment, light commercial vehicles and television sets.

There are, of course, a number of VERs between the governments of member states of the European Community and Japan (and also between member states and other countries). These become an essential part of the story to be told below. Moreover, Community VERs have been negotiated with Japan within the framework of the Coal and Steel Treaty. The VCR restriction, together with that for television tubes, was the first Community VER outside of the bounds of that Treaty.

2.   The complaint must have possessed a certain piquancy for the Japanese. The Community had earlier made an Article XXIII complaint against Japan, which in considerable part was based on the assertion that as a result of cultural bias and a difficult language, the Japanese often buy Japanese goods. Article XXIII, however, is concerned with nullification and impairment, which presumably implies that something has happened to change a position reasonably expected at some past time. The Japanese complaint against the Community was rather better based.

3.   The Commission did issue a reasoned opinion (a warning of forthcoming legal action) to the French government on the basis that the Poitiers action was impeding the free circulation of goods within the Community (the action was with respect to all VCRs entering France, including those of European origin). It could, of course, have referred the issue to the European Court of Justice. That is a long procedure. The interval between a decision of the Court and the compliance of a member state can also be lengthy.

4.   See Hindley (1985a) for a fuller account of this activity. The account in the text may give the Commission a too passive role. I do not want to commit myself to that view. Without reliable inside information, it is difficult to know which of the players in a drama of this kind are active and which passive. The Commission - or particular members of it - may have instigated more of the activity than is apparent on the surface.

5.   There was a prospective French interest in the

manufacture of complete VCRs via Thomson. It is difficult to see that the Poitiers action would have assisted Thomson in any degree commensurate with its costs except through its effect in procuring Community-wide protection.

6.   Though there is also a manufacturing facility for Video 2000 in Austria.

7.   That Europeans should be taxed largely for the benefit of Japanese producers of VCRs but not be able to obtain information on the tax system is, to say the least, curious. This may in the long run be the worst feature of the VER system.

8.   BEUC (1983) reported that V2000 sales in 1982 held about 15 per cent of a total Community market of over 5 million units. The Economist (15/12/84) reports that sales in 1984 were estimated to be between 600,000 and 700,000. Unofficial figures from the Department of Trade and Industry in London give sales of 770,000 in 1983 and 900,000 (including VHS sets manufactured under licence) for 1984. Presumably Thomson sets now figure in the European target, but information as to how and in what quantity is not available.

9.   Though a report giving minimum prices for the three categories appeared in the Times of 15/8/84.

10.   The classic reference is Harry G. Johnson (1965). A discussion in the specific context of VCRs is contained in Hindley (1985a) pp.53-54.

11.   These figures were supplied verbally by officials of the Department of Trade and Industry. The Financial Times (26/10/84), reporting on the opening of a new Japanese plant for the manufacture of video components, comments that 'employment in Japanese video plants is set to rise to 1,100 people.' This figure, however, appears to refer to component manufacture as well as assembly.

12.   The underlying issue, of course, is the relation between protection and employment under a floating exchange rate. Mundell (1961), using a Keynesian model, argued that a tariff would reduce aggregate employment. For a recent survey of the literature on this proposition, see Krugman (1982).

13.   Philips has links with Matsushita dating back to its role in the reconstruction of the Japanese company after 1945. Without the VER, V2000 might have been abandoned more rapidly, but had Philips wanted it, a licence from Matsushita to manufacture VHS sets for the European market - such as Philips had for other markets, and now has

for Europe - presumably would have been available.

References
BEUC (1983), Video Tape Recorder Prices (Brussels: Bureau Européen des Unions Consommateurs)

Bhagwati, J. (1969), "On the Equivalence of Tariffs and Quotas" in Bhagwati (Ed.), Trade, Tariffs and Growth (London, Weidenfeld and Nicolson)

Falvey, Rodney E. (1979), "The Composition of Trade within Import-restricted Product Categories", Journal of Political Economy pp.1105-14

Feenstra, Robert C. (1984), "Voluntary Export Restraints in U.S. Autos, 1980-81" in Robert E. Baldwin and Anne O. Krueger (eds), The Structure and Evolution of Recent U.S. Trade Policy (University of Chicago Press for the National Bureau of Economic Research)

Hindley, Brian (1985a), "A European Venture: VCRs from Japan" in David Greenaway and Brian Hindley, What Britain Pays for Voluntary Export Restraints (London: Trade Policy Research Centre)

Hindley, Brian (1985b), "Voluntary Export Restraints and Imperfect Competition", (Unpublished: available from author)

Krugman, Paul (1982), "The Macroeconomics of Protection with a Floating Exchange Rate", Carnegie-Rochester Conference Series on Public Policy 16 (Amsterdam: North Holland)

Johnson, Harry G. (1965), "Optimal Trade Intervention in the Presence of Domestic Distortions" in R.E. Caves, H.G. Johnson, and P.B. Kenen (Eds), Trade, Growth and the Balance of Payments (Chicago)

Mundell, R.A. (1961), "Flexible Exchange Rates and Employment Policy", Canadian Journal of Economics and Political Science

Part Three

COUNTRY STUDIES

Chapter Ten

DOES FRENCH PROTECTION DISCRIMINATE AGAINST LDCs?

Patrick A. Messerlin

1. INTRODUCTION

This paper tries to investigate whether French trade policies discriminate against LDCs exports to France during the last decade. At a first glance such an investigation may appear somewhat odd; since the introduction of the EC Generalized System of Preferences (hereafter GSP) it is largely believed in France - and in Europe - that trade rules established with the Third World countries are "fair" for the LDCs. However a similar belief in Australia was shown to be erroneous by Warr and Lloyd (1982): the Australian system of protection remained biased against LDCs exports even after the introduction of the Australian GSP. Is such a result also verified in the French case?

The French trade with LDCs is important: it represents around 30% of non-EC French imports and exports, or roughly 15% if we include intra-EC trade flows. Three interesting points about French trade with LDCs emerge from Table 10.1. First, since 1973 the share of LDC imports (not coming from Middle East countries) in total French imports from outside the EC increased by 24%: particularly significant is the growth of imports from export oriented Asia (Korea, Taiwan, Hong-Kong, Macao and Singapore) and to a lesser extent Northern Africa and Latin America. Second, the net effects of the EC agreements with ACP countries on French trade with LDCs look modest: (1) the share of imports from Africa (where most of the ACP countries trading substantially with France are concentrated) is stable despite the very low level of

Table 10.1: French Trade with Selected Zones and Countries (1973-1984), in percentages (a)

	A. Imports			B. Exports		
	1973	1983	1984	1973	1983	1984
Northern Africa	2.68	4.39	4.33	4.41	5.77	5.63
Export-Oriented Asia	0.49	1.23	1.31	0.64	1.27	1.32
Other LDC (Low Income)	5.20	4.80	5.24	5.21	5.87	5.51
Africa	4.74	4.45	4.89	4.63	5.24	4.81
Southern Asia	0.46	0.35	0.35	0.58	0.63	0.70
Other LDC (High Inc.)	4.22	4.78	4.71	4.82	5.27	4.06
South-East Asia	1.08	0.81	0.79	0.87	1.33	0.79
Latin America	2.25	3.13	3.06	2.35	2.74	2.01
Southern Europe	0.89	0.84	0.86	1.60	1.20	1.26
TOTAL I	12.59	15.20	15.59	15.08	18.18	16.52
Middle East	7.42	7.63	6.19	2.65	5.75	6.43
TOTAL II	20.01	22.83	21.78	17.73	23.93	22.95
Italy	9.40	10.36	9.85	11.29	10.26	10.89
Spain	2.25	3.38	3.40	2.76	3.06	3.22
Portugal	0.28	0.66	0.64	0.69	0.73	0.70
Greece	0.20	0.38	0.48	1.02	1.03	0.86
TOTAL III	12.13	14.78	14.37	15.76	15.08	15.67
TOTAL I + III	24.72	29.98	29.96	30.84	33.26	32.19

(a) All commodity imports as a percentage of French non-EC trade.

Source: DNSCE, Own computations.

protection enjoyed by these exports to France. Third, the growth of the French imports from the main EC competitors of LDCs (Italy, Greece, Portugal and Spain) is similar to the growth of the trade with the LDCs growing the most rapidly: indeed the share of the three Mediterranean European countries joining the EC (Greece, Portugal and Spain) has been increasing at a similar rate as the share of Northern Africa and of export oriented Asia (NICs).

In order to investigate possible bias against LDCs exports to France this paper provides quantitative estimates of the French system of protection during the last decade (2). The paper is organized as follows. In a second section the tariff protection is examined under two different points of view: nominal tariffs and "implicit" tariffs (i.e. tariffs measured such that specific distortions against the LDCs exports towards France can be fully revealed if existing). The main result of this first approach is that EC tariffs undoubtedly discriminate against LDCs when applied to French imports. The third and fourth sections face the difficult non-tariff barriers (NTBs) problem by considering respectively non-tariff protection at the French borders and French non-border protection. It can be argued that NTBs are more suited to protect against imports from other developed countries than against imports from LDCs because NTBs offer a better control on imports of differentiated goods which are close substitutes to the domestic ones (as often between developed countries) and because NTBs make retaliations from the exporting countries more difficult and therefore more costly and unlikely. The results of Sections 3 and 4 however suggest that the observed discrimination against LDCs exports due to tariff protection would not be offset by non-tariff and non-border protection so that French protection would seem ultimately to discriminate against LDCs exports.

2.   TARIFF PROTECTION

Since the successive Trade Rounds of the 60s and 70s tariffs are generally considered to be too low to represent substantial barriers to trade. This view rests upon data on duties and imports which are aggregated over all goods. However the full logic of tariff protection against LDCs can only be grasped when inserted in the following dynamic perspective: LDCs have to face the highest tariffs for the goods for which they are expected (or are in the process) to become more and more competing with domestic producers of industrial countries. In other words, any tariff structure, even if it looks free trade oriented at a given period of time because it is full of zero tariff rates for goods in which LDCs currently have no or massive comparative advantages, (3) is conservative in the sense that it tends to freeze existing specialization between trade partners and to inhibit changes in existing specialization. Such a dynamic perspective is particularly crucial for EC state members - like France - which are the closest competitors of the NICs among the EC members. Indeed the EC Common External Tariff gives good examples of our argument: its highest rates are in textiles and cars (around 10%), electronics (14%) and apparel (15%), all industries booming in LDCs and NICs and representing 25.5% and 28.2% of the French manufacturing output in 1974 and 1984 respectively. Definitively such tariff rates cannot be qualified as negligible.

The fact that tariffs of EC countries are decided at Brussels does not mean that a study at the member state level is not meaningful. Indeed EC member states constantly keep close control over the evolution of the Common External Tariff. A good illustration of this point is the recent changes in the tariff rate decided for VCRs and electronical components: these "European" decisions closely reflect the suggestions made by Thomson (for not talking about Philips) and the French (and Dutch) Government.

2.1 **Nominal tariff protection**

Table 10.2 shows average tariff rates for French imports in 1974, 1979, 1981 and 1984. These rates are "aggregated sectoral" rates since they are computed for each industrial sector by dividing duties collected at all rates by total imports (i.e. dutiable as well as non-dutiable since our data didn't allow to distinguish between them) entered at all rates. Basic data are provided by the French Customs Office and they are available for given sets of countries and groups of industrial sectors. In what follows these sectors will be presented according to the French Standard Industrial Classification, mostly under the relatively aggregated version (NAP 40). Four different sets of countries will be distinguished: EC countries, OECD non-EC countries, French Franc Zone (mainly African countries) and the Rest of the World. In what follows we will consider the OECD non-EC countries as representing the DCs and the Rest of the World as representing the LDCs. (4)

These DCs and LDCs zones are not totally homogeneous in terms of preferential arrangements because France is imbricated in a complex network of preferential arrangements (5) as illustrated by the French Customs Books which exhibits no less than eleven basic trade zones.(6) It is easy to understand that these agreements can easily influence imports even if they don't directly deal with imports because often trade partners strongly insist on bilateral trade balance.

Table 10.2 provides three interesting results. (7) First, tariffs imposed on LDCs exports are now higher than those applied to DCs. That confirms a similar result found by Balassa and Balassa (1984) at the EC level. (8) Second, relative distortions against LDCs exports to France are concentrated in few industries and are high: glass, electronics, textiles and clothing, leather and shoes (except in 1984), wood and miscellaneous (toys and musical instruments) industries. On the other hand relative distortions against DCs exports towards France are small and disseminated over many industries. It is interesting to note that the "excess" tariffs imposed on LDCs exports (i.e. the differences between tariffs on LDCs exports and tariffs on DCs exports of the same goods) are significantly and positively correlated to the ratio of LDCs over DCs French imports. (9) Third, distortions against LDCs exports to France arose since 1980. As is well known, a consequence of the successive Trade Rounds is that tariff barriers between industrialized countries are decreased further than those between DCs and LDCs: our results suggest that the EC GSP was not sufficiently powerful for counterweighting this evolution and stopping the deterioration of the relative situation of LDCs with respect to DCs in terms of tariff protection. (10)

2.2 "Implicit" tariff protection

Warr and Lloyd (1982) developed a new concept of protection by focusing on the following point: a given exporter will be more or less harmed by a given tariff structure when it is more or less specialized in exports on which high tariff rates are imposed by the importing country. Warr and Lloyd call "indirect" discrimination this

Table 10.2: Tariff Protection at the French Borders

Industries (b)	in percentages (a) Developed countries (c)				Less Developed Countries (c)				LDC/DC Import Ratio (1984)
	1974	1979	1981	1984	1974	1979	1981	1984	
T07. Steel	2.5	1.6	1.0	0.9	1.0	1.8	1.4	1.8	0.40
T08. Non-ferrous ind.	0.7	0.6	0.8	0.5	0.0	0.0	0.1	0.3	0.90
T09. Stones, Ceramics	1.7	1.0	1.2	0.9	0.4	0.9	0.8	0.8	0.81
T10. Glass	7.0	4.4	4.1	3.9	9.7	8.2	6.9	6.3	0.21
T11. Basic chemicals	4.9	2.7	2.2	1.7	2.0	1.8	2.0	1.6	0.29
T12. Pharmaceuticals	7.7	5.2	5.0	3.8	3.5	3.0	1.7	1.2	0.09
T13. Foundries	4.6	2.8	3.0	3.1	5.5	4.5	3.6	2.8	0.30
T14. Machine Equipment	4.9	3.3	3.2	4.6	6.5	3.4	2.2	3.0	0.11
T15. Electronics	5.9	5.1	4.9	4.4	6.8	5.7	6.2	4.5	0.19
T16. Cars	5.0	4.3	4.3	4.0	4.9	3.9	3.3	3.0	0.12
T17. Aircraft, Ships	0.3	0.3	0.2	0.2	0.1	0.1	0.1	0.1	0.09
T18. Textile, Clothing	6.4	4.4	4.5	3.1	5.8	6.4	6.5	5.1	1.56
T19. Leather, Shoes	4.1	3.2	3.5	9.7	4.2	5.7	6.8	5.8	2.00
T20. Wood, Miscellaneous	2.9	2.0	2.0	1.7	2.5	3.0	3.2	3.0	0.61

Table 10.2: continued

Industries (b)	in percentages (a) Developed countries (c)				Less Developed Countries (c)				LDC/DC Import Ratio (1984)
	1974	1979	1981	1984	1974	1979	1981	1984	
T21. Paper, Cardboard	3.9	2.7	2.0	0.6	2.2	1.2	0.9	0.7	0.09
T22. Printing	1.5	1.8	1.9	1.6	1.2	0.5	0.4	0.4	0.19
T23. Rubber, Plastics	7.7	4.8	4.6	7.5	5.0	4.1	3.4	23.6	0.20
All Manufacturing (d)	3.7	3.2	3.0	3.1	2.2	3.1	3.2	3.3	0.35

Notes:
(a) Average tariff rates (%) for each item. See text.
(b) French Standard Industrial Classification "NAP 40". (See the Annex).
(c) For the definition of DCs and LDCs see text.
(d) i.e. from T07 to T23.

Source: DNSCE, Own calculations.

way of looking at tariffs which focuses on the "adequacy" between tariff structure of the importer and specialization structure of the exporting partner. Such "indirect" discrimination gives rise to "implicit" tariff protection against the different trade partners. Warr and Lloyd suggested an index for measuring this implicit tariff protection. (11) By using this index we estimated the level of protection a given exporter towards France has to face, given the French-EC tariff structure and the export structure of this exporting country.

Table 10.3 shows the values of the Warr-Lloyd index for different sets of exporters to France and for several years between 1974 and 1982. The highest rates are systematically imposed to export oriented Asia and to a lesser extent to Northern Africa and Southern Europe since the second half of the seventies. A second interesting point is the relative situation of Japan and the United States: the results clearly suggest that the EC tariff system applied on French import structure discriminates against Japan in contrast to the USA.

Table 10.3: Nominal Rates of French Implicit Tariff Protection, in percentages (a)

	1974	1976	1978	1980	1982
Northern Africa	2.7	3.9	3.3	3.4	3.7
Export-Oriented Asia	5.5	5.4	3.7	4.6	4.5
Other LDC (Low Income)					
Africa	1.4	1.5	1.5	1.2	1.2
Southern Asia	3.8	3.7	3.0	4.1	4.0
Other LDC (High Inc.)					
South-East Asia	1.7	2.3	2.1	2.4	3.0
Latin America	2.1	2.3	2.4	1.9	1.7
Southern Europe	3.5	4.4	3.5	3.4	3.8
Developed Countries					
Japan	3.6	4.6	3.4	4.3	4.2
United States	4.0	3.9	2.8	3.1	3.1

(a)   see text for the definition of 'implicit' tariff protection and the method of calculating the percentages (especially footnote 11).

Source: DNSCE. Own computations.

All these results confirm evidence that the French-EC tariffs try to harm more the "rising" competitors than the old-established economies.

3. NON-TARIFF BARRIERS AT THE BORDERS

It is important to note that information in this section is different by nature from what it is in section 2. While section 2 provides a precise identification of tariffs and the corresponding value of the granted protection, this section deals only with an attempted identification of existing NTBs at the borders. No estimate of the value of the protection granted can be directly drawn from this collected information. Indeed some of the identified NTBs may have no restrictive effects at all on French imports: NTBs "inefficacy" is a possibility which has always to be kept in mind in this section.

3.1 **NTBs creation as a result of contradictory bureaucratic behaviour**

French bureaus continuously hesitate between two contradictory behaviours concerning non-tariff protection at the borders. On the one hand the desire of more power pushes them to consider any new field of action with sympathy: new forms of protection are then welcome. On the other hand costs of enforcing protectionist measures as well as some reluctance to become a too close friend of the French industry (and to appear as being "a captured regulator") induce French bureaus to limit the scope of their actions.

In other words, and contrary to the well defined tariff protection, protection through NTBs at the borders has upper and lower bounds which are in line with one of these two behaviors. Non-tariff protection moves around within these two limits according to the political and economic forces at the national and international levels. (12) A good overview of the NTBs at the borders cannot therefore be given by one measure. To give separate estimates of the upper and lower bounds of the bureaucracy willingness to impose and enforce NTBs looks then to be the more appropriate approach.

Table 10.4: NTBs at the French Borders, in percentages (e)

Industries (a)	Import quota coverage (b) Z.1 (e)	Z.2 (e)	All zones (e)(f)	Sensitive imports (c) DC (g)	LDC (g)	DC+LDC (e)	Nogués et al. (d) DC	LDC
T04. Coal	35.5	44.8	100.0					
T05. Oil	42.5	34.7	89.7				78.2(h)	78.1(h)
T06. Electricity	100.0		100.0					
T07. Steel		5.2	5.4	40.9	20.9	31.6	78.1	35.1
T08. Non ferrous ind.				5.8	0.8	4.2		
T09. Stones, Ceramics		1.8	2.6	13.1	7.8	7.8		
T10. Glass				14.3	3.9	4.0		
T11. Basic chemicals	4.3	0.7	5.2	16.6	12.5	16.3		
T12. Pharmaceuticals	1.0	0.1	1.1	7.9	10.3	8.1		
T13. Foundries		0.2	0.2	44.4	38.6	43.4		
T14. Machine Equip	4.7	3.0	7.9	25.4	31.6	26.3	42.8	35.5
T15. Electronics	11.9	5.9	18.0	54.2	24.1	49.8		
T16. Cars	21.5	6.0	27.6	8.0	3.3	7.5	45.6	29.0
T17. Aircraft, Ships							21.9	64.6
T18. Textile, Clothing	33.1	12.4	52.8	22.7	26.6	24.9		
T19. Leather, Shoes				72.5	74.5	73.3	0.3	11.3
T20. Wood, Miscellaneous	0.6		0.9	22.4	27.2	26.2		

Table 10.4 continued

Industries (a)	Import quota coverage (b)			Sensitive imports (c)			Nogués et al. (d)	
	Z.1 (e)	Z.2 (e)	All zones (e)(f)	DC (g)	LDC (g)	DC+LDC (e)	DC	LDC
T21. Paper, Cardboard	35.1	0.1	35.6	65.3	86.7	66.9		
T22. Printing	11.7	0.2	0.2	0.0	0.0	0.0		
T23. Rubber, Plastics				2.7	0.7	2.4		
All Manufacturing (i)	9.1	3.2	13.1	28.4	22.2	26.7	25.0	33.0
All industries (j)	23.6	17.0	46.7					

Notes:
(a) French Standard Industrial Classification "NAP 40" (see the Annex).
(b) For the definition of official quotas see text.
(c) For the definition of "sensitive" imports see text.
(d) See Table 4C in Nogués et al. (1985).
(e) Imports under quotas or sensitive imports as a percentage of non-EC imports for each sector.
(f) For Zones 1 to 4. Quotas in steel roughly estimated to 66%.
(g) For the definition of DCs and LDCs see text.
(h) Figures for "all fuels".
(i) From T07 to T23.
(j) From T04 to T23.

Sources: DNSCE, DREE, Journaux Officiels, Nogués et al., own computations.

303

3.2 The lower bound estimate: official import quotas

Lists of the official import quotas ("produits contingentes a l'importation") are regularly published in the "Journal Officiel" by the French authorities. (13) Such lists undoubtedly provide a good estimate of the lower bound of the French NTBs at the borders. Since the 30s and until very recently French governments didn't largely resort to NTBs at the borders other than quotas: (14) in their Table 2c Nogués, Olechowski and Winters (1985) show that quantitative restrictions in 1983 still represent 83% of the level of protection achieved through NTBs (47.2% over 57.1%) in France against 53% for the whole EC (11.8% over 22.3%). The EC "Journal Officiel" (1982) in which are published all the national import quotas officially recognized by the EC Commission shows that France kept 122 national quotas versus 65 for the UK and 31 for Germany (but 127 for Italy which is the closest EC member to France and Greece in these matters): more importantly 47 of these 122 French import quotas concern commodities which are not subject to such restriction by any other EC member state.

French import quotas are not specified country by country but instead by groups of countries called "zones de liberation". We are essentially interested here in two of the four "zones de liberation" defined by the French Customs, namely zones 1 and 2. (15) Zone 1 covers the OEEC (the OECD predecessor) and therefore includes mainly Canada, the United States and most of the Western European countries with most of their colonial dependencies, at that time. Zone 2 covers all the other countries of the world belonging to GATT. Quotas imposed on the imports coming from Zone 1 are also imposed on the imports from Zone 2 which is subject to additional restrictions: in other words the French quota system is by construction biased against the past and current NICs and LDCs since Zone 2 includes such countries in particular. Moreover for some goods (textiles, clothing and electronics) some countries belonging to Zone 1 are now classified in Zone 2 which means an increasing bias of the French import quota system against the NICs-LDCs. (16)

Estimates of the lower bound of NTBs imposed on Zone 1 (Zone 2) are obtained by dividing imports from Zone 1 (Zone 2) under quota by the total non-EC imports for each industry (specified in NAP 40) including the items under quota: (17) these results are reported in the "Z.1" ("Z.2") column of Table 10.4. Estimates of the coverage of the French quotas for all the zones which are computed by dividing the sum of the four zones imports under quota again by the non-EC imports for each industry are also given.

As shown by Table 10.4 French official import quotas roughly concern 13% of the French total non-EC manufactured imports and 47% if energy is added to the manufacturing sector. (18) Such figures can be considered as the "hard bottom" of the French non-tariff protection at the borders although quotas on steel products are not included since they are not officially published at the EC or French levels (according to most of the sources these steel import quotas would cover two-thirds of French non-EC imports at least).

Tariff discrimination against LDCs exports appears reinforced by import quotas. As the French quota system is biased against Zone 2 which mainly comprises NICs and LDCs, imports subject to quota represent 33% of the total imports from Zone 1 (mainly industrialized countries) against 53% for Zone 2. (19) Secondly, quotas appear to be concentrated in LDCs traditional industries (energy and textiles) and NICs-LDCs "sunrise" sectors (steel and electronics) as well. Thirdly, French bureaus systematically favor domestic producers when acting as importers against any other kind of importers (the so-called "preference pour l'industriel") in quota allowance procedures.

3.3 The upper bound: "sensitive" imports

Lists of so-called "sensitive" imports are jointly established by several French bureaus interested in foreign trade among which Direction des Relations Economiques Exterieures (DREE) is the most influential. Such lists are based on two criteria. The first one is rather mechanical since it refers to import pressures during the last years as measured by penetration ratios. The second criterion is more flexible since it refers to the rather vague concept of the "strategic" value of the industry. These two criteria lead to interpret these lists as showing the largest scope for future potential bureaucratic interventions on imports: the first criterion because penetration ratios are the most usual tool of the mercantilist approach, the second one because it gives the necessary degree of freedom to the bureaus for reacting to pressure groups and picking up the industries they want to "help". Lists of "sensitive" imports indicate therefore all the products the French bureaus agree to be ready for considering potential "trade actions", and represent therefore the best estimates of the upper bound of French bureaucratic actions through all kinds of NTBs. (20) Sensitive imports are identified at the most detailed level (NAP 600) of the French Industrial Classification by the bureaus concerned. Sensitive items (for DCs and LDCs separately) were aggregated at our usual level of classification (NAP 40) and then divided by the corresponding total imports of each corresponding industry for DCs and LDCs separately.

Results are presented in Table 10.4. (21) Imports considered as "sensitive" by French bureaucracy in 1981-82 concern 28.4% of the total French manufactured imports from DCs (OECD nonEC countries) and 22.2% of the total French imports coming from LDCs (agriculture, energy, aircraft, ships and armament are not included in these two estimates). This result is interesting because it is the first time French protectionism seems to hurt imports from DCs more than imports from LDCs. However it has to be underlined that this protection differential is largely related to two sectors only (steel and electronics) and concerns a protectionist instrument which can be considered as weak (since it is from a "surveillance" kind) as it follows two powerful protectionist instruments (tariffs and quotas).

Our "upper bound" estimates show potential expansion of NTBs considered by the French bureaus and therefore are conceptually close to what the UNCTAD inventory would describe as "surveillance" measures. Comparisons between our estimates and the estimates of Nogués, Olechowski and Winters (1985) which are reported in Table 10.4 as well show convergence of the two sets of estimates with four exceptions: cars, shoes, wood and paper. The reason is that NTBs examined in this section are exclusively imposed at the borders while NTBs of Nogués et al. take into account NTBs which are directly imposed on domestic markets.

3.4 French NTBs at the intra-EC borders

The efficacy of all the NTBs described first depends on how different are protection levels granted by other EC member states: French nontariff protection could be ineffective and only generate traffic distortions if other EC members are significantly less protectionist than France. To measure possible gaps between different EC member states' protection would require a separate study. Second the efficacy of French non-tariff protection depends on the existence of French protection at the intra-EC borders. Under the Treaty of Rome this protection can only consist of NTBs at the intra-EC borders or of non-border protection. Leaving non-border protection for the next section we want to investigate now if French NTBs at the intra-EC borders exist.

The Treaty of Rome and the "adhesion" treaties signed when new member states joined the EC give two instruments for "managing" intra-EC trade: the safeguard clause and Article 115. The safeguard clause which is banned by the Treaty but authorized by some "adhesion" treaties is scarcely used. However it has to be noticed that France was the first country to use such a clause vis-a-vis Greece in 1981 freezing French imports of Greek cotton at the level of 1980 with a "reasonable margin of growth".

Much more important is Article 115 according to which an EC member state can be authorized to introduce some kind of "surveillance" on intra-EC trade flows when it can prove that commodities under quotas penetrate its domestic market under the umbrella of the intra-EC preference. Use of Article 115 can lead to a freeze of intra-EC trade of the goods considered. It is initiated by the EC member state concerned but it requires the agreement from the EC Commission. Table 10.5 gives a complete record of all the French demands and of all the actions accepted by the EC Commission under this article between 1981 and 1984. A correct interpretation of the use of Article 115 by French authorities requires a comparison between the commodities under quotas given in Table 10.4 and the goods under Article 115.

Three groups of goods can be distinguished. First there are goods under French national quotas with no use of Article 115: energy, steel, basic chemicals, aircraft-ship-armament, paper and printing. For this first group there clearly are alternative solutions to Article 115 which are less visible and risky than the use of Article 115: it is non-border protection for energy and aircraft-ship-armament, cartellized production and trade quotas under the EC Commission umbrella for steel (22), "cooperative" behaviours of few firms and public authorities for basic chemicals, paper and printing. The second group of goods concern industries under French national quotas with a massive use of Article 115: machine equipment, electrical-

Table 10.5: The French Use of Article 115 (1981-1984)

Industries		in numbers (a)							
		Actions engaged (a)				Actions accepted (a)			
		1981	1982	1983	1984	1981	1982	1983	1984
T14. Machine Equip. Clocks (quartz)	DC	0	0	0	1	0	0	0	1
	LDC	0	3	2	9	0	2	2	9
T15. Electronics, of which Radio-sets	DC	2	2	2	2	2	2	2	2
	LDC	7	5	6	6	7	4	6	5
TV-sets	DC	3	3	3	1	3	3	1	0
	LDC	2	4	2	0	2	3	1	0
Others	DC	2	0	3	1	0	0	0	0
	LDC	0	0	0	0	0	0	0	0
T18. Textile, Clothing Textile Group 1	DC	0	0	0	0	0	0	0	0
	LDC	35	44	43	29	25	35	29	22
Textile Group 2	DC	0	0	0	0	0	0	0	0
	LDC	43	31	21	9	30	21	12	4
Umbrellas	DC	0	0	0	0	0	0	0	0
	LDC	5	3	3	1	4	3	3	1
T.20 Wood and Others (toys)	DC	2	4	2	0	2	3	0	0
	LDC	6	12	7	0	5	9	1	0
Total	DC	9	9	10	5	7	8	3	3
	LDC	98	102	84	54	73	77	54	41

(a) numbers refer to cases of actions engaged and accepted, respectively.

Source: Own computations.

electronic equipment, wood and others (toys). In these industries no cheap alternative to Article 115 exists and indeed the use of Article 115 is concentrated on French national quotas since for all the observed cases Article 115 is used for goods belonging to the 47 commodities for which France is the only one EC member state to impose quotas. (23) The third group of goods to be examined are commodities under EC quotas, i.e. mainly textiles and apparel under MFA. As well known these quotas are officially negotiated by the EC Commission for the whole EC and they are split between the different EC member states which are fictitiously considered as EC "regions". In this third case the use of Article 115 is more a matter of legality than a tool of economic substance. Some evidence can be drawn from the textile products of Group I (MFA categories 1 to 9) since they represent a high share (40 to 50%) of the French actions under Article 115. For each of these nine MFA categories EC quotas allocated to France in 1983 represent (on the average in 1983 for instance) 11% of the total EC quotas for each category (except for category 4 where the share is 21%). These relatively stable shares over time have to be compared with the share of the French GNP in the EC GNP (roughly 18%) which is generally used as a yardstick for such type of "burden sharing". It can then reasonably be argued that the use of Article 115 reflects more the implementation of a French specific trade policy within the EC framework than a purely legalistic implementation of the EC trade policy concerning textiles.

To' summarize, Article 115 appears to be substantially (if not totally) used by the French authorities as a "legal" NTB at the intraEC borders. (24) Table 10.5 shows that LDCs are much more concerned by Article 115 than DCs, especially since the only DC country harmed by Article 115 is Japan, i.e. a former NIC. This conclusion follows from two facts. Only 10% of the demands concern DCs. There is some evidence of a deliberate French policy of "harassment" for some goods and countries, as for instance for clocks, radios and TV sets coming from Pacific Asia. (25)

Finally it can be briefly mentioned that partial inquiries by two independent private bodies (The European Council of American Chambers of Commerce (1985) and "Industriradet" (1985), the Danish Council of Industry) interestingly suggest that France is one of the massive users of NTBs on intra-EC trade since she is the most frequently mentioned both for border delays (12 times over 34 cases versus 8 times for UK and 7 times for Italy the immediate followers) and for technical barriers at the borders (such as certificates of origin, requirements concerning extensive use of French, compliance with technical standards, environmental regulations, national price controls, etc.) (13 times over 42 cases versus 11 times for Italy and 6 times for UK). Still, interestingly these surveys mention that such NTBs are the most frequent precisely for the industries our general approach picked up: chemicals (cosmetics, raw materials for plastics, cables, hollow fibre dialysers), machines (sawing and drilling), printing, electronic goods (computer products), toys and gifts.

4. NON-BORDER PROTECTION

Instruments of non-border protection are so numerous that a complete overview seems impossible. In addition some of these instruments have a rather ambiguous theoretical status, like for instance export subsidies, the role of which is underlined by the recent economic literature on monopolistic competition with product differentiation and scale economies. Despite these difficulties an overview of the four following key instruments would give a useful glance on French non-border protection: domestic taxes on goods which are not produced domestically, domestic subsidies with special emphasis on export subsidies, public procurements and quotas on domestic sales.

4.1 **Domestic taxes**
No systematic information is available for domestic taxes but three examples will show how important protectionist effects of such taxes can be in the French case. During the last ten years indirect taxes on oil amounted to 50% (fuel for domestic heating) and to 220% (gasoline). Secondly, French indirect taxation on VCRs consists of the highest possible VAT rate (33%) plus a "special" specific tax imposed each year: these taxes together represent roughly 120% of the French retail price of a standard VCR which would be used during five years. The last example is provided by the set of specific taxes on cars which depend on several characteristics of the engine and introduce a systematic and significant bias against some EC car makers. It has to be underlined that two of these three examples concern goods exported by LDCs and "sunrise" industries in

these countries.

4.2 Domestic subsidies

Domestic subsidies are expected to have powerful protectionist impacts. As is well known these subsidies are extremely difficult to estimate and they are likely to be biased towards underestimation because of many reasons: empirical definition of subsidies, constraints due to national accounts and public accounting, special accounting rules for the most subsidized French industries (like shipyards for instance), complex channels for financial aids, bureaucratic tastes for secrecy, lack of knowledge about local financial aids, etc. These usual difficulties are reinforced by two institutional features of the French economy: first, long term contracts between nationalized firms can incorporate potential subsidization of one firm by the other as we shall see later: second, the fact that the banking system is quasi completely nationalized and the particularly complex channelling of "soft" loans makes the use of such soft loans for all purposes especially easy and discrete.

Estimates of public aids to the industry between 1979 and 1981 (26) are reported in Table 10.6 under the form of a percentage of the output (added value) for each industry; they take into account four main types of aids: reliefs of operating costs (including those for labour costs), investment aids, public capital funds granted to firms and public revenues abandoned to firms (among which there are export credits). According to these estimates "successful (for getting subsidies) lameducks" are concentrated in four industries: coal, electricity, steel and aircraft-ship-armament. Two of these industries (steel and ships) being NICs import competing. However these estimates are averages over 1978-1981, i.e. three years characterized by some efforts from the Barre Government to keep under control subsidies as much as possible. Between 1981 and 1985 however the successive French governments were in favour of an "active" industrial policy and didn't hesitate to substantially increase public financial aids to the industry so that the 1978-81 figures in Table 10.6 are likely to be underestimates. Tentative updated estimates are therefore provided for the period 1982-1984, at least for the most subsidized industries. Needless to say these updated estimates are not perfectly similar to the preceding ones but they are sufficiently close for the common year

Table 10.6: French Non Border Protection: Some Facts (1979-84)

Industries	Domestic Subsidies (a)	(b)	Export Subsidies (c)	Public Procure- ments (d)	Nationalized Firms (e)	(f)
T04. Coal	53.0	60.0			99.3	99.4
T05. Oil	1.5	nsc			39.7	0.1
T06. Electricity	11.7	nsc			88.8	99.8
T07. Steel	34.0	38.0	1.9		56.5	60.0
T08. Non-ferrous ind.	3.0	nsc			60.2	66.6
T09. Stones, Ceramics	1.0	nsc			10.9	22.6
T10. Glass	2.0	nsc			34.7	26.2
T11. Basic chemicals	3.0	nsc			48.8	50.7
T12. Pharmaceuticals	1.0	nsc			14.6	16.5
T13. Foundries	1.0	nsc	1.2		10.3	16.1
T14. Machine Equip.	2.0	4.0	1.7	7.4	11.8	11.2
T15. Electronics	3.0	10.0	1.8	30.0	28.1	33.6
T16. Cars	2.0	5.0	1.4		31.4	36.4
T17. Aircraft, Ships	20.0	40.0	7.0	45.0	70.3	72.7
T18. Textile, Clothing	2.0	5.0			0.8	1.5
T19. Leather, Shoes	1.5	nsc			0.0	0.0
T20. Wood, Miscellaneous	1.5	nsc			1.2	2.1

Table 10.6 continued

Industries	Domestic Subsidies (a)	(b)	Export Subsidies (c)	Public Procure- ments (d)	Nationalized Firms (e)	(f)
T21. Paper, Cardboard	3.0	nsc			7.6	12.3
T22. Printing	2.0	nsc			0.3	0.6
T23. Rubber Plastics	1.0	nsc	0.3		6.8	8.6
Total Manufacturing	5.0	6.0	1.5	15.7	22.5	32.1

Sources and Notes:
(a) As a % of value added (1979–81). Source: Dutailly (1984).
(b) As a % of value added (1982–84), nsc: no significant change. Source see text.
(c) As a % of value added (1978–81). Source: Messerlin (1986a).
(d) As a % of value added (1980). Source: Ponssard and de Pouvourville (1982).
(e) As a % of value added (1979). Source: Ministere de l'Industrie (1982).
(f) As a % of total exports (1979). Source: Ministere de l'Industrie (1982).

313

available (1982) for authorizing interesting comparisons. Subsidies heavily increased in seven sectors between 1982 and 1985: coal, steel, machine tools (essentially due to the consequences of the bankruptcy of Creusot-Loire), electronics, carmakers, textile and clothing, and last but not least aircraft-ship-armament (keeping apart armament, the proportion of subsidies to the value added appears to be close to 40% for aircraft and to 50% for ships). (27) In addition to these seven industries three other industrial sectors benefited from increasing state generosity although to a lesser extent: chemicals (because of nationalized firms in difficulty: CdF-Chimie and EMC), wood and paper (Berger, 1985).

Seven of these ten happy few "successful lameducks" can be easily considered as competing with the LDCs and NICs exports: steel, electronic goods, cars, textiles and clothing, ships, chemicals and wood. In other words the protectionist bias against LDCs seems to have been recently increased.

4.3 Export subsidies

Export subsidies play a crucial role in the French system of public aids to industry: the subsidy equivalent of medium and long-term export credits represents one fourth of the total subsidies to the manufacturing sector between 1979 and 1981. It is then useful to give estimates separate from all the other domestic subsidies. As the Dutailly's estimates of export subsidies are not available we give our own estimates in Table 10.6 in terms of the value added. (28)

The main sectors concerned by export credits can't be systematically considered as competing with LDCs traditional exports. But they are certainly competing with NICs sunrise industries: indeed export subsidies are mainly granted to supposingly infant industries while the other domestic subsidies look more specialized in mature industries. However, it is interesting to note that if French export subsidies hurt LDCs competing industries they tend also to mechanically favour some LDCs industries using goods produced by the subsidized French industries as inputs.

4.4 Public Procurements, Quotas on Domestic Sales and Nationalized Firms

Public procurements are the third important instrument of non-border protection: for 1980 they are estimated to 92 billions of francs, i.e. 15% of the total state budget or 16% of the total value added of the manufacturing sector (excluding energy). Table 10.6 gives the few estimates available by industry except for two manufacturing industries (oil and paper) where public procurements are substantial but where no information is available for splitting the total value of these procurements among these sectors. (29) Again figures are given as a percentage of value added for making comparisons easier with other nonborder protection instruments. The general feeling from these estimates is that public procurements are completing what domestic and export subsidies begin to do: they concern the same industries as those protected by subsidies; they restrict the French demand of the goods concerned and distort the remaining demand in favour of domestic firms the supply of which is artificially expanded by subsidies.

The last instrument of nonborder protection consists of quotas imposed on sales on the French markets. To our knowledge such quotas are so far limited to very few cases. The only significant one concerns the sales of Japanese cars in France which are limited to 3% of the total car sales on the French market. (30) However it has to be underlined that some bureaus at the French Ministry of External Trade recently appeared to be in favour of a more systematic use of such quotas: so far these suggestions were not seriously considered by the French governments. (31)

French nonborder protection (and particularly public procurements and quotas on domestic sales) cannot be fully described without some measure of the importance of the nationalized firms in domestic production and exports. Some appraisal of the role of the public sector is necessary for two reasons. First the public procurement policy has a natural extension in long-term contracts between nationalized firms. It can be argued that corresponding long term contracts which mainly involve firms operating as energy producers or consumers can be observed in other countries. However, the point is that the French public authorities exert pressures on such contracts and don't hesitate to introduce some kind of subsidization of one firm by the other, as for instance in the contract between Electricité de France and Charbonnages de France. Secondly, no French government would hesitate to use non-border protection in order to help nationalized firms under increasing import pressures. Table 10.6 provides the shares of nationalized firms exports in the total (EC and non-EC) French exports and the share of nationalized firms outputs in value added by industry. (32)

It can be noticed that non-border protection and nationalized firms are concentrated in the same industries as before: energy, steel, basic chemicals, electronic goods, cars and aircraft-ship-armament. (33) Such a result can be hardly considered as a surprise since in France national-ization has two main motives: either to solve problems of senile industries which lose money or to build "national champions" in infant industries. Obviously these two motives have direct references to protection against foreign competition.

4.5 Again the bias against LDCs exports

To summarize, non-border protection creates may be the most serious obstacle to freer trade in France, as in other industrialized countries presumably. This third kind of protection seems again to hurt more LDCs than DCs exports for two reasons although it is probably not specially designed for achieving such a result.

First, it seems clear that a substantial part of non-border protection (domestic subsidies, indirect taxes, quotas on domestic sales) is devoted to protect industries where NICs are now efficient producers (steel, basic chemicals, electronics, cars and textiles and clothing) while the other part (export credits and public procurements) tends to inhibit potential growth of new industries (equipment goods and electronics) in LDCs by artificially increasing French production and decreasing French demand. Secondly, non-border protection appears to be much more difficult to be overcome by LDCs than by DCs: EC state members can use the Treaty of Rome (EC Court of Justice) for limiting the effects of such a protection; the United States and Japan can use their bargaining power and retaliating possibilities; it remains then few DCs and all the NICs or LDCs which have no powerful means for reducing the impacts of such a protection on their exports.

Notes

I would like to thank Carl Hamilton, Mike Finger, Jacob Kol, Loet Mennes, Jean Waelbroeck and all the participants at the Workshop on "European Trade Policies and the South", The Hague, 13-14 September 1985, for helpful comments on earlier drafts. I would also like to thank S. Becuwe for helpful research assistance.

1. For greater detail see Neme (1985), Roy (1984) and Brochart (1985). This evolution seems mainly due to the fact that over the period considered changes in tariffs favored more heavily ACP countries located in Latin America or in English-speaking African than French-speaking African countries which benefited from bilateral agreements and the first Lome Conventions.

2. To our knowledge no such work has been done before. Bobe's study (1983) stressed the mechanisms of French protection rather than presenting quantitative estimates of the French barriers to international trade.

3. These low rates are mostly granted for limited amounts of imports because of quotas free of tariffs.

4. The NAP 40 contains 1 item for agriculture, 2 for food industries, 3 for energy, 17 for manufacturing activities and the rest for services while the most disaggregated level (NAP 800) contains some 300 industrial sectors. The Annex presents a rough correspondence table between NAP 40 and ISIC to two digits.

5. See Wolf (1987) for an acute analysis of the preferences policy of the EC and its effects on the world trade system. The main preferential agreements involving France are the following ones. First EC and EFTA form a free-trade zone for most of the goods. Secondly, the EC developed its GSP as early as 1971 and incorporated the British, Danish and Irish GSPs in its own system after 1974. In 1984 no less than 127 independent states and 22 non-independent territories benefited from the EC GSP which is a unilateral trade convention granted by the EC to LDCs. However only 56 (among them China, Romania and Yugoslavia) of these 127 countries are really concerned by the EC GSP since all the other states benefit from other preferential agreements. Among these 71 other states 64 belong to the so-called ACP (African-Caribbean-Pacific) zone and benefit from the Lome III Convention which is a more favourable trade treaty negotiated between the EC

and these 64 independent countries which are generally former European colonies. The 7 remaining states (all located in the Mediterranean area) enjoy bilateral trade arrangements with the EC. In addition to these EC agreements many countries in the world have signed direct bilateral agreements with France which can have substantial impacts on trade relationships since they deal with financial operations, French investments, export credits and French public aid. For instance 40% of the ACP countries and most of the Mediterranean countries benefit from such bilateral agreements. Moreover some of these agreements concern crucial trade flows such as oil (with Algeria or Gabon) or armament (France is the third world exporter of arms). For more details on all the trade-related agreements between France and LDCs, see Cadenat (1983) and Nguyen-Duy-Tan (1985).

6. The eleven zones are the following: TEC (Common External Tariff), GSP (reduced duties and/or quotas free of tariffs), ACP (and other territories known as PTOMA), Greece and Turkey, Maghreb, Israel, Spain, EFTA and Faroe Isles, Cyprus, Machrak, Malta and Yugoslavia. Because we use data allowing only to distinguish between DCs (OECD nonEC countries) and LDCs our results can't catch all the effects of this complex set of agreements: for instance LDCs regroup countries benefiting from Lomé Convention with the socialist countries and all the other LDCs, some of them benefiting from the EC GSP.

7. Average tariff rates given in Table 10.2 are systematic underestimates of the tariff protection since duties levied are divided by all imports some of which are benefiting from preferences and not only by the imports supporting these duties.

8. As Balassa and Balassa (1984) weighted tariffs by imports, they were able to exclude nondutiable imports.

9. The equation tested gives: X 0.71(-1.66) + 1.54(2.98)Y, R2=0.37 where X represents the tariff differentials and Y the import ratios for 1981 and where the figures in parenthesis (.) are t-statistics.

10. However, when a more detailed classification (NAP 600) of the goods is used, some nuances can be introduced. On the one hand for a selection of 86 industries with LDCs export shares of more than 5 per cent of all French nonEC imports average tariff rates were quite stable for the imports coming from the DCs but doubled for the corresponding imports from the LDCs between 1974 and

1984. On the other hand average tariff rates exhibit a stable dispersion for LDCs in 1974 and 1984 while the dispersion of the corresponding rates for the DCs exports to France increased between 1974 and 1984. As Nugent (1974) showed that for a given tariff average the protective effect of tariffs is the higher, the greater is their dispersion, the observed changes in the dispersion of the tariffs imposed on imports from DCs and LDCs suggest that unfavourable evolution for LDCs exports is entirely mirrored by the changes in average tariff rates while a good appreciation of the corresponding evolution for DCs exports would require consideration concentration among tariffs.

11.   This index is defined as "the weighted sum of nominal rates of protection for various commodities with the weights reflecting for each trading partner the proportion of the value of its total exports to the importing country which consist of the commodity concerned" (Warr and Lloyd (1982), page 14). It can therefore be expressed as:

$$t_i \cdot (x_{ij}/X_j)$$

where t_i is the French average tariff rate for the industry i, x_{ij} the exports (towards France) of commodity i by the considered exporting country j and X_j the total exports of this country j towards France. For computing this formula we used "aggregate" average tariff rates for t_i and the export data provided by the French Customs Office (consistent with the import data). The level of disaggregation used for the considered industries is the NAP 100 in order to introduce relatively differentiated tariff rates while keeping a reasonable size to data base.

12.   From the bureaucracy point of view such changing forces introduce an element of uncertainty which may favour the bureaus since it may raise the costs of acting for all the other participants (foreign exporters as well as domestic importers and producers) by more than it raises the costs for bureaus.

13.   French bureaucracy makes subtle distinctions between "contingentements", "quotas" and "VERs". We shall use the word quota for all these different legal statuses.

14.   Since 1982 new trends appear in the French bureaucracy trying to introduce technical norms "à l'allemande" and financial constraints "à l'italienne" on importers.

15.   Zone 3 covers all the socialist countries except

East Germany which is the only one country in Zone 4.

16. There doesn't exist a perfect correspondence between countries of Zone 1 and our DCs on the one hand and countries of Zone 2 and our LDCs on the other hand since definitions of Zones 1 and 2 were dependent upon historical political circumstances. Indeed Zone 1 includes some countries which were dependent territories of the European countries when OEEC was created (like Hong Kong, Macao, Malaysia, Nigeria and Singapore). Similarly correspondence between Zone 2 and LDCs is not perfect since Zone 2 includes three DCs, namely Australia, Japan and New Zealand, in addition to many NICs and LDCs: these three industrialized countries represent one fourth of the Zone 2 exports to France while the LDCs within Zone 2 represent 40% of all the LDCs exports to France. Finally some countries are classified in Zone 2 for some quotas: that is the case for Hong Kong for items 6601, 8515 Aex III and 9703, i.e. three items which the French authorities put systematically under the pressure of Article 115 of the Treaty of Rome as we shall see in Section 4.

17. Import quotas are published by the French bureaus under the form of a four digit tariff classification with additional characters (letters). This procedure which is traditional doesn't help to clarify the situation. Our estimates are based on data established at the four digit level of Nimexe which introduces a systematic bias towards overestimation. However such bias seems to us interesting since it allows us to cover possible "zealous" interpretation by the French bureaus of import quota classification.

18. Computations of import quotas concerning aircraft, ships and armaments (T17) give ratios of roughly 28% for all zones together. Such a ratio looks very low. That can be explained by two reasons: the way military imports are treated in the Customs data and the fact that imports of civil airplanes and ships are blocked by NTBs directly imposed on the domestic market (through technical specifications and public procurement rules). No official import quotas are imposed on steel products (T07) while quotas on cars (T16) are imposed on domestic sales as we shall see in Section 4.

19. These percentages are the ratios of imports under quotas (agricultural products excluded) by the total non-EC imports from the respective zones (agricultural goods included). These figures therefore are not reflected in Table 10.4. This obviously introduces a downward bias. Ratios of

import quotas over domestic demands are sometimes suggested for describing quota coverages in order to circumvent systematic downward biases introduced by considering effective imports under quotas which by definition are lower than the imports which would have existed under free trade, these last ones giving the accurate measure of the protectionist effects of the quotas. However these consumption-import ratios would take into account the evolution of domestic demands which can be a source of difficulties when broad definitions of industries are used and when domestic demands decrease. These two conditions apply precisely to our study.

20. It has to be underlined that the "upper" bound doesn't refer to a precise set of NTBs: consequently French bureaus may well decide to use non-border non-tariff barriers in order to try to stop "sensitive" imports. Such a choice will depend on the preferences of the "dominant" bureaus.

21. In addition to separate estimates for DCs and LDCs Table 10.4 provides the ratio of sensitive imports for both DCs and LDCs as a percentage of total non-EC imports in order to get figures comparable with import quota coverages for all the zones. No figures are provided for energy sectors and for aircraft-ship-armament because trade flows in these industries are already so controlled by French bureaus that additional regulation is hard to imagine. However trade quotas on oil products are changing (decreasing) since December 1985 since now French retailers of gas and fuel can import from non-EC refineries. According to our first rough estimates new percentages will be 31% for DCs and 55% for LDCs.

22. It was argued (Messerlin, 1985) that the Treaty of Paris which is still ruling the European Community of Steel and Coal (ECSC) was not designed to establish a true free trade zone or a true common market. It was rather designed to establish a free trade "en trompe l'oeil" since it introduced the "basing point system" in Europe, imposed investment controls and maintained national trade policies for the ECSC member states, i.e. three measures which favored the "status quo" on the national markets and prohibited any deep specialization. It was relatively easy for the EC Commission to use the Treaty of Paris in order to establish a "managed" trade in steel as complete as possible within the so called Davignon Plans: in 1985 more than 80% of the ECSC steel was under quota systems. It is only since

mid 1985 that the EC Commission is seriously thinking about liberalizing steel trade and production.

23.   Concerning non-MFA goods Article 115 is quasi exclusively used for radio-TV sets (Item 8515 AIII in EC trade and tariff classification), electronic measure instruments (item 9028), quartz clocks (item 9101) and toys (item 9703 A and exB).   Clocks are the best example of harassment. In 1982 Hong Kong was the only one to be hurt but, in 1984, there were Macao, Taiwan, Japan, China, India, Singapore, Philippines and Pakistan.

24.   Since 1981 the EC Commission requires more information for examining a demand for the use of Article 115 and gives no more authorization of freezing intra-EC trade for short periods (one or two months).

25.   French authorities don't seem to engage actions against DCs under Article 115 in order to prove some "commitment" towards these countries. The rate of success (i.e. the number of actions accepted over the demands) recovers less completely from the drop of 1983 for the DCs than for the LDCs.

26.   See Dutailly (1984). Before this study the main other sources were the Parliament Reports on public funds granted to industry. Since 1982 there have been two other special reports one from the Commissariat General du Plan and the other from Direction de la Prevision (published by Le Foll (1985): their results confirm Dutailly's ones.

27.   These last results may appear surprisingly high. They are however confirmed in the shipyard case by observed differentials between production costs of a standard ship built in French and Korean shipyards: French shipyards exhibit costs which represent 284% of the corresponding Korean costs. What is striking is that these cost differentials are not only due to labour cost differentials (660%) but also to intermediate good differentials (168%) (Le Monde, 24.01.1984). For details on subsidies to newly nationalized firms, see Messerlin (1986b).

28.   This ratio is not only useful because it allows direct comparisons with all other instruments of protection but also because it is difficult to argue that subsidies granted to Thomson for exporting sophisticated electronic goods don't serve to finance (by "general equilibrium" effects) Thomson's efforts for producing French VCRs or semi-conductors. For details on export credits, see Messerlin (1986a) and Melitz and Messerlin (1987).

29.   Information of Table 10.6 is based on Ponssard

and de Pouvourville (1982) and on Notes Bleues (several issues). It has to be underlined that information is limited since only public procurements of some importance (more than 10 millions of Francs in Table 10.6) are systematically registered by our sources.

30.   For details on the impacts of this quota, see Messerlin and Becuwe (1985).

31.   For more details on these suggestions, see Nguyen Duy-Tan (1985), p. 107.

32.   Data are drawn from the Ministry of Research and Industry (1982): figures are estimates of the shares in 1978 for all the firms nationalized before and since 1981.

33.   Some more examples are provided by Hager and Taylor (1982).

References

Balassa, Bela and Balassa, Carol (1984), Industrial Protection in the Developed Countries, The World Economy, June (179-196).

Berger, Guy (1985), Faut-il condamner la politique industrielle?, Commentaire, Hiver (1220-1224).

Bobe, Bernard, (1983), Public Assistance to Industries and Trade Policy in France, World Bank Staff Working Papers, No. 570.

Brochart, Françoise (1985), Evaluation des effets de la Convention de Lomé sur les exportations des Etats ACP vers la Communauté Européenne, in Lassudrie-Duchene, Bernard and Reiffers, Jean-Louis, Editors, Le protectionnisme (527-544), Economica (Paris).

Cadenat, M. (1983), La France et le Tiers-Monde: vingt ans de coopération bilaterale, Notes et Etudes documentaires, La Documentation Française, No. 4701-4702.

Dutailly, Jean-Claude (1984), Aides aux entreprises: 134 milliards de francs en 1982, Economie et Statistiques, Septembre (3-12).

European Commission (1982), Official Journal, 9 Fevrier, No. L-35.

European Council of American Chambers of Commerce, (1985), Survey on the Free Movement of Goods within the EC, mimeo.

Hager, Wolfgang et Taylor, Robert (1982), Pratiques et tendances du protectionnisme dans la OEE, European Research Associates.

Industriradet (1985), Industriens eksport og international-
isering, mimeo.
Le Foll, Jean (1985), Les aides publiques à l'industrie:
éléments d'évaluation, Economie et Prevision, No. 70
(7-41).
Melitz, Jacques and Messerlin, Patrick A. (1987), The
Macroeconomic Aspects of Export Subsidies, mimeo.
Messerlin, Patrick A. (1985), Comment on the EC-US Steel
Crisis, in Tsoukalis, Loukas, Editor, Europe, America
and the World Economy, Basil Blackwell.
Messerlin, Patrick A. and Becuwe, Stephane, (1985), French
Trade and Competition Policies in the Car Industry,
Organisation For Economic Co-operation and
Development, Committee of Experts on Restrictive
Business Practices, mimeo.
Messerlin, Patrick A. (1986a), Export-credit Mercantilism,
The World Economy, Vol. 9, No. 4, pp.385-408.
Messerlin, Patrick A. (1986b), The French Industrial Policy,
in Duchene, Francois and Shepherd, Geoffrey, (eds),
Managing Industrial Change in Europe: the Experience
of Germany, France, Italy and the UK, forthcoming.
Ministry of Research and Industry (1982), Le secteur public
dans l'industrie avant et après les nationalisations,
STISI, No. 25.
Neme, Colette (1985), Bilan du système de préférences
généralisées: l'exemple du schéma communautaire, in
Lassudrie-Duchene, Bernard and Reiffers, Jean-Louis,
(eds), Le protectionnisme (545-584), Economica (Paris).
Nogués, Julio J., Olechowski, Andrzej and Winters, L. Alan,
(1985), The Extent of Non-Tariff Barriers to Industrial
Countries Imports, World Bank Discussion Paper,
January, mimeo.
Nguyen Duy-Tan, Joele (1985), Le commerce exterieur de la
France, Notes et Etudes documentaires, La
Documentation Française, No. 4798.
Nugent, Jeffrey (1974), Economic Integration in Central
America, The Johns Hopkins Press.
Ponssard, Jean-Pierre et de Pouvourville, Gerard (1982),
Marchés publics et politique industrielle, Economica.
Roy, M. (1984), La Communauté Européenne et le Tiers
Monde (hors Convention de Lomé), Notes et Etudes
documentaires, La Documentation française, No. 4773.
Warr, P.G. and Lloyd, P.J. (1982), Do Australian Trade
Policies Discriminate Against LDCs?, The Australian
National University, Discussion Paper No. 50.

Wolf, Martin (1987), An Unholy Alliance: The European Community and Developing Countries in The International Trading System, <u>This book.</u>

Annex
Correspondence table between ISIC (3 digits) and NAP40 (French industrial Classification)

NAP	ISIC
04	21
05	220, 353
06	400
07	230p, 371p, 372p
08	230p, 371p, 372p
09	290, 369
10	362
11	351
12	352
13	371p, 381
14	382p, 385
15	382p, 383
16	384p
17	382p, 384p
18	321, 322
19	323, 324
20	331, 332, 390
21	341
22	342
23	355, 356

This Table is only indicative. The symbol p means that it is only a part of the ISIC item which corresponds to the NAP item.

Chapter Eleven

GREEK ACCESSION AND EC COMMERCIAL POLICY TOWARD THE SOUTH

Alexander Sarris

1. INTRODUCTION

Greece formally joined the European Communities (EC) on January 1, 1981 in the middle of a worldwide stagnation and rise of protectionist sentiments. As the accession negotiations were carried out within a spirit of political urgency, not much effort was put by the Greek side to assess the impact of the EC common policies on the Greek economy and negotiate compensation for potential damage. As a consequence Greece agreed to adopt without change all the existing EC common policies.

Since, however, the existing EC common policies were negotiated with the absence of Greece, and since the Greek economy is structurally quite different from the economies of most of the other nine EC partners, it is probable that these policies are not compatible with the national economic Greek interests. This divergence could potentially increase the tendency in any future change in the common policies, to reflect more the Greek viewpoints.

The purpose of this paper is to examine the potential influence of Greek accession in the future shaping of the EC common commercial policy (CCP), and in particular the EC's CCP toward the "South", namely the developing countries.

The paper is organized as follows. The evolution of the structure of Greek production and trade is examined first. Then trends in Greek sectoral protection, import penetration and export propensity are exhibited in order to bring out potential strains. An analysis of similarity of Greek and developing country exports to the EC is then

326

made in order to identify possible conflicts, and finally some early post-accession trends are analysed. In the concluding section an overall assessment is made about the future of the EC's CCP toward the South.

2. THE STRUCTURE OF GREEK FOREIGN TRADE AND PROTECTION

2.1 Trade

In this section we exhibit a brief overview of the structure of Greek foreign trade.

Table 11.1 shows the sectoral breakdown of Greek exports and imports in 1983, to and from the world, the EC and the developing countries. The EC-9 accounts for about half of Greek imports and exports. The developing countries account for 28% of Greek imports, most of which is mineral fuels (petroleum), and 27% of Greek exports, of which food products and basic manufactures constitute the bulk. About 53% of Greek imports is manufactures, 27% fuels and the remaining is agricultural products and raw materials. However, more than 74% of imports from the EC is manufactures. Turning to exports, about 52.5% of the total is manufactures of which 54% is absorbed by the EC (53.6% of total exports to the EC). Greece, however, exports mostly manufactures to the developing countries (65.6% of total exports to class 2 countries). A substantial portion of Greek exports is agricultural products (about 37% of the total) of which about 57% is absorbed by the EC. An analysis of revealed comparative advantage in manufacturing products by Donges et al. (1982) showed that Greece's trade resembles that of a less industrialized labour-abundant country.

Table 11.2 presents the distribution of Greek domestic manufacturing value added (MVA) and of exports among twenty manufacturing sectors over time. The table gives at a glance the dynamic picture of that changing industrial structure in Greece. It appears that the industries with increasing shares in both domestic production and exports are mostly those producing intermediate products (refinery products, non-metallic minerals (chiefly cement), basic metallurgy, and electrical machinery). On the other hand, many of the traditional industries are either losing shares both domestically and in exports (food, tobacco, leather, non-electrical machinery) or at best staying at the same

Table 11.1: The Structure of Greek Foreign Trade in 1983 (in millions ECU)

SITC Section	Imports by origin			Exports by destination		
	World	EC	LDCs (a)	World	EC	LDCs (a)
0 Food and Live Animals	1278	978	132	1107	635	282
1 Beverages and Tobacco	82	76	2	270	85	44
2 Crude Materials except Fuels	668	151	139	337	163	17
3 Mineral Fuels etc.	2977	124	2564	348	85	64
4 Animal and Vegetable Oils and Fats	15	13	1	288	250	22
5 Chemicals	907	706	28	215	97	85
6 Basic Manufactures	1801	1306	78	1517	688	624
7 Machinery and Transport Equipment	2695	1587	65	174	46	113
8 Miscellaneous Manufactures	381	258	28	730	585	68
Total (b)	10863	5212	3041	5028	2639	1357

Table 11.1: continued The Structure of Greek Foreign Trade in 1983 (in percentages)

SITC	% of total imports by origin			% of total exports by destination		
Section	World	EC	LDCs (a)	World	EC	LDCs (a)
0 Food and Live Animals	11.8	18.8	4.3	22.0	24.1	20.8
1 Beverages and Tobacco	0.8	1.4	0.1	5.4	3.2	3.2
2 Crude Materials except Fuels	6.1	2.9	4.6	6.7	6.2	1.3
3 Mineral Fuels etc.	27.4	2.4	84.3	6.9	3.2	4.7
4 Animal and Vegetable Oils and Fats	0.1	0.2	0.0	5.7	9.5	1.6
5 Chemicals	8.3	13.5	0.9	4.3	3.7	6.3
6 Basic Manufactures	16.6	25.1	2.6	30.2	26.1	46.0
7 Machinery and Transport Equipment	24.8	30.4	2.1	3.5	1.7	8.3
8 Miscellaneous Manufactures	3.5	5.0	0.9	14.5	22.2	5.0
Total (b)	100.0	100.0	100.0	100.0	100.0	100.0

(a) LDCs: Class 2 countries according to Eurostat classification.
(b) Total includes SITC section 9: Commodities not classified elsewhere.

Source: Eurostat, Analytical Tables of Foreign Trade SITC, 1983.

relative share (textiles). It is interesting to note that sectors whose share in value added has increased while the share in exports declined or stayed constant (which might be characterized as import substituting sectors) include many of the more traditional manufacturing sectors (beverages, wood and cork, rubber and plastics, chemicals, transport equipment). There are two sectors which appear to be gaining export shares while losing domestic shares. These are shoes and clothing as well as products of metal. This could possibly be the result of trade diversion in the EC.

In the early sixties the manufacturing export pattern of Greece was highly specialized in four industries (food, textiles, leather and chemicals) accounting for about three quarters of total manufacturing exports, albeit only 38% of manufacturing value added. In the twenty year period 1960-1980, however, there has been a gradual diversification in both the domestic production pattern but mostly in the export pattern. By 1980 those same four industries accounted for only 37% of total manufacturing exports while three other industries (shoes and clothing, refinery products, and basic metallurgy) accounted for another 43.3%.

The conclusions from this brief exposition reinforce the conclusions reached earlier by Donges et al. (1982): Greece still exhibits the production and trade pattern of a developing labour-abundant economy.

As far as the central question of this paper is concerned, however, namely the impact of Greek accession in EC trade policy toward the South, the exposition here showed that the developing countries do not supply Greece many items competing with domestically produced goods. On the other hand, they provide fairly large markets for Greek manufacturing exports. If these markets are to expand it might not be of interest to Greece to push for increased protection of EC markets from developing country exports. However, as will be analysed below, these tendencies might have to be balanced against the threat of competition to Greek exports by developing countries on the EC markets.

2.2 **Protection**

Until the early 1960s Greece, in conjunction with a general push toward industrialization, followed a commercial policy biased toward import substitution. In the 1960s and especially in the 1970s, however, export promotion became a major objective. A catalytic factor in this shift was the signing in 1962 of the association agreement with the EEC which included among its stipulations a substantial liberalization over a 22 year period of the protective structure of Greece.

Only a general description of the various means of protection and export promotion existing in Greece in the 1970s will be made here. For details, the reader is referred to the thorough description in Papageorgiou (1983) and Voloudakis and Fylaktos (1982).

Besides tariffs, the fiscal structure of Greece includes an array of ad valorem and specific taxes such as turnover tax, luxury and consumption taxes, stamp fees, wage bill taxes, specific import taxes etc. While most of these taxes have fiscal objectives and are applied on both domestic production and imports, the differential application to domestic production and imports renders many of them in effect protective in nature. Besides taxes, the Greek protective system in the 70s included other instruments, the most prominent of which were import licensing and advance deposit requirements.

As already mentioned the association agreement stipulated for a gradual reduction in tariffs on imports from the EC as well as a gradual alignment of Greek tariffs with the Community's common external tariff (CET) toward third countries. Table 11.3 shows the evolution of average ex-post tariffs and border taxes (1) on Greek imports from the EC and non-EC sources. Total duties collected at the border are just the sum of tariffs and non-tariffs taxes.

Indeed the average collected tariff on all imported items (dutiable and non-dutiable) from the EC had declined from 13.2% in 1960 to 3.3% in 1980 just before accession and in 1983 it stood at barely 1.4%. After the full transition period this rate will presumably be very close to zero. Substantial also is the decline of the average Greek tariff on imports from nonEC countries from an average of 7.9% in 1960 to 2.3% in 1983. This is mainly the result of alignment with the CET, as well as the Kennedy and Tokyo rounds of trade liberalization. A portion of these trends might also be due to substitution toward lower tariff imports within fairly broad categories. To assess this, however, would require exceedingly detailed data and would carry us beyond the purpose of this paper.

The same decline, however, does not seem to be

Table 11.2: Distribution of Manufacturing Value Added and Manufacturing Exports Among Twenty Sectors in Greece, 1960-1980

CCCN Code (b) Sector		% of Manufacturing Value Added			% of Manufacturing Exports		
		1960	1970	1980	1960	1970	1980
20	Food	14.9	13.4	12.8	27.5	14.7	12.3
21	Beverages	3.1	3.2	4.1	2.2	2.4	0.8
22	Tobacco	6.1	2.3	1.5	0.4	0.0	0.0
23	Textiles, Yarns	16.7	14.0	16.6	9.5	11.3	12.1
24	Shoes, Clothing	13.4	9.4	8.6	1.5	4.8	11.7
25	Wood and Cork	3.1	3.3	3.8	1.0	0.3	0.6
26	Furnitures	2.9	2.9	1.6	0.2	0.1	0.1
27	Paper Products	1.7	1.7	2.1	0.5	0.7	1.3
28	Printing and Publishing	2.5	2.9	2.8	2.0	0.5	0.2
29	Leather Goods	1.8	1.5	0.8	8.5	5.2	2.3
30	Rubber and Plastics	1.8	2.8	2.8	0.3	0.9	0.2
31	Chemicals	4.6	6.0	6.2	28.7	14.2	10.3
32	Refinery Products	1.9	2.3	2.8	0.0	2.0	20.0
33	Non-Metallic Min.	6.0	7.6	8.9	3.8	2.2	7.0
34	Basic Metallurgy	1.8	7.4	5.6	4.3	35.0	11.6
35	Products of Metal	7.2	5.6	5.4	1.3	1.4	4.3
36	Non-Electr. Mach.	2.7	2.5	1.7	4.6	0.4	0.7

Table 11.2: continued

CCCN Code		% of Manufacturing Value Added			% of Manufacturing Exports		
(b)	Sector	1960	1970	1980	1960	1970	1980
37	Electr. Machinery	2.6	4.6	3.8	0.2	1.6	2.4
38	Transport Equipment	3.3	5.3	6.9	1.2	0.9	0.9
39	Other	1.1	1.1	1.1	2.3	1.4	1.3
	Total (a)	100.0	100.0	100.0	100.0	100.0	100.0
	Percent of MVA in Total VA and percent of ME in Total Exports	16.3	19.2	19.5	4.9	36.6	54.5

(a) Totals might not add to 100.0 because of rounding.
(b) CCCN = Customs Cooperation Council Nomenclature.

Source: Computed from Data Compiled by the Center for Planning and Economic Research (KEPE).

Table 11.3: Evolution of Average Greek Tariff and Non-Tariff Border Taxes, 1960-1983

	Tariffs as % of value of Dutiable Imports (3)		Tariffs as % of value of Total Imports (3)		Taxes as % of value of Dutiable Imports	
	From EC (1)	From Non-EC	From EC(1)	From Non-EC	From EC(1)	From Non-EC
1960	21.1	19.0	13.2	7.9	-	-
1965	17.5	19.1	11.6	10.1	12.5(2)	12.7(2)
1970	12.9	18.3	8.9	7.5	14.5	9.9
1975	11.8	9.8	5.9	3.3	21.8	9.0
1980	5.0	5.8	3.3	2.7	15.4	6.5
1981	3.6	8.9	2.2	2.5	16.8	13.3
1982	3.2	8.5	2.0	2.6	22.3	20.1
1983	2.3	7.6	1.4	2.3	19.6	17.1

Table 11.3: continued

	Tariffs as % of value of Total Imports		All Duties and Taxes as % Value of Total Imports	
	From EC (1)	From Non-EC	From EC(1)	From Non-EC
1960	—	—	—	—
1965	8.1(2)	7.4(2)	19.7	17.5
1970	9.9	4.1	18.8	11.6
1975	11.0	3.9	16.9	7.2
1980	10.2	3.0	13.5	5.7
1981	10.4	3.7	12.6	6.2
1982	13.6	6.1	15.6	8.7
1983	11.8	5.3	13.2	7.6

Notes:
1. For years before 1973 EC refers to the original 6 EC members. For later years EC refers to the 9 members.
2. 1964.
3. Imports comprise all commodities and are classified as those for which there is some tariff duty and/or tax and those which enter completely tariff and tax free. The first set of figures is obtained by dividing total collected tariffs or taxes by the cif value of imports subject to tariff and/or tax, while the second set is obtained by dividing the same realized tariff or tax proceeds by the cif value of total imports, from the respective sources.

Source: Computed from data of Ministry of Economics.

happening with border taxes. While as far as third countries are concerned, the average ad-valorem border tax had declined before accession by more than 50%, it seems to have risen after accession. On imports from the EC, however, border taxes do not show any clear pattern.

The last column of Table 11.3 shows that the average total duty on Greek imports from the EC has always been and still is substantially higher than on imports from non-EC countries, the major reason for this being that most of the non-EC imports are mineral fuels which are subject to very low duties.

While as far as tariffs are concerned the decline has been by design, the results as far as average border taxes are concerned could very well be due to the changing product mix of imports. The main Greek border taxes are the turnover tax, the luxury tax and the consumption tax. While the turnover tax is the same fixed ad-valorem rate, for all products, the others differ by product categories. This could also account for the rather large difference in average border tax rates between imports from EC and imports from third countries. A breakdown of the average ex-post border tax rates for dutiable imports by 2-digit SITC categories for 1983 showed indeed that the rates differ widely among product classes from zero up to 94%.

Turning now to protection by sectors, the evolution of sectoral protection over time brings out the different liberalization pressures felt by the various branches of Greek industry during the pre-accession period. To assess this evolution we work with nominal protection coefficients.

The methodology used is the following. Denote by ϕ the rate of taxes levied on the production of some sector, and by ε the rate of production subsidies on the same sector. Then $\chi = \phi - \varepsilon$ is the net tax rate on the product of the sector if it is produced locally. Let further τ be the tariff rate. The real nominal rate of protection of import substituting production is then equal to

$$NP = (\frac{1 + \tau}{1 + \chi} - 1) \cdot 100$$

The rates τ and χ have been computed for all twenty CCCN industrial branches for the years 1960-1980. (2)

Table 11.4 shows the evolution of industrial sector

protection in Greece from 1960 to 1980. Note that while in most industrial sectors nominal real protection has declined in the last twenty years, there are five where protection has increased. These are textiles and yarns (CCCN 23), wood and cork (CCCN 25), rubber and plastics (CCCN 30), refinery products (CCCN 32), and basic metallurgy (CCCN 34). Three industries had no important change in protection: food (CCCN 20), products of metal (CCCN 35), and electrical machinery (CCCN 37). All the other twelve industries experienced significant declines in protection over time.

Table 11.4: Evolution of Protection in the Manufacturing Sectors of Greece, 1960-1980

CCCN Code (b)	Sector	Real Nominal Rate of Protection (a) in percentages of the price		
		1960	1970	1980
20	Food	31.7	43.6	31.2
21	Beverages	608.8	251.0	101.9
22	Tobacco	340.8	69.9	-35.0
23	Textiles, Yarns	32.9	44.2	45.6
24	Shoes, Clothing	72.9	60.6	21.8
25	Wood and Cork	22.7	31.0	46.5
26	Furnitures	158.1	53.4	25.1
27	Paper Products	22.5	20.3	15.6
28	Printing & Publishing	18.6	4.1	3.8
29	Leather Goods	12.7	-2.2	0.4
30	Rubber and Plastics	22.2	38.0	31.4
31	Chemicals	21.3	20.8	13.4
32	Refinery Products	-32.7	-37.9	12.0
33	Non-Metallic Minerals	33.2	11.6	19.0
34	Basic Metallurgy	-10.9	7.4	4.3
35	Products of Metal	37.7	31.6	22.0
36	Non-Electrical Machinery	8.9	-0.7	-2.9
37	Electrical Machinery	25.1	21.9	16.2
38	Transport Equipment	21.4	17.3	15.1
39	Other	24.5	20.6	12.3

(a) For a definition of this concept see text.
(b) CCCN = Customs Cooperation Council Nomenclature.

Source: Data from the Ministry of Economic Affairs; data on trade (see text).

Table 11.5: Import Penetration and Export Propensity Ratios for the Greek Manufacturing Sectors, 1960-1980. Figures in percentages

CCCN Code (b)	Sector	Import Penetration (a)			Export Propensity (a)		
		1960	1970	1980	1960	1970	1980
20	Food	4.8	4.5	7.3	1.4	3.9	12.3
21	Beverages	0.5	1.2	2.0	0.9	4.6	3.6
22	Tobacco	0.0	0.1	0.8	0.1	0.1	0.0
23	Textiles, Yarns	10.9	10.3	9.3	0.9	5.3	14.4
24	Shoes, Clothing	0.6	0.7	3.7	0.2	2.7	30.4
25	Wood and Cork	29.6	23.0	11.9	0.5	0.6	2.8
26	Furnitures	0.4	1.6	4.4	0.1	0.4	1.6
27	Paper Products	32.7	30.8	35.6	0.3	1.5	7.9
28	Printing and Publ.	3.3	6.5	7.2	2.2	1.7	1.6
29	Leather Goods	2.6	21.5	48.6	2.3	16.3	39.2
30	Rubber and Plastics	29.1	15.2	13.9	0.3	2.4	1.5
31	Chemicals	45.4	42.0	56.3	6.6	10.8	19.9

Table 11.5: continued

CCCN Code (b)	Sector	Import Penetration (a)			Export Propensity (a)		
		1960	1970	1980	1960	1970	1980
32	Refinery Products	24.1	20.7	7.4	0.0	3.4	31.9
33	Non-Metallic Min.	9.3	9.8	10.6	1.5	2.6	19.2
34	Basic Metallurgy	74.6	41.1	44.5	1.8	27.4	24.2
35	Products of Metal	8.9	19.2	21.8	0.2	1.9	13.8
36	Non-Electr. Mach.	65.2	75.3	80.3	1.4	0.3	2.0
37	Electr. Mach.	45.8	31.4	42.5	0.1	1.5	8.2
38	Transport Equipment	52.7	41.5	42.2	0.5	0.9	2.5
39	Other	61.1	56.7	68.8	3.3	6.3	14.2

(a) Definition of concepts see text, formulae (3) and (4).
(b) CCCN = Customs Cooperation Council Nomenclature.

Source: See footnote 3.

Note that the formerly highly protected tobacco industry has in fact ended up being taxed by 1980. Also, the most highly protected sector over time remains the beverage industry.

2.3 Market penetration
In order to understand better the experience of the producers in the Greek economy from protection, reported on in the previous section, the present section analyses import penetration and export performance for the various sectors. (3)

Denote by X_i the value of production of sector i, M_i imports of products similar to or competing with those of sector i, and by E_i the exports of products of sector i.

The import penetration ratio is defined as the ratio of imports M_i to total apparent domestic consumption of products of sector i.

$$IP_i = \frac{M_i}{X_i + M_i - E_i} \qquad (3)$$

The export propensity is defined as the ratio of exports of sector i to total apparent supply of sector i goods

$$EP_i = \frac{E_i}{X_i + M_i} \qquad (4)$$

There are several well-known caveats in using these indices mentioned in Hughes and Thirlwall (1977), Blades and Simpson (1985) and GATT (1974, appendix IV). Keeping these observations in mind, the values of the indices IP and EP were calculated. Table 11.5 presents the evolution of import penetration and export propensity ratios for twenty 2-digit CCCN Greek manufacturing sectors from 1960 to 1980.

It can be noted that import penetration is high in the more sophisticated manufacturing sectors (chemicals, basic metallurgy, non-electrical and electrical machinery, transport equipment, and other manufactures). This is expected for a country at the level of development of Greece. Notice also the low levels of export propensities in the 60s and the substantial increase in these ratios during the 70s. This reflects to a large extent the vigorous export promotion policies of Greece after 1970. (For more details on this, see the studies by Papageorgiou (1983) and

Voloudakis and Fylaktos (1982).) Almost all sectors exhibit an increasing export propensity, except CCCN 22, 28 and 36, where it is unchanged.

Relatively strong sectors in terms of declining import penetration combined with a rising export propensity appear to be textiles (23), wood and cork (25), rubber and plastics (30), refinery products (32) and basic metallurgy (34). These sectors were found in the previous section to have experienced increased protection over the same twenty year period. Sector 38 (transport equipment) seems to be somewhat of an exception. On the other hand quite a few sectors (nrs. 21, 22, 24, 26, 28, 29 and 36) experienced increased import penetration with decreasing protection. It thus appears that there is a strong association between increasing protection and decreasing import penetration and also vice versa.

Two of the five sectors mentioned above, namely wood and cork (25) and rubber and plastic (30) appear to have been characterized by import substitution policies; the absolute level of their export propensity albeit slowly rising is still less than 3%, while import penetration has declined dramatically. In the three other sectors, textiles (23), refinery products (32) and basic metallurgy (34) export propensity has increased substantially. Apparently, export promotion seems to be the prevalent policy there, especially in textiles where import penetration went down only slightly. Indeed this sector is crucial for Greece accounting for almost 17% of manufacturing value added and 11.3% of total exports in 1981 (9.9% in 1983). Furthermore, the bulk of textile exports goes to the EC (81.7% of total textile exports in 1983).

Two sectors experienced large increases in export propensity, while their protection went down and import penetration of their products went up. These sectors are clothing and shoes (24) and leather (29); these developments might indicate that these sectors are becoming quite competitive internationally. They might hold out under further liberalization.

3. GREEK AND LDCs EXPORTS ON THE EC MARKET

3.1 Similarity of Export Patterns
To investigate the potential source of friction of Greek with LDCs exports to the EC market we have computed the

Table 11.6: Similarity of EC imports from Greece and Various Groups of Developing Countries, 1983

| | | Finger-Kreinin Index | | | | | |
| | | Similarity between Greece and Country Group | | | | | |
SITC Code	Product Category	LDCs	ACP	Mediterranean	Arab	Maghreb	Central and South America
0	Food and Live Animals	34.9	19.1	26.9	64.1	30.8	27.4
1	Beverages and Tobacco	78.9	82.7	45.9	39.9	71.2	91.1
2	Crude Materials Except Fuels	35.2	42.8	28.4	27.8	30.9	40.0
4	Animal, Vegetable Oils and Fats	20.9	46.8	30.1	93.0	24.3	46.4
5	Chemicals	33.7	18.9	26.6	26.0	41.6	46.7
6	Basic Manufactures	34.0	18.0	28.5	45.1	30.9	31.0
7	Machines, Transport Equipment	48.8	46.2	45.7	39.3	42.0	31.2
8	Miscellaneous Manufactures	52.1	43.8	23.9	52.6	28.5	46.0
(0-8) -3	All the Above	36.8	23.0	23.1	35.6	26.6	28.5

Source: Computed from Data in Eurostat: Analytical Tables of Foreign Trade (SITC). Country groupings defined in same source, LDCs comprise all class 2 countries (Eurostat classification).

Finger-Kreinin (1979) index of export similarity between Greece's exports to the EC and several groups of developing countries at the three-digit SITC level. Table 11.6 shows the results reported for each one-digit class and all classes together for 1983. We have also computed the index for the years 1979, 1980 (years before Greece's accession) and 1982 to check for spurious effects but the results were fairly similar. The value of the Finger-Kreinin index is bounded below by 0, indicating complete dissimilarity and from above by 1 indicating perfect similarity.

In general, examining the aggregate figures it appears that the degree of similarity between Greek and developing country exports to the EC is fairly small. However, there are important subcategories of products where the similarity is fairly high. In the food and live animals class (SITC 0) we notice fairly high similarity between Greece and the group of Arab countries. This is due primarily to both sources' large exports of fruits and vegetables to the EC. Sector 1 (beverages and tobacco) appears to be a sector with very high degrees of similarity between Greece and most groups of developing countries. Despite the bias that can be induced by the fact that SITC 1 includes only four 3-digit SITC subcategories, the high degree of similarity is due to the inclusion of wines and unprocessed tobacco, two fairly important Greek export products.

The high similarity between Greece and the Arab Countries in SITC 4 is due to the inclusion in SITC 4 of olive oil which is a very important Greek export product and also for Tunísia. In SITC category 6 which includes textiles (SITC 65) it is quite interesting to note the low degree of export similarity between Greece and almost all groups of developing countries (except perhaps the Arab countries). There appears to be a higher degree of similarity in categories such as SITC 7 (machines and transport equipment) and SITC 8 miscellaneous manufactures including clothing (SITC 84) and footwear (SITC 85). The low similarity in category 6 could be attributed to the fact that it is a highly diverse category of which textiles is only one subcategory. If we examine the individual figures it turns out that while textiles accounts for 56% of total Greek exports to the EC in this category, they account for only 19% of total developing country exports in SITC 6 to the EC.

The moderate similarity observed in SITC 7 might be spurious as exports of Greece in this category account for less than 2% of total Greek exports to the EC (cf. Table 11.1). On the other hand the reasonably high similarity in SITC 8 is due to the subcategories clothing and shoes which constitute some of Greece's major exports to the EC.

Juxtaposing the results of Table 11.7 with the figures of Table 11.1, which highlights the relative importance to Greece of the various export categories, and given the observations just made, it appears that the major areas where Greece might be in conflict with developing countries as far as access to the EC market is concerned, are on the one hand certain agricultural products (mainly fruits and vegetables, wine, tobacco and olive oil), and on the manufacturing products side mainly clothing, shoes and textiles.

Wine, tobacco and olive oil are already fairly well protected in the context of the Common Agricultural Policy (CAP) of the EC. However, given the recent financial woes of the CAP and the large stocks of Greek olive oil and tobacco accumulated with EC funds, as well as the well known EC wine lakes, the pressure, which Greece will resist, will be to lower overall support and protection for these products. As far as fruits and vegetables are concerned, the support provided by the CAP is not as high as the support provided to northern products (cereals and meat). This fact coupled with the results of Sarris (1983) and Hunt (1979) that foresee a medium term decline in relative international prices of fruits and vegetables - due to excess international supply - indicate that the pressures in the EC will be toward a more balanced CAP, favoring Mediterranean products. This means pressures for increased protection against imports of fruits and vegetables from developing countries.

Turning now to <u>textiles and clothing</u>, these products were seen to constitute a fairly large share of Greek exports to the EC. Apart from the Multifibre Arrangement, the EC has established certain preferences for developing countries in these products in the context of its system of GSP. It is interesting to examine the similarity between exports to the EC of developing countries and Greece in the subcategories enjoying preferences. (4)

The results are shown in Table 11.7. There is some similarity in the sensitive MFA products of annex A. EC imports from Greece in groups I, II and IV of annex A account for 734.5 million ECUs in 1983 or 89% of total EC imports from Greece in all product categories of Table 11.8. EC imports from all developing countries in the same groups

Table 11.7: Similarity of Greece with Class 2 Developing Countries in their Exports to the EC of Textile Products Covered by EC Preferential Arrangements with Developing Countries, 1983.

Annex (1)	Group (2)	Similarity Index
	I	39.5
	II	45.6
A	III	11.4
	IV	43.7
	V	1.4
	III	10.9
B	IV	36.0
	V	1.2
	VI	0.0
C	VII	10.0
	VI	0.0
D	VII	3.9

(1) The annex categories refer to those mentioned in the EC preferential agreement (EC (1981)). They refer to the following categories.
Annex A: MFA textile products subject to Community tariff ceilings allocated among Member States.
Annex B: MFA textile products subject to Community tariff ceilings not allocated among Member States.
Annex C: Non-MFA products subject to Community tariff ceilings allocated among Member States.
Annex D: Non-MFA products subject to Community tariff ceilings not allocated among Member States.

(2) The Groups I-VII refer to MFA group classification with decreasing degrees of "sensitivity".

Source: Computed from Data in Analytical Tables of Foreign Trade NIMEXE.

amount to 5,562 million ECUs or 82.9% of EC imports from developing countries in all the product categories of Table 11.7, or 10.6% of total EC-9 non-oil imports from class 2 developing countries. Given the importance of textiles and

Table 11.8: Greek Exports to the EC as Per cent of Total Greek Exports, Before and After Accession, Selected Products, 1978-1983.

			In percentages	
SITC Code	Product	Per cent of Total Greek Exports 1981-1983	Exports to EC Per cent of Total	
			1978-1980	1981-1983
05	Fruits and Vegetables	15.2	54.0	63.6
112	Alcoholic Beverages	0.8	62.7	68.4
121	Tobacco, unmanuf.	4.3	30.9	24.4
263	Cotton	0.9	5.8	30.5
278	Other Crude Minerals	1.8	55.4	55.8
423	Fixed Vegetable Oils	3.2	68.1	80.2
598	Misc. Chemicals	1.4	59.7	73.9
651	Textile Yarn	6.6	81.3	82.4
652	Cotton Fabrics	1.1	79.6	78.1
658	Articles Made-Up of Textiles	1.1	72.9	74.8
653-657, 659	All other Textiles and Yarn	1.5	80.1	69.0
84	Clothing	10.8	89.2	90.4
851	Footwear	1.4	53.4	37.8
0-9	All Products	100.0	48.9	48.3

Source: Computed from Data of the Greek Statistical Service: Foreign Trade of Greece. Various Years.

clothing for the Greek economy and its exports it is fairly clear that there will be pressures from the Greek side not to enlarge the scope of EC preferences toward developing countries in the textile and clothing sector and especially in the sensitive product categories of the MFA.

3.2 Trade developments since accession

The analysis of similarities between Greek and LDC exports to the EC markets has identified some of the main sectors where conflicts might arise. In this section we exhibit the initial post accession changes in the direction of Greek exports in these sectors. Although not much time has elapsed to indicate firm conclusions, tentative inferences are nevertheless possible.

Table 11.8 presents the average shares of Greek exports going to the EC in total Greek exports in the three year periods just before and just after accession for products and sectors where potential conflicts were identified. The products considered constitute 50% of total Greek exports in the period 1981-1983. For only some products the share of Greek exports going to the EC has increased after accession. This increase is particularly pronounced in fruits and vegetables, cotton and olive oil (the main export under SITC 423) and miscellaneous chemicals while in most manufactured exports that compete with LDCs the share going to the EC has increased only slightly and in some (notably footwear and tobacco) it has declined.

An examination of EC shares in Greek imports (figures not shown) in the three years just before and after accession revealed that the aggregate EC share has increased from 44.5 to 48.7% with most pronounced increases in the food sector (SITC 0) (from 31.5 to 74.2 per cent with the bulk of this shift due to increased beef imports from the EC) and the basic manufactures sector (SITC 6) (from 60.5 to 71.6 per cent with the bulk of the shift due to increased furskin and iron and steel imports from the EC).

In conclusion, the early indications after Greek accession seem to reinforce the tentative conclusion reached earlier, namely that the resistance to a more liberal EC preferential trade policy toward developing countries might increase, especially for agricultural products.

4. SUMMARY AND CONCLUSIONS

This paper has investigated developments in trade and protection of the Greek economy in the last twenty five years. It has attempted to pinpoint the sectors where conflicts are likely to arise between the interests of Greek producers and those of developing countries. As far as the Greek import market is concerned we have shown that accession will not have much impact on developing country exports to Greece because of the small shares of Greek non-oil imports from these countries. The major conflict is bound to arise in products which both Greece and developing countries export to the EC. We have identified the main sectors which will face problems in the shaping of a more liberal trade policy of the EC toward the "South". Among agricultural products these are wine and olive oil, further fruits and vegetables and possibly tobacco. Among industrial products, textiles and clothing were identified as products where Greek interests are many and rather vital. Diversification of Greek manufactured exports to the EC away from the present concentration on textiles and clothing might be needed to arrive at a more lenient attitude to be expected from Greece towards liberalization of the EC trade policy on these products.

However no strong tendency of diversification was found in the period before 1980; still, upon accession the direction of Greek exports seems to be shifting more toward the EC. This means increased competition for the established producers in the EC-9 especially in textiles and clothing. Hence, the need for adjustment in those sectors, which might be felt even more after the accession of Spain and Portugal, will impose on them strains that might necessitate more protection against competing imports from developing countries.

It therefore appears that the EC enlargement is likely to reverse the trend toward a more generous EC preferential trade policy toward the South.

Notes

I would like to thank D. Amallos, J. Anastassakou, P. Kalfaoglou, S. Lazaridis, P. Livas, N. Touribabas, E. Mane, J. Vartholomeos and V. Vassilopoulou for assistance at various stages of this project. I would also like to thank the participants of the seminar on European Trade Policies and the South held in the Hague on September 13-14, 1985 for helpful comments and in particular D. Greenaway, C. Hamilton and J. Waelbroeck.

1. In this paper ex-post tariffs and taxes are computed by dividing the value of collected duties by the cif value of imports. Ex-ante tariffs or taxes are the ones prescribed in the tariff legislation. Because of various temporary exemptions on imports of some items or on imports by specific origins the ex-post tariffs or taxes are not exactly equal to ex-ante ones.

2. Denote by P^p and P^b the producers and world price of the product respectively, including marketing

margins. Given rates for net taxes (χ) and for tariffs (τ) the sales prices become for domestically produced products P^{cd} = $P(1+\chi)$ and for imported products P^{cm} = $P^{b}(1+\tau)$. For perfect substitutes then: P^{cd} = P^{cm}; this implies P^{p}/P^{b} = $(1+\chi)/(1+\tau)$, which constitutes the formula for the nominal rate of protection (NP). Use has been made of Ministry of Economic Affairs ex-post data on tariffs, taxes and subsidies compiled by the Center for Planning and Economic Research (KEPE) and matching industrial sector classification with SITC classifications. The value of production data were compiled from industrial censuses by KEPE. Clearly, the methodology accounts for the differential impact of tax rates on imports and domestic production. Since the data used is ex-post, the rates of domestic taxation are effective, namely realized, and are of course different from nominal rates because of various exemptions allowed to business. The subsidy data do not include investment incentives or other fiscal incentives such as accelerated depreciation allowances. The ex-post border tariff and tax data also do not account for quantitative restrictions and other protective measures such as advance deposit requirements. Hence, the figures exhibited must be regarded as lower bounds of the actual protective rates. However, what is of interest at this juncture is the evolution over time and not the absolute level of protection.

3.   Data on values of production, imports and exports by industrial branch is available from the Center for Planning and Economic Research (KEPE).

4.   To do this we obtained from the EC Official Journal the detailed six digit (with the NIMEXE classification) subcategories of textile and clothing products for which some kind of preference was granted to developing countries. Then, from the Eurostat analytical tables of foreign trade NIMEXE we observed the imports of the EC-9 from Greece and from all developing countries of class 2 in these subcategories. We then computed the Finger-Kreinin index of similarity between exports of Greece and class 2 countries in various groups of textile products mentioned in the annexes to the EC regulation.

References

Blades, D. and Simpson, W. (1985), "The OECD Compatible Trade and Production Data Base", OECD Economics and Statistics Department, Working Paper No. 18, January

1985.

Donges, J.B., Krieger, C., Langhammer, R.J., Schatz, K.W., and Thoroe, C. (1982), The Second Enlargement of the European Community: Adjustment Requirements and Challenges for Policy Reform, Kieler Studien No. 171, Institute for World Economics, University of Kiel, Tübingen, 1982.

EC (1981), "Commission Proposal for a Council Regulation Opening, Allocating and Providing for the Administration of Community Tariff Preferences for Textile Products Originating in Developing Countries and Territories", Official Journal, Volume 24, C273, October 26, 1981.

Finger, J.M. and Kreinin, M.E. (1979), "A Measure of Export Similarity and its Possible Uses", Economic Journal, Vol. 89, No. 356, December, 1979.

GATT (1984), Textiles and Clothing in the World Economy, Geneva, July 1984.

Hunt, R.D. (1979), "Fruit and Vegetable Exports from the Mediterranean Area to the EEC", World Bank Staff Working Paper, No. 321, Washington, 1979.

Hughes, J.J. and Thirlwall, A.P. (1977), "Trends and Cycles in Import Penetration in the U.K.", Oxford Bulletin of Economics and Statistics, Vol. 39, November 1977.

Papageorgiou, D. (1983), Export Promotion Policies in Greece, Unpublished Study, World Bank, March 1983

Sarris, A.H. (1983), "European Community Enlargement and World Trade in Fruits and Vegetables", American Journal of Agricultural Economics, Vol. 65, No. 2, May 1983.

Voloudakis, E. and Fylaktos, P. (1982), Greek Exports: Determinants and Policies 1960-1979, Mimeographed, Center for Planning and Economic Research, Athens, 1982.

NOTES ON THE CONTRIBUTORS

David Greenaway is Professor of Economics at the University of Buckingham. He has been Visiting Professor at Lehigh University (1982) and at the Graduate Institute of International Studies in Geneva (1981).

He has authored, co-authored and edited books on international trade issues and commercial policy. He has authored and co-authored articles in a number of journals including The Economic Journal, the European Economic Review, Kyklos, the Scottish Journal of Political Economy and Applied Economics.

Carl Hamilton is Senior Research Fellow and acting Director of the Institute for International Economic Studies of Stockholm University. He also worked at the World Bank.

He has published on international trade theory and commercial policies, in particular issues related to the theory and measurement of non-tariff barriers to trade. Articles appeared in among others the European Review of Agricultural Economics, The World Economy, Weltwirtschaftliches Archiv, The Scandinavian Journal of Economics and the Journal of International Economics.

Brian Hindley is Senior Lecturer at the London School of Economics and Counsellor for Studies at the Trade Policy Research Centre in London. He has authored books and articles on international trade and industrial policy. Articles were published in among others the Journal of World Trade Law and The World Economy.

Ad Koekkoek is Senior Lecturer at Erasmus University Rotterdam. He has taught development economics at the University of Lagos in the years 1973-1975. He has written on international trade and commercial policy. Articles have been published in among others the Journal of World Trade Law and Weltwirtschaftliches Archiv.

At present he is temporarily attached to the Ministry of Foreign Affairs of the Netherlands at the Directorate General for International Cooperation.

Jacob Kol is Senior Lecturer at Erasmus University Rotterdam. He has authored and co-authored articles on international trade and policy issues in among others Economie Appliquée, the European Economic Review and the Journal of International Economics.

Loet Mennes is Professor of Development Planning at Erasmus University Rotterdam and Director of the Netherlands Economic Institute. Previously he was employed at the Central Planning Bureau (The Hague) and the European Economic Community (Brussels).

He has authored and co-authored books on regional planning, economic integration, project appraisal and investment planning. He is author and co-author of articles in Econometrica, Weltwirtschaftliches Archiv, Journal of World Trade Law and Journal of International Economics.

From 1983 to 1986 he was special adviser to the Netherlands Minister for Development Cooperation.

Patrick Messerlin is Professor of Economics at the University of Paris XII and Senior Research Fellow at the Foundation Nationale des Sciences Politiques in Paris. At present he is working at the World Bank in the International Economic Research Division. He has published on trade policy issues and on industrial organization. Articles appeared in The World Economy and Weltwirtschaftliches Archiv.

Alexander Sarris is Professor of Economics at the University of Athens. At present he is Chairman of the Board of Directors of the Centre for Planning and Economic

Research in Athens. He has taught at the University of California, Berkeley.

He has published on applied international economics, agricultural and development economics in among others the American Journal of Agricultural Economics.

He has been consultant for international organizations such as the FAO, World Bank and others.

Mathew Tharakan is Professor in the Department of Economics at the University of Antwerp. He has been Visiting Professor at the Catholic University of Louvain (1985), Jayewardena University in Sri Lanka (1982), the Institute for International Economic Studies at the University of Stockholm (1979) and at the National Institute for Bank Management in Bombay (1975).

He has authored, co-authored and edited books on international trade and commercial policy issues. Articles appeared in among others the European Economic Review and Weltwirtschaftliches Archiv.

Wouter Tims is Director of the Centre for World Food Studies at the Free University in Amsterdam. He has been working at the World Bank till 1976, lastly as Director of the Economic Analysis and Projections Department.

He authored and co-authored books and articles on development issues, economic modelling and agricultural economics in among others the Journal of Agricultural Economics.

He is adviser to the Netherlands' Ministeries of Agriculture and of Foreign Affairs on development cooperation.

Jan Waelbroeck is Professor of Mathematical Economics and Econometrics at the Université Libre de Bruxelles, where he is President of the Centre for Econometrics and Mathematical Economics (CEME). He is Member of the Centre of Operations Research and Econometrics (CORE) at the Catholic University in Louvain-la-Neuve and also Senior Research Fellow of the Centre for European Policy Studies in Brussels.

He has published numerous articles and books on general equilibrium modelling, mathematical economics and trade policy issues. Articles have appeared in among others The American Economic Review, Economie Appliqueé and The World Economy.

He is Editor of the European Economic Review.

Martin Wolf is Director of Studies at the Trade Policy Research Centre in London. He was a staff member of the World Bank from 1971 to 1981, where among other things he was member of the core team for the first World Development Report.

He has written on commercial policy and economic development. His work has been published by the World Bank and by the Trade Policy Research Centre, especially in the Thames Essays Series and in The World Economy as well as in other books and journals.

THE HAGUE GROUP

The Hague Group consists of economists, mainly from European countries, who cooperate in research in the area of trade relations and protection. The work of the group is policy oriented. Its aim is to carry out research that is useful to decision makers. To that end the work of the group has a strong empirical content. Its work is not merely descriptive but uses in addition techniques of quantitative analysis.

The Dutch Minister for Development Cooperation and the World Bank have provided support to make the group's cooperation feasible.

A list of members of the Hague Group as they particpiated in the work of the group from 1985 onwards is given below.

World Bank
*Mike Finger (Chief International Economic Research
    Division
Enzo Grilli (Deputy Director Economic Projections
    Department)
Helen Hughes (at present: Australian National University)
Paul E. Holmes (International Economic Research Division)
Deepak Lal (Research Adviser)
Costas Michalopoulos (Director Economic Policy Analyais
    and Coordination)
Andrzej Olechowski (International Economic Research
    Division)

The Hague Group

Belgium
Mathew Tharakan (University of Antwerp)
* Jean Waelbroeck (Universite Libre de Bruxelles)

France
Gerard Lafay (CEPII, Paris)
Patrick Messerlin (University of Paris XII)

Federal Republic of Germany
Juergen Donges (Inst. fuer Weltwirtschaft, Kiel)
Egbert Gerken (Inst. fuer Weltwirtschaft, Kiel)

Greece
Alexander Sarris (University of Athens)

The Netherlands
Ad Koekkoek (Erasmus University, Rotterdam)
Jacob Kol (Erasmus University, Rotterdam)
*Loet Mennes (Erasmus University, Rotterdam)
Wouter Tims (Centre for World Food Studies, Amsterdam)

Sri Lanka
Lal Jayawardena (at present: Director WIDER, Helsinki)

Sweden
Carl Hamilton (Inst. for International Economic Studies,
Stockholm)

Thailand
Ch. Isarangkun (Government of Thailand)
Boontipa Simaskul (Ministry of Commerce, Bangkok)

United Kingdom
David Greenaway (University of Buckingham)
Brian Hindley (Trade Policy Research Centre, London)
Martin Wolf (Trade Policy Research Centre, London)

* Steering Committee

356

AUTHOR INDEX

INDEX

Printed in the United States
by Baker & Taylor Publisher Services